KT-238-517

8 9)

M D S
(G r a)

0669819840

PROBLEMS IN
EUROPEAN CIVILIZATION

The Cold War

A Conflict of Ideology and Power

Second Edition

Edited and with an introduction by

Norman A. Graebner

The University of Virginia

D. C. HEATH AND COMPANY
Lexington, Massachusetts Toronto

CONTENTS

INTRODUCTION

What characterized American thought on the cold war, especially that which bridged the years from mid-century to the late sixties, was the profound absence of agreement on every aspect of postwar Soviet-American relations. Almost thirty years of struggle with the Kremlin produced no consensus on the meaning of even the most elemental aspects of those relations. The Richard Nixon-Henry Kissinger search for détente in the seventies assumed a mutual Soviet-American interest in avoiding war and thereby blunted many of the fears and anxieties of previous years. Still the continuing enigma of Soviet behavior sustained the divisions among the people of the United States regarding the role of both Russian and American policy in determining the character of the East-West relationship. So incompatible were the conclusions of many Russian experts on matters of Soviet intent that Paul Winterton's poignant observation seemed perennially valid: "There are no experts on the Soviet Union, merely varying degrees of ignorance."

Despite the enormous variety of individual viewpoints, studies of the cold war fell consistently into two competing groups. One important body of scholarship viewed Russia as essentially a powerful nation pursuing traditional policies designed to secure a maximum of security against one or more proven antagonists. For proponents of this limited concept of the cold war, Soviet policy was circumscribed by the concrete factors of power politics and national interest. They believed, moreover, that an imperialistic Russia could be contained successfully through coalition diplomacy without resort to suicidally dangerous strategies. To another equally knowledgeable group of American writers the Soviet Union represented a massive assault on the institutions and values of the free world. In the absence of any relief from the multiple pressures exerted by the U.S.S.R. on world politics, they could assume only that the Kremlin harbored some sinister blueprint that aimed at world domination. For them the cold war had evolved into a limitless contest between freedom and tyranny, a totally revolutionary struggle propelling history down its final, dangerous course.

Fundamental to the continuing debate on the nature of the cold war was the question of origins. That the triumph of the Bolsheviks under Lenin in 1917 inaugurated a deadly and all-encompassing struggle between the U.S.S.R. and the Western democracies seemed clear enough from the dire predictions of Lenin, Stalin, and Khrushchev, repeated through that succeeding half century with disturbing arrogance and regularity. For those historians, political scientists, journalists, and politicians who viewed the Soviet-American conflict as a war of ideologies, what mattered in 1917 was the victory of a well-organized minority of revolutionaries over a populous and potentially aggressive nation and that minority's subsequent inauguration of a war against capitalism and democracy, to be pursued by whatever means came to hand. The continuing conflict in the postwar world was merely the extension of an ideological assault on the embattled forces of freedom everywhere which began with the Russian Revolution itself.

Those who accepted the more traditional concept of the Soviet-American rivalry likewise recognized the existence of some tension during the interwar years. But they attributed this tension less to the Bolshevik declaration of ideological warfare on the West than to obvious Western enmity toward the Red regime. The Allied effort to intervene in the Russian Revolution in 1919 through an invasion of white armies was frustrated by a combination of war-weariness and the strength of the Red Army under Trotsky. This overt Allied hostility, however, aggravated a traditional Russian distrust of the West, a distrust partially relieved by United States recognition of the Soviet government in 1933. During the late thirties, moreover, Soviet leadership resented the efforts of Western diplomacy to isolate the U.S.S.R. from the main currents of European diplomacy despite the fact that the Soviet Union alone among the major powers of the world favored a realistic program of collective security to limit German and Japanese aggression. For a troubled Kremlin the refusal of Britain, France, and the United States to counter the aggressions of the thirties revealed simply a clandestine Western acceptance of Hitler as a first line of defense against Soviet power and ideology.

If United States-Russian relations during the thirties were marred occasionally by distrust, those relations were generally favorable until the Nazi-Soviet Pact of 1939. Neither nation threatened the vital interests of the other. Both were fundamentally status quo powers, devoted to preserving European stability as defined by the Versailles system. Only a dramatic shift in the balance of power appeared capable of bringing the interests of the United States and the U.S.S.R. into sharp conflict. When the German armies invaded Russia in mid-1941, the alacrity whereby the United States accepted the Soviet Union as an ally denied the existence of any recognizable conflict of purpose between the two nations. Yet the Nazi assault on Russia itself damaged irreparably the mutuality of interest which existed in American-Russian relations, for the deadly struggle for existence between the two giants of the Eurasian continent—Germany and Russia—made it certain that with peace the world would not return to the status quo of the interwar years which had favored the position of the democracies. Only the common concern of the Allies in destroying Nazi power sustained until 1945 the illusion that the traditional European balance of power would survive the war. That Russia, unlike both the United States and Great Britain, suffered incalculable physical destruction and twenty million deaths at the hands of the invading German forces assured the disruption of mutual Allied interests vis-à-vis Central and Eastern Europe once Hitler's armies were defeated.

Throughout the war Stalin faced the hard choice between working for postwar cooperation with the Western democracies and establishing absolute dominion over those peoples and territories occupied by the Red Army, in defiance of the principles of the Atlantic Charter. The first decision might have gained some support for the reconstruction of the Soviet economy, but it would have conceded Slavic Europe again to the control of non-Communist and perhaps anti-Soviet forces. Stalin's clear warning that he would tolerate only governments friendly to the U.S.S.R. along Russia's western frontier proved to be a critical issue even before the United States entered the European war. The exiled Polish government in London, known to be anti-Soviet, demanded guarantees of national self-determination from the United States as early as the autumn of 1941.

This Polish reliance on the West merely created a determination in the Kremlin to control the Polish political structure through the eventual establishment of a Communist regime.

For the American Secretary of State, Cordell Hull, it was unthinkable that the United States would condone any transfer of political authority in Eastern Europe from the Nazi invaders to the Soviet government. Unable to gain any guarantees for self-determination from Stalin during the war, American officials simply kept the burgeoning and inescapable conflict over the future of East-Central Europe out of sight by postponing all territorial settlements until the conclusion of the war. Through their conduct of the war against Germany, ironically, American leaders encouraged the establishment of the Soviet sphere of influence; then, in turn, they refused to sanction the existence of any portion of it through formal diplomatic arrangement. Stalin, no longer anticipating any agreement with the United States which might recognize a Soviet hegemony over Eastern Europe, began as early as November 1944 to prepare the Soviet people for the forthcoming break with the democracies. He reversed the Soviet party line by dropping the wartime mood of tolerance for the West and its values and returned to the harsh insistence that once Hitler was defeated the U.S.S.R. would resume its attack on its chief enemy, the capitalist system. The first selection in this volume, by Staughton Lynd, analyzes in detail the impact of American wartime decisions on subsequent United States-Soviet relations.

II

With the collapse of Soviet-American unity following the Yalta Conference of February 1945, largely over the issue of Poland, the U.S.S.R. established what Churchill termed an Iron Curtain from Stettin to Trieste as an initial defense maneuver both to control the political structure of Eastern Europe and to prevent the reestablishment of a free and united Germany. Western diplomacy at Potsdam in July–August 1945 attempted to undo the new Soviet hegemony through a variety of diplomatic pressures. Tragically the West had few practical alternatives available, for there was no way that it could regain control of East-Central Europe except through a war against the Soviet Union. Indeed, the Western democracies could not have defeated Germany except for the unlimited support of those Soviet troops which in 1945 occupied all areas in dispute. Yet the United

States, assuming the leadership of the West in its diplomacy with the Kremlin, persistently refrained from recognizing the Soviet sphere of influence. Washington preferred to quarrel over issues totally under Russian control, even to the disruption of the wartime alliance, rather than desert the principle of self-determination. For this unprecedented interest in the welfare of Slavic Europe the reasons were clear enough. The wartime experience itself had reawakened not only an American interest in world affairs but also a widespread commitment to the liberal-democratic principles of Woodrow Wilson now embodied in the Atlantic Charter. If the Roosevelt and Truman administrations admitted privately the virtual elimination of Western influence from Eastern Europe, the actual record of Soviet repression, reported in detail by American representatives, rendered the recognition of the Soviet hegemony increasingly difficult.

Unable either to accept or to deflate the Soviet sphere, Western spokesmen could only resort to a moralistic attack on the U.S.S.R. in an effort to arouse Western sentiment against Soviet action. Employing what Secretary of State James F. Byrnes termed "patience with firmness," they attempted in numerous conferences to argue the Soviets back to their 1939 boundaries. Soviet officials responded to Western efforts to eliminate their power from Eastern Europe with increasing hostility and resentment. In parrying the persistent Western recital of previous wartime agreements, the Kremlin revealed a pattern of deviousness which taxed the patience of American and British diplomats. In the second selection James B. Reston traces the breakdown of Allied diplomacy and suggests its significance for future Western security.

Questions of ideology had played no demonstrable role in the breakdown of the Grand Alliance. Western diplomacy throughout 1945 was directed at the achievement of political change in areas under the control of Soviet arms. The notion that Russia's forward position was only an initial step in a general assault on the free world was scarcely in evidence. It was Western policy, with its avowed purpose of ending Soviet hegemony, that maintained a spirit of aggressiveness. Soviet ambition still appeared limited to regions already under the dominance of the Red Army. Soviet intransigence from Potsdam to the Paris conferences of 1946 was more productive of frustration than of fear. That the Kremlin presented a challenge to American diplomacy was obvious, but beyond acknowledging a divided world Washington officials could not agree on either the character or the magnitude of the Russian danger. To adapt policies to the unanticipated conditions of international life, Western leadership was compelled both to evaluate the capability of the West to protect its interests in a new era of conflict and to define the long-range motivations, intentions, and capabilities of the U.S.S.R.

By early 1946 a new Soviet rhetoric revealed a disturbing confidence and determination anchored to the Marxist-Leninist promise of ultimate Communist victory. This Soviet anticipation of ever greater triumphs in the future reflected, first, the unprecedented power status of the U.S.S.R. in European affairs. "Today," declared Soviet Foreign Minister V. M. Molotov in February 1946, "no great issues of international relations can be solved without the Soviet Union or without listening to the voice of our Fatherland." Second, the Kremlin's aims reflected a Marxist faith in the imminent collapse of the capitalist system. Soviet analysts announced that the Western economies could not survive their internal inconsistencies, that industrial prosperity in the capitalist-dominated world was false and destined to be short-lived. Rising prices and falling wages would soon lead to another depression. Unfortunately for world peace, this incipient crisis in capitalism, ran the official Soviet judgment, could be reversed only through another war. Since the U.S.S.R. was the world's chief opponent of war, to save its economy, the United States had arrived at the conclusion that war must be organized against the U.S.S.R. and the other partisans of peace.

Stalin shook the complacency of Western officials completely with his radio address of February 9, 1946. Recalling the Communist dogma regarding war, he attributed the recent struggle to political and economic forces unleashed by monopoly capitalism. "Our Marxists declare," said Stalin, "that the capitalist system of world economy conceals elements of crisis and war, that the development of world capitalism does not follow a steady and even course forward, but proceeds through crises and catastrophes. The uneven development of the capitalist countries leads in time to sharp disturbances in their relations, and the group of countries which consider themselves inadequately provided with raw materials and export markets try usually to change this situation and to change the position in their favor by means of force." Perhaps a periodic redistribution of the world's markets and raw materials could prevent conflict, but such peaceful adjustments, continued Stalin, were impossible "under the present capitalist development of world economy." He then asserted that the Russian victory in World War II demonstrated the vitality and popularity of the Soviet system. "The war has shown," the Soviet leader declared, "that the Soviet multinational state system has successfully stood the test, has grown still stronger during the war and has proved a completely vital state system. . . . The point now is that the Soviet state system has proved an example of a multinational state system where the national problem and the problem of collaboration among nations are solved better than in any other multinational state."

This Soviet division of the world into two competing systems appeared complete in Andrei Zhdanov's report at the reestablishment of the Cominform at Warsaw in September 1947. No previous statement revealed better the depth of Soviet hostility toward the Western world. Declared Zhdanov:

> *The fundamental changes caused by the war on the international scene and in the position of individual countries have entirely changed the political landscape of the world. A new alignment of political forces has arisen. The more the war recedes into the past, the more distinct become two major trends in postwar international policy, corresponding to the division of the political forces operating on the international arena into two major camps: the imperialist and anti-democratic camp, on the one hand, and the anti-imperialist and democratic camp, on the other. The principal driving force of the imperialist camp is the USA. Allied with it are Great Britain and France. . . . The cardinal purpose of the imperialist camp is to strengthen imperialism, to hatch a new imperialist war, to combat Socialism and democracy, and to support reactionary and anti-democratic pro-fascist regimes and movements everywhere.*
>
> *The anti-fascist forces comprise the second camp. This camp is based on the U.S.S.R. and the new democracies. It also includes countries that have broken with imperialism and have firmly set foot on the path of democratic development, such as Rumania, Hungary and Finland. . . .*

III

After 1946 the ubiquitous Soviet rhetoric of Communist superiority, added to Soviet propaganda and diplomatic aggressiveness which lapsed occasionally into warlike actions such as the Berlin blockade of 1948, demonstrated that the U.S.S.R. harbored hostile intentions toward the West. Yet neither Soviet words nor Soviet belligerency necessarily conveyed an accurate judgment of the Kremlin's intention or ultimate purpose. Soviet words, whatever the sweeping nature of the goals which they envisaged, required no price of the nation. Perhaps they were meant less for foreign than for domestic consumption. There remained the possibility, moreover, that Soviet policy itself, as divorced from the verbal assumption of ultimate Communist victory, had not transcended the traditional goals of the Tsars—the quest for warm-water ports and maximum security against invasion from the West. It remained the contention of many American scholars that the Soviet Union confronted the West, not with the prospects of world revolution, but rather with historic policies of imperialism.

There was much in the United States-Soviet conflict that flowed logically from the past. Such extended struggles had been common enough in history, for great nations had usually found themselves in competition for prestige and security, sea lanes and natural resources, markets and even empires. That such a rivalry would eventually embrace the United States and Russia had been predicted for over a century. In the 1830s Alexis de Tocqueville, the brilliant French critic of American democracy, pointed to the two nations as the great powers of the future, and observed that "each of these seems to be marked out by the will of heaven to sway the destinies of half the globe." In the next decade Alexander Herzen, the noted Russian writer, denied that human destiny was nailed to Western Europe. He saw in the United States and Russia two young, vigorous nations which were preparing themselves to wield the power that once belonged to Europe. It seemed inescapable that these two aspiring giants, with their extensive territories, temperate climates, energetic populations, and abundant resources, would come to the forefront of world politics as major contestants for prestige and power. In a sense the Soviet-American conflict in the postwar world was a traditional struggle, conducted in a historic context, the mere fulfillment of prophecy. Richard W. Van Alstyne, in the third selection, has traced United States-Russian relations from the early nineteenth century, accepting, in the context of long-established diplomatic relations, the finite nature of the cold war.

Another significant body of historians, the New Left revisionists, viewed the burgeoning Soviet-American conflict less as a finite confrontation reflecting predictable big-power rivalry than as the product of misguided United States expansionism. Writing largely in the 1960s, this group condemned the United States government for not recognizing Soviet security interests in Eastern Europe. They attributed the hard-line policy, aimed at the elimination of Soviet political and economic dominance from East-Central Europe, not to the American principle of self-determination—the desire to extend the borders of freedom—but to the perennial American resistance to exclusive trading practices wherever they might exist. As Walter LaFeber expressed it, "Since becoming a major power, the United States had viewed anything resembling Stalin's fence as incompatible with American objectives." For some revisionists it was the country's capitalist economy and its addiction to overproduction that compelled it to adopt expansionist policies. For others the responsibility for United States aggressiveness toward Eastern Europe lay less in American capitalism than in the nation's postwar leadership.

Revisionists accused President Truman of reversing Roosevelt's wartime approach to Russia and inaugurating the new era of toughness. What compelled Truman and his associates to reject spheres of influence, according to the revisionist model, was the fear that any regional hegemony would limit United States commerce and plunge the nation into a postwar depression. "We cannot go through another 10 years like the 10 years at the end of the twenties and the beginning of the thirties," Dean Acheson told a congressional committee in 1944, "without having the most far-reaching consequences upon our economic and social system. . . . So far as I know, no group which has studied the problem . . . has ever believed that our domestic markets could absorb our entire production under our present system." William Clayton, Assistant Secretary of State for Economic Affairs, warned Congress in March 1945 that unless the United States exported three times as much as it exported before the war, it would not keep its industry running at capacity. Still, any policy aimed at Eastern Europe had no chance of success. The United States had no economic or security interests in that region worth the price of another war. This fact alone would destroy the effectiveness of any threat, even one anchored to the American atomic monopoly, designed to free the Slavic states of Soviet control. Thus the New Left charged not only that the hard line failed to achieve its objectives but, even worse, that it revealed an American aggressiveness toward the U.S.S.R. which eventually broke up the Big Three alliance. William Appleman Williams develops this revisionist theme in the fourth selection.

Whether the judgment of American scholars followed the more orthodox revisionism of those who defined the Soviet challenge in historic Russian terms or the unorthodox revisionism of those who interpreted Soviet behavior as a response to United States aggressiveness, the judgment argued that the U.S.S.R. was a limited, largely nonideological threat to Western society. By early 1946, however, many American officials and writers viewed the danger posed by Russia as ideological, global, insatiable, and limitless. During January James V. Forrestal, Secretary of the Navy, confided his fears of the Soviets to his diary: "Our task is . . . complicated by the fact that we are trying to preserve a world in which a capitalistic-democratic method can continue, whereas if the Russian adherence to truly Marxian dialectics continues their interest lies in a collapse of this system." Forrestal wondered whether columnist Walter Lippmann was correct in assuming that communism and democracy could coexist satisfactorily. "To me," he addressed Lippmann on January 7, "the fundamental question . . . is whether we are dealing with a nation or a religion—a religion after all being merely the practical extension of philosophy." William C. Bullitt, former ambassador to Russia, expanded this view in his book of 1946, *The Great Globe Itself.* "As conquest of the earth for Communism is the objective of the Soviet Government," he wrote, "no nation lies outside the scope of its ambitions."

Prompted by Stalin's ominous speech of February 1946, which called for a huge arms program to defend the U.S.S.R. against any eventuality, the State Department asked Goerge F. Kennan, then Chargé d'Affaires at the American Embassy in Moscow, to produce an analysis of Soviet behavior. Before the end of February, Kennan wrote from Moscow: "The Kremlin's neurotic view of world affairs is the traditional and instinctive Russian sense of insecurity. . . . Russian rulers . . . have learned to seek security only in patient but deadly struggle for the total destruction of rival power, never in compacts and compromises with it." The discrepancies between official Soviet propaganda and the obvious facts of international life indicated, wrote Kennan, "that the Soviet party line is not based on any objective analysis of the situation beyond Russia's borders; that it has, indeed, little to do with conditions outside of Russia; that it arises mostly from inner Russian necessities which existed before the recent war and exist today." The dogma of "insoluble social conflict" was designed less to defend objectives abroad than to keep the Soviet despotism in power at home. Soviet motivations, Kennan explained, resulted from the same sense of instability and insecurity which beset the Tsars. "Russian rulers," he wrote, "have invariably sensed that their rule was relatively archaic in form, fragile and artificial in its psychological foundation, unable to stand comparison or contact with political systems of Western countries. For this reason they have always feared foreign penetration, feared direct contact between the Western world and their own, feared what would happen if Russians learned the truth about the world without or if foreigners learned the truth about the world within."

Kennan warned the administration in Washington that the Kremlin would exert unrelenting pressure on the international system in an effort to undermine its opposition. It would accept no permanent modus vivendi with the United States until it had achieved the disruption of Western society. "This political force," ran Kennan's conclusion, "has complete power of disposition over the energies of one of the world's greatest peoples and the resources of the world's richest national territory." No longer, he believed, could the West escape a long-term struggle for power and position with the Soviet Union, especially since the Kremlin leaders believed victory throughout the world predetermined and inevitable, but he carefully avoided any suggestion of policy that would terminate the struggle on Western terms. Kennan elaborated these views in his noted Mr. "X" article which appeared in *Foreign Affairs* (July 1947). This perennially relevant evaluation of the Soviet problem comprises the fifth selection.

IV

Increasingly the strident references to an ideology that promised no less than ultimate global victory for communism created an intellectual dilemma in the non-Soviet world of vast proportions, for an adequate Western response to the Soviet challenge demanded a reasonably accurate knowledge of not only the Kremlin's intention but also of the relationship between that intention and actual Soviet power. Students of the Soviet Union searched the Russian record to determine the respective roles of Tsarist tradition and Soviet dogma in directing the considerable energies of the U.S.S.R. in that nation's conflict with the Western world.

American writers, editors, politicians, and officials, unable to establish any consensus on either the nature of the Soviet danger or the resultant demands which the U.S.S.R. imposed on United States performance, disagreed violently over the matter of a proper national response. The containment policies of the Truman administration—especially the Truman Doctrine, the Marshall Plan, and NATO—comprised the fundamental strategy of the United States in the cold war. Prompted by the fear of further Soviet expansion in the late forties, these policies aimed at the unification and strengthening of the West as the surest means of preventing aggression and avoiding war. They assumed, moreover, that the containment of Soviet power over a reasonable period of years would produce tensions within the Soviet structure, force modifications in Soviet ambitions, and eventually permit the West to achieve a world that satisfied both its security requirements and its principles of self-determination. The Truman leadership based its posture vis-à-vis the U.S.S.R. on the assumption that the advantages of time and purpose favored the West. Containment implied the eventual rollback of the Iron Curtain. This anticipation of success ruled out the necessity of negotiating with the Kremlin on the basis of spheres of influence.

Unfortunately the military containment of Russia failed to achieve the grandiose expectations attached to it. The moral and physical power required to frustrate Soviet purpose in most European areas of dispute proved to be illusive. The United States demonstrated its capacity to maintain the status quo where it appeared essential; it did not demonstrate the power to alter it appreciably. Containment offered nothing to a divided Germany or Korea. Nor had it any applicability to the revolutionary upheavals of Asia and Africa which sprang from indigenous conditions rather than Communist aggression. Containment evolved into a package of means without any clearly defined body of ends which might be achieved through the mere possession of military power.

When military containment failed to bring freedom automatically to the Iron Curtain countries, critics charged that the Truman policies merely relegated the captive peoples of Europe to permanent suppression. John Foster Dulles, who became Secretary of State in January 1953, represented the burgeoning conviction that the United States could do better. He possessed a deep sense of the importance of moral force in international affairs and supreme confidence in the ultimate triumph of principle. In his article, "A Policy of Boldness," published in *Life* on May 19, 1952, he developed the concept that the nation had available moral resources that could topple the Soviet imperial structure. He cast aside the Truman administration's concept of limited power and long-range expectation as inadequate for the nation. Mr. Dulles charged that American policy was not even de-signed to win a conclusive victory in the cold war. It was conceived less to eliminate the Soviet peril than to live with it "presumably forever." The time had come, he wrote, to develop a *dynamic* foreign policy that conformed to *moral* principles. American policy must move beyond containment; it must anticipate the "liberation" of those who lived under compulsion behind the Iron Curtain.

Again in the Republican platform of 1952 Mr. Dulles promised a program that would "mark the end of the negative, futile and im-moral policy of 'containment' which abandons countless human be-ings to a despotism and godless terrorism which in turn enables the rulers to forge the captives into a weapon for our destruction." Mr. Dulles made clear his program as Secretary of State in an address before the Four-H Clubs Congress in November 1954: "Liberation normally comes from within. But it is more apt to come from within if hope is constantly sustained from without. This we are doing in many ways." The concept of liberation demanded above all that the United States shun any settlement that would recognize Soviet control over alien peoples. To that extent liberation varied little in the realm of diplomacy from the established precepts of containment. Moreover, the concept of liberation so completely overlooked the essential ele-ment of means that it could not serve as the basis of national action even when supported by massive revolutions behind the Iron Curtain. Major uprisings in both Poland and Hungary in 1956 demonstrated its total inefficacy as national policy.

The perennial failure of either containment or liberation to dispose of any of the cold war issues dividing the world sent Americans during the late fifties in search for alternative courses of action. For some, such as George F. Kennan, who expected less of American policy, disengagement in Europe offered a feasible program for allay-ing world tensions. If the Soviet system possessed an unanticipated resiliency to internal and external change, plus the technology and industrial power to compete successfully with the West in the har-nessing of destructive power and even to surpass the United States in some areas of rocketry, then liberation could be achieved only on Soviet terms. To alter the status quo and bring an element of free-dom to the nations of Eastern Europe, Kennan in his Reith Lectures over the BBC late in 1957 argued for a Soviet and Western with-drawal of military forces from a neutralized belt across the heart of Europe. One concomitant of such an agreement would be a unified, but neutral, Germany. Western leaders, however, preferred the stability which military containment, guaranteed by actual American involvement in Europe, assured a divided continent, to the more flexible and less predictable concept of disengagement.

Others, accepting Soviet ideology as a long-term, mortal threat to all liberal and democratic values, attacked postwar American policy because it had not undermined the enemy. They interpreted Soviet diplomatic intransigence as evidence of an inner Soviet conviction that history was on its side. Indeed, Russian obstinacy brought to mind the Bolshevik Revolution and the disturbing phrases of Marx, Lenin, and other proponents of world revolution. For many Americans the Kremlin was merely taking its cue from the precepts of Marx published in the *New York Tribune* on September 18, 1952:

> *Surprise your antagonists while their forces are scattering, prepare new successes, however small, but daily; keep up the moral ascendancy which the first successful rising has given to you, rally those vacillating elements to your side which always follow the strongest impulse, and which always look out for the safer side; force your enemies to retreat before they can collect their strength against you; in the words of Danton, the greatest master of revolutionary policy yet known, de l'audace, de l'audace, encore de l'audace!*

Marx's exhortation, "You have a world to win," comprised for James Burnham, in *The Struggle for the World* (1947), a succinct and accurate statement of Soviet intent. It was essential, he declared, that the American people take the threat at face value. The world was ripe for revolution and the Soviet leaders were driven toward its accomplishment by both the considerable power at their disposal and the need to divert the attention of the Russian people from their domestic problems. Such characterizations of Soviet motives and strategy predicted that the Kremlin would maintain an interminable pressure on the free world until either communism dominated the earth or more aggressive, purposeful Western policies penetrated and undermined the Soviet structure. In a global struggle the United States had no choice but to win totally or be destroyed. For that reason an enduring and meaningful peace could come only when the power of communism had been uprooted.

Bertram D. Wolfe presented his estimate of the Soviet Union in *The New Leader* of January 26, 1959: "It is a deadly enemy. It is a deadly enemy because never for a moment does it abandon its two basic aims: to remake man, and to conquer the world. It is particularly our enemy—not because we so choose, but because it has chosen. It regards the strength and the way of life of the United States as the chief obstacle to its plan to. remake its own people and to remake the world in the image of its blueprint." Any effort of the United States to disengage itself from an area of conflict, Wolfe warned, would merely move the battle closer to American shores. Because the Soviets would never concede their goal of world conquest, every maneuver to mitigate tension was tantamount to undermining the will of the Western world to protect its own interests and freedoms.

At the heart of the continuing search for the meaning of the Soviet challenge was the question of the role of ideology in determining actual Soviet behavior. Neither experience nor the accumulation of knowledge in any manner mitigated the Western argument on this central question. Few would deny that ideology had some significance, if only that it rendered any reasonable settlement of cold war issues exceedingly difficult. But whereas some insisted that dogma comprised the only valid indication of Soviet intention, others attributed to ideology the task of rationalizing policies determined by fundamental interests and necessities. Three readings (six through eight), selected from a voluminous and impressive body of literature on the Soviet Union, illustrate three major, if not all-encompassing, concepts of the Soviet enigma.

V

Nikita Khrushchev's new course in international affairs after 1956 reflected a pragmatic evaluation of the world scene. Plagued by unending criticism from within the Soviet structure, the Russian leader never presented his program as a complete body of thought. Yet the essentials of post-Stalinist Soviet foreign policy were quite identifiable. Khrushchev recognized that Soviet expansion had reached a dead end under the decisions of the late Stalin era. Western policies of containment had brought considerable stability to Europe. What remained among Kremlin objectives still within the realm of the achievable was the further consolidation of the empire. Unlike Stalin, Khrushchev was prepared to recognize the legitimacy of neutralism among the Afro-Asian nations and to come to terms with their nationalist governments as the only means whereby he might direct their energies against the West. Khrushchev, moreover, was determined to end the open Soviet conflict with Yugoslavia and the scarcely hidden tension with China. Actually the dramatic switch to the policy of de-Stalinization in February 1956 shook the unity of the Communist ranks abroad to a degree which Khrushchev had not anticipated.

Fundamentally Khrushchev's innovations reflected a conviction that military policy was meaningless under conditions of nuclear stalemate. Further Soviet triumphs in the international realm, therefore, required the avoidance of armed conflict and the confining of the cold war to a peaceful competition between the socialistic and capitalistic systems in the area of actual performance. As Khrushchev declared before the Austrian-Soviet Society in July 1960:

> *I have said many times in my speeches that it is necessary to insure peaceful coexistence, irrespective of the basis—capitalist or socialist—on which the statehood of this or that people is built. In our time the capitalist and socialist countries must coexist in order to prevent war, so that all disputes are settled peacefully, through discussion and not through war.*

In demilitarizing Soviet policy Khrushchev gave it an unlimited objective, for he again promised the Communist conquest of the globe, not through the limited efficacy of military might or even the gospel of Marx and Lenin, but through the superior technology and productivity of the U.S.S.R., operating abroad through policies of trade, aid, and investment, This new doctrine of "peaceful coexistence," with its assurance of ultimate Soviet victory, Khrushchev explained fully in *Foreign Affairs* (October 1959). This exposition is presented in the ninth selection.

For those who took the global threat of Soviet ideology seriously, Khrushchev's proposal of "peaceful coexistence" comprised little but a more determined, more varied, and more insidious assault on the free world. Peaceful coexistence, they warned, meant only the ultimate triumph of the Communist system. It would not lead to peace or even to coexistence. Those who would accept the Soviet challenge simply underestimated the nature of the enemy, his power, his ruthlessness, his determination to conquer the world and refashion human society. What was especially troublesome to those who studied the Soviet rhetoric carefully was the identification of coexistence in Asia and Africa with the encouragement of wars of national liberation. "The Communists fully support such wars," Khrushchev admitted in 1961, "and march in the front rank with peoples waging liberation struggles." Clearly Khrushchev's definition of coexistence legitimized the limited employment of force in the turbulent subcontinents. Soviet strategy of coexistence seemed obvious enough. By keeping alive the threat of nuclear destruction, the Kremlin would retain maximum maneuverability in limited war situations. In the tenth selection Philip E. Mosely revealed the aggressive mood and limitless expectation of the Soviet concept of peaceful coexistence and suggested its uselessness as a means of eliminating the cold war from world politics.

In the eleventh selection, on the other hand, Frederick L. Schuman again limited the Soviet challenge to considerations attributable to historic Russian fears and ambitions. For him the United States had no available alternative except war to coexistence even on Soviet terms. Nor did this more conservative evaluation of the cold war regard either the values or the security of the United States necessarily jeopardized by the acceptance of Khrushchev's challenge of coexistence, defined by G. L. Arnold in *The Pattern of World Conflict* (1955) as "competitive attempts to alter the balance of power without overt resort to force."

VI

Khrushchev's policies, with their broadened techniques and extended reach, were far more ambitious than those of Stalin. Still, Khrushchev's most troublesome behavior, especially his threats that created the Berlin crisis of 1958–1959, reflected Soviet fears of a united, nuclear-armed West Germany and an increasingly antagonistic China. When John F. Kennedy assumed the American presidency in January 1961, the chief disruptive issues in United States-Soviet relations were still Berlin, the two Germanies, and the continued Soviet control of the Slavic states. Despite the defensive quality in Khrushchev's European policies, Kennedy viewed the U.S.S.R. as an immediate danger to American security. Preoccupied with the building of a more balanced defense force, he spent much of his first two presidential years in fanning the tensions of the cold war. His inaugural address sounded the alarm of the Soviet danger; his State of the Union message even more so. His approval of the Bay of Pigs invasion demonstrated a fear of Soviet encroachment. In May 1961, he warned newspaper editors and publishers assembled at the White

House that the United States was in the most critical period of its history. His reaction to Khrushchev's ultimatum on Berlin at Vienna in June was traumatic. His report to the American people was so terror-ridden that it produced a war psychology. Such anti-Sovietism caused many to question the President's judgment.

Why Washington perpetuated the cold war rhetoric amid conditions of growing international stability is clear enough. Two factors had circumscribed the Soviet-American antagonism: the absence of vital interests in conflict and the fear of mutual extinction. Successive Washington administrations, in emphasizing the deterrent effect of nuclear arsenals, had placed United States security on the altar of power. Unfortunately the external gains of power—whether economic or military—can be measured only in the diminution of the challenges which prompted the initial creation of power. Inasmuch as the Soviet danger of the immediate postwar years never lent itself to tested, precise definition, the changes wrought in Europe by more than a decade of containment conveyed convictions of security only to those who had always regarded the U.S.S.R. as fundamentally a status quo power, at least in its postwar relationship to Europe. But for those Americans—many of them in high places—who identified United States security with the uprooting of Communist power as well as Communist intent, the gains of twenty years had augmented Western security little if at all.

As late as the sixties many United States officials refused to accept the considerable normalization of Europe's political and economic life as a measure of increased security or a demonstration of limited Soviet ambition. To them ten years of European stability had not undermined the Kremlin's continuing ideological imperative to wage war on the capitalist states by all means short of military force. Senator Barry Goldwater's perennial demand for total victory in the cold war reflected such an assessment of the Soviet threat. Washington's failure to pursue victory openly, he charged, exposed "an official timidity that refuses to recognize the all-embracing determination of communism to capture the world and destroy the United States." In his inaugural President Kennedy warned, "We dare not tempt them [the Russians] with weakness. For only when our arms are sufficient can we be certain beyond doubt that they will never be employed." Secretary of State Dean Rusk declared as late as September 1963: "There can be no assured and lasting peace until Communist leaders abandon their goal of world revolution." As long as Soviet leaders sustained their verbal commitment to world domination, many Americans would regard competitive coexistence synonymous with cold war.

Still, Kennedy, burdened with the responsibility of managing the nuclear deterrent, moved toward negotiations with the Russians on the issues of nuclear testing and proliferation. But what created the turning point in the Kennedy-Khrushchev relationship was the Cuban missile crisis of October 1962. Why the Soviet leader accepted the risk of a nuclear confrontation by planting intermediate-range missiles on Cuban soil is not certain. Stalinist forces in Russia demanded a tougher Soviet posture toward the United States; the Cubans pushed for a Soviet guarantee against an American invasion. Perhaps more important to Khrushchev, however, was the hope that a strategic advantage in Cuba might enable the Kremlin to force some American concessions on Germany. Kennedy's deliberate countermeasures were forceful enough to eliminate the missiles, but not enough to force a showdown with Khrushchev. Both men recoiled from the nuclear brinkmanship, conscious of the responsibility which they carried for humanity. Thereafter both Kennedy and Khrushchev spoke more insistently of the need to avoid nuclear war. By 1963 Kennedy had become aware of the greater fluidity in international life and had made clear his determination to bring United States policy into conformity with it.

Increasingly the record of coexistence on terms generally acceptable to the major powers of the world questioned the seriousness of the assumptions of ultimate victory encompassed by the war of words. The prospects for diplomatic settlement which would recognize formally the essential requirements for successful coexistence continued to appear elusive if not necessarily unattainable, for both Washington and Moscow still pursued revisionist goals totally unacceptable to the other. Yet as long as neither side actively sought war, some room existed for the reduction of tension through highly skilled diplomacy. "To succeed," Barrington Moore, Jr. wrote as early as 1950, "this diplomacy would have to part company with the parochial moralism that has characterized much American negotiation and free itself from the miasma of dogmatic suspicion likely to become chronic on the Russian side." In the absence of any genuine diplomatic settlements, the cold war could terminate either in war or in the gradual erosion of the ambitions of one or both contestants through the process of endless retreat from goals established by national dogma. Norman A. Graebner, in the twelfth reading, notes both the historic elusiveness of peace based on destructive power alone and the futility of avoiding negotiation on issues that could be eliminated only through war.

The erosion of ambitions that gradually eased the tensions of United States-Soviet relations first occurred within the Communist bloc itself. During the sixties it became increasingly clear that the earlier assumptions of unity in world communism, which in turn sustained images of Soviet power that extended far beyond the reach of Russian armies, had never been particularly accurate. The loss of Yugoslavia in 1948, the repression of Hungary in 1956 and Czechoslovakia in 1968, demonstrated that the authority of the U.S.S.R. extended as far as its tanks would go. That the Soviets could sustain a Communist monolith on free consent was always an illusion. The decision of Leonid Brezhnev, Khrushchev's successor, to repress the Czech government made clear the power of the Kremlin to impose some measure of conformity on Eastern Europe in defense of its own interests. The Brezhnev Doctrine of November 1968 carried Soviet pretensions in Eastern Europe beyond any previous declaration. Said the Soviet leader: "When the internal and external forces hostile to Socialism seek to turn back the development of any Socialist country toward the restoration of the Capitalist order . . . this is no longer only a problem of the people of that country, but also a common problem of concern for all Socialist countries." The doctrine warned the westerly Communist states against edging too far either toward political and economic liberalization, as had Alexander Dubček's Czechoslovakia, or toward excessive commercial and political relations with the West. But if Slavic Europe remained the Kremlin's private preserve, it was not monolithic. Rumania, Hungary, and Poland, careful not to threaten Soviet security with anti-Soviet policies or ideologies, had long enjoyed some degree of independence.

Elsewhere the Soviet Union still controlled a number of parties out of power, but the degree of control was inversely proportional to the importance of these parties in the life of their own countries, to the size of their membership, and to the influence of their leaders. The differences which existed between Communist leaders on matters of foreign policy, organization, and strategy, as well as the opportunities which dissension created for individual Communist parties to express their national preferences, suggested that what remained of international communism would never recover its cohesion. "Indeed," wrote Alex Nove of the University of Glasgow in 1970, "not only is the world Communist movement no longer monolithic, but it is arguable whether it exists at all." Similarly Klaus Mehnert, editor of *Osteuropa,* concluded: "I find it easier to imagine all Christians accepting Pope Paul VI than all Communists following Brezhnev. . . ."

If much of the change within the Soviet bloc was organizational, the important Sino-Soviet split reflected historic and ideological conflicts as well. The split did not necessarily weaken either Russia or China militarily, but it created for each a new powerful antagonist and thereby reduced the image of both as dangers to Western interests. Policies justified in terms of international communism seemed increasingly divorced from reality. Hans J. Morgenthau, in the thirteenth reading, has delimitated both the restraints and the issues that encompassed United States-Soviet relations at the dawn of the seventies.

VII

Behind the march to the summit meetings of the seventies was a half decade of accumulating conviction that the cold war drift had ceased to serve the interests of either the United States or the U.S.S.R. The overriding concern of the two superpowers was the avoidance of nuclear war. Beyond that was the mutual desire to curb the ruinous arms race. For the Kremlin the questions of economics and security included as well greater access to Western technology to close the overall scientific-technological gap between the U.S.S.R. and the United States, Western Europe, and Japan. The Soviets, moreover, desired trade agreements, with ample American credits and most-favored-nation status, to compensate for Russia's grain shortages. During the late sixties China emerged as a special threat to the Soviet Union. The perennial danger of confrontation along the Sino-Soviet frontier exposed Russia's western flank where the Soviet hegemony contributed little security against West Germany. In 1969 one young Russian complained of Soviet policy: "In two world wars, [the Germans] nearly defeated us even while fighting on two fronts. But now, it is we who have arranged to have enemies on two fronts—7,000 miles apart—and to have antagonized nearly all the nations of the world capable of helping our sick economy." It was not strange that Moscow favored détente with the United States and Western Europe.

For the United States also the cold war had become a costly endeavor. The expenditure of some $1.3 trillion over a quarter century had purchased neither peace nor security, and the end of the expenditure was nowhere in sight. Despite the cold war demands on American resources and emotions, responsible officials no longer agreed in the late sixties on what the effort could or should accomplish. Twenty years of cold war tensions and expenditures did not eliminate Russian power or the Soviet hegemony from Eastern Europe. Nor was it clear what policies would recognize Russia's legitimate security interests or best reassure Europe against the power and ambition of a united Germany. Self-determination was not selective enough to serve as a guide for Western policy. Soviet ideology continued to create an ambivalence in the American willingness to accept coexistence in principle. Still the West could neither eliminate the Soviet adherence to Communist dogma nor identify its interests with the success or failure of the Soviet experiment. Finally, the decades of cold war without victory over either Soviet power or Soviet ideology demonstrated that American security and well-being, as well as that of most countries of the world, did not require the restoration of the Versailles order after all. In Europe containment had won. As an end it had stabilized the division of Europe with vengeance. As a means to an end—the negotiation of a new order in Europe—it had failed simply because no Western military structure could undo the Soviet political and territorial gains which flowed from Hitler's collapse.

Despite such ubiquitous pressures for a Soviet-American détente, the Moscow summit of May 1972 came hard. As early as his nomination in 1968 Richard M. Nixon promised that his administration would move from confrontation to negotiation with the U.S.S.R. But was Washington prepared to offer terms that recognized the interests and the world position of the Soviet Union? Certainly the Kremlin would not capitulate to the principle of self-determination, and yet the new President quickly made clear that he expected no less. For Nixon the nation's interests demanded the worldwide acceptance of the axiom that national aggrandizement, to be legitimate, had also to be peaceful. "Only a straightforward recognition of that reality," he said, ". . . will bring us to the genuine cooperation which we seek and which the peace of the world requires." But during 1970 the new Soviet aim of increased cooperation with the West became more and more apparent. Brezhnev's speech before the Communist Party Congress in March 1971 established the new direction of Soviet policy. Nixon responded cautiously, determined to work on the broadest possible range of issues to establish relaxation of tension on all fronts.

Meanwhile Western revisionism received its first challenge in West German Chancellor Willy Brandt's *Ostpolitik*. During 1970 Brandt signed treaties with both Moscow and Warsaw which recognized the postwar frontiers of Central Europe. Nixon followed that precedent. During 1971, negotiations in Washington and Moscow settled a number of secondary issues. In May the President announced that an impasse in the Strategic Arms Limitation Talks (SALT) had been broken. Then in August the Big Four, after long and tedious negotiations, reached an agreement on West Berlin. Finally on October 12 the President announced: "In light of the recent advances in bilateral and multilateral negotiations involving the two countries, it has been agreed that a meeting [between the leaders of the United States and the Soviet Union] will take place in Moscow in the latter part of May, 1972." During the spring of 1972 Kissinger flew to Moscow to work out guidelines for the summit conference. Much of this pre-summit negotiation remained highly confidential, but these careful preparations were indispensable to the smoothness and efficiency of the Moscow meeting itself. That the United States and the U.S.S.R. shared a mutuality of interest in going to the summit received reaffirmation, at least in part, in the cordiality which characterized both the private and the formal exchanges between Nixon and Brezhnev.

If the agreements signed were scarcely overwhelming, they were impressive enough. The Soviet and American leaders pledged to strive for a better relationship by binding their two countries together so tightly with joint commitments and projects that only with difficulty could remote conflicts of interest disrupt their mutual resolve to avoid direct confrontations. In a special communique the two leaders accepted a body of principles to guide their countries toward a new era of peace. To achieve a more stable balance of terror at existing nuclear levels the negotiators at Moscow signed two nuclear arms pacts. One limited defensive missiles to two locations; the second froze offensive weapons at current levels for five years. In large measure this nuclear formula had been reached during previous months at the SALT talks. The Nixon-Brezhnev summits of 1973 and 1974 extended the aura of cordiality and the area of agreement on a wide variety of secondary issues.

Certainly a major landmark in the history of changing Soviet-American relations was the summit meeting held at Helsinki, Finland, in late July of 1975. There President Gerald Ford joined 34 other heads of state to sign a lengthy document produced over the two previous years by the Conference on Security and Cooperation in Europe. The U.S.S.R. and its Warsaw Pact allies had pushed for the all-European conference since 1954, but not until 1971 did they agree to United States and Canadian participation. The document was a statement of intent; it was not a treaty nor a binding agreement under United States constitutional usage. It included ten principles on European security, among them the nonuse of force, the inviolability of frontiers, territorial integrity, nonintervention in the internal affairs of other nations, respect for human rights, and the fulfillment of international obligations. The document provided for economic, scientific, technical, and environmental cooperation; for the freer movement of people and ideas; and for a review conference in Belgrade in 1977. In recognizing officially for the first time the Soviet status in postwar Europe, the United States operated under the assumption that détente, to endure, had to be beneficial to all sides.

VIII

For many writers, scholars, and even statesmen the cold war died amid the trends and events of the sixties and seventies. The changes wrought by a quarter century of relative peace and stability were profound. Whether they eliminated the cold war remained a matter of definition. Those who could not agree on the meaning of the cold war could scarcely agree on the moment of its beginning or ending, especially when the specific objects pursued in the name of the cold war had hardly been achieved at all. Obviously the cold war had ended for those who believed that the world had reached a desirable state, at least in terms of national intent and capabilities. If the cold war meant, as many argued, a struggle for the destruction of the power, ambition, and ideology of either the United States or the U.S.S.R., then the struggle had no foundation in reality; it never existed or would never end. Even the more limited goals of world leadership and absolute security proved to be beyond reach, and with the failure of such purpose came, for many, a failure of pretension. Accepting this analysis Ronald Steel could write in September

1972: "The Cold War is dead and the autopsies have begun." Senator Mike Mansfield concluded in July 1973 that Nixon and Brezhnev had changed the international climate sufficiently to put an end to the cold war.

Other Americans were not convinced. Whereas the Soviets had always behaved prudently, many analysts denied that the U.S.S.R. had become a status quo power. While the United States had retreated from many of its cold war ambitions, some warned, the U.S.S.R. had increased its commitments. The Soviet Union continued to proclaim an ideology hostile to Western principles and to maintain its passion for secrecy, its preoccupation with internal security, its suspicion of foreigners, and armed forces much larger than any visible danger seemed to justify. Some charged that the chief Soviet purpose was to mislead the West and gain preponderance over the United States militarily and politically. Even behind the new civility and sophistication in Soviet diplomacy, one American official complained, was always the search for "the marginal advantage." Nothing in the East-West experience had established an atmosphere of openness and mutual trust. What accounted for this failure, in part, was the Soviet system itself. In terms of human rights the Soviet Union had made little progress; and a leadership was scarcely trustworthy that did not trust its own people.

Some American experts doubted that the U.S.S.R. had any interest in an orderly world. Harvard Professor Richard Pipes warned the Senate Subcommittee on Arms Limitations: "The Soviet elite tends to think in terms of perpetual conflict pitting right against wrong, from which only one side can emerge victorious. . . . Russian ideology with its stress on class warfare culminating in a vast revolutionary cataclysm neatly reinforces this. . . . Soviet behavior is motivated by fear . . . only the fear is not of other people but of its own and for that reason it is incapable of being allayed by concessions. Fear breeds insecurity which in turn expresses itself . . . in aggressive behavior." In a similar vein, Columbia University's Zbigniew Brezezinski wrote that "the fear of contagion . . . makes the Communist systems of the Leninist-Stalinist variety, which thrive on hostility, shrink away from unrestricted East-West collaboration." Professor Leonard Schapiro of the London School of Economics warned Americans in July 1970: "Soviet policy is unremittingly dynamic. It is not directed toward achieving equilibrium, or balance of forces, or peace, or collective security, or certain specific concrete objectives; its ultimate aim is 'victory,' which means Communist rule on a world scale.''

Critics feared that the Kremlin's softer approach was designed to encourage Europe's historic forces of rivalry and fragmentation. Anthony Eden warned in January 1973: ''It must never be forgotten that Russia's objective is to pry apart the countries of NATO and to establish herself as the dominating power over Europe. The continuing buildup of Russian military power in Europe by land, sea and air supports this purpose and cannot be explained otherwise.'' The West, declared proponents of Western unity, was in danger of overstressing its adversary relations at the price of undermining the established community of the developed nations. Such analysts believed that strong economic and military ties among the world's great trading states—especially the United States, Western Europe, and Japan—remained the key to enduring world stability. For them the cooperative community of the capitalist countries still merited higher priority than did détente with the U.S.S.R.

Soviet naval expansion in the sixties posed an unprecedented, yet vaguely understood, threat to Western leadership by transforming Russia for the first time into a truly global power. By the early seventies new, sleek Soviet warships and submarines had established a strong Russian presence in the Mediterranean and South Asia particularly. Nowhere were the prospects bright for confining Soviet influence. Senator Henry Jackson, Democrat of Washington, warned the nation in 1970 that the U.S.S.R. ''is now, for the first time in Russian history, a *global military power.* Looking ahead, the somber prospect is a Soviet Union increasingly bolder in its policies and more disposed to throw its military weight around to support its great power interests and to extend Soviet influence into new areas of the world.'' Others, however, believed that Moscow's desire to avoid conflict would dictate restraint and the avoidance of abrasive situations. To George F. Kennan, writing in the fourteenth selection, the U.S.S.R. was behaving like a great power—something which that country, no less than the Western naval powers, had a right to do. Beyond that he believed the constraints on Soviet policy had eliminated the danger of war and the rationality for the Soviet-American military rivalry.

Finally, some Americans questioned the significance of détente. Except for some reassurance to Americans who were tired of overseas burdens and desired greater international stability, détente seemed to offer few clear benefits to the United States. The SALT agreements stabilized the arms race at a lower threshold of anxiety, but they had little effect on the United States military budget. Trade increased, but without a mutually beneficial commercial relationship, for Soviet goods would find few markets in the United States. Perhaps the United States lost little in legitimatizing the Soviet hegemony, but George W. Ball believed that American policy should have displayed at least a color of morality. As he wrote in a *Newsweek* article of August 4, 1975: "It is one thing to refrain from starting World War III over Prague; it is quite another to drink toasts to the division of Europe and implicitly sanctify with banal phrases Germany's continued amputation. Should we not, at least, insist on the evil nature of the Berlin wall—that it is not a fortification to keep invaders out; it is a cage the Russians built to imprison peoples who would opt for freedom?" Kennan reminded the nation that every administration since the thirties had favored some improvement in United States-Russian relations. If the results under Nixon were more favorable, they were largely attributable to favorable changes in circumstances. The summit meetings themselves, he thought, contributed little to the improvements. European leaders, who generally deplored the public relations aspect of international diplomacy, tended to respond with cynicism, anxiety, or admonitions of caution.

Washington officials defended détente by noting that the avoidance of a major war turned on the Soviet-American relationship. Whatever the nature of the big-power antagonisms or the character of the U.S.S.R., there still was no alternative to peace. The existence of the United States depended on an environment in which competitors could regulate and restrain their differences. Secretary of State Kissinger repeatedly reminded the nation that the Nixon and Ford administrations harbored no illusions about the Soviet system. Both administrations, he insisted, judged every movement in United States-Soviet relations, not by agreements signed, but by responsible international conduct. It was the premise of détente that neither the United States nor the U.S.S.R. could expect to impose its will on the other without running an intolerable risk. To those who questioned both the wisdom and the morality of recognizing the Soviet hegemony in Eastern Europe, Kissinger replied in a news conference of late July 1975: "What is more helpful for a humane evolution: a policy of confrontation or a policy of easing tensions; whether peoples can realize their aspirations better under conditions in which there is . . . a threat of military conflict, or under conditions in which the two sides are attempting to settle their disputes and ease tensions. . . ."

Perhaps détente came too late. For the world of the seventies had already grown too complex, too economically interrelated, the underdeveloped world too demanding, allies too independent to be harnessed by superpower diplomacy. Neither Washington nor Moscow had the competence to deal with problems of inflation and financial chaos, depression and unemployment, impoverishment and famine. Long before the mid-seventies, moreover, it was clear that the superpowers could not prevent lesser nations from asserting their primary interests. Détente could not terminate the Vietnam war before Saigon's collapse; nor could it control events elsewhere. Still, for Marshall D. Shulman, in the fifteenth and final reading, the new issues which plagued international society permitted the United States no escape from responsibility, for any economic and political disintegration within the Western states would create opportunities for exploitation by the Kremlin. The Soviet challenge to Western institutions still lay in their ability to dispose of domestic social and economic problems realistically, and to respond hopefully to the prodding of the less affluent countries. The United States possessed the physical and intellectual resources to meet the Soviet danger with reasonable and adequate success. Whether the American people possessed the necessary national purpose and resolution to accept the burdens imposed by the challenges of energy, inflation, food, and resources remained the crucial and still unanswered question.

Perhaps the trends in world politics after the mid-sixties did not eliminate the cold war, but they diverted the course of the conflict. The conversion of the historic East-West confrontation into a condition of genuine stability required at some time a transfer of emphasis from deterrence to adjustment. The Great Contest, whether sustained by fear or ambition, still prevented both the United States and the U.S.S.R. from limiting their essential requirements to the existing order. But a myriad of mutually beneficial negotiations had circumscribed what remained of the lingering competition. For the new diplomacy clarified the interest of all nations in peaceful cooperation and elevated the price they would pay for undermining the gains of a quarter century for greater international stability.

I WARTIME ORIGINS OF THE COLD WAR

Staughton Lynd

HOW THE COLD WAR BEGAN

Staughton Lynd finds the inescapable foundations of the Soviet-American conflict in the moralism which underlay the wartime attitudes of the Roosevelt administration toward the postwar status of Eastern Europe. He is especially critical of Secretary of State Cordell Hull's dogged adherence to the principle of self-determination of peoples long after it had been rendered irrelevant by the clearly stated will of a powerful, determined, and essential ally. Throughout the struggle against Germany, Stalin warned the Western governments that he would never again accept a cordon sanitaire of anti-Soviet states along Russia's western periphery. By clinging to the abstract phrases of the Atlantic Charter, Hull consistently promised the Slavic peoples of Europe what no Allied military victory, however decisive, could achieve for them. Through their refusal to pursue a realistic course, concludes Lynd, United States officials set the stage for the predictable break with Russia which followed the collapse of Germany in the spring of 1945.

At the banquet which closed the Yalta Conference, Roosevelt, Churchill, and Stalin all offered toasts. When it came Churchill's turn, he

> *addressed himself to the years ahead. He felt, he said, that all were standing on the crest of a hill with the glories of great future possibilities stretching before them; that in the modern world the function of leadership was to lead the people out from the forests into the broad sunlit plains of peace and happiness. He felt that this prize was nearer their grasp than at any time in history, and that it would be a great tragedy if they, through inertia or carelessness, let it slip from their grasp. History would never forgive them if they did.[1]*

We live today amid the ruins of that hope. Any responsible inquiry into the present controversies between the United States and the Soviet Union must find its way back, from the U-2 to Hungary and Suez, thence to Korea, Czechoslovakia, the Marshall Plan, and the Truman Doctrine, and so, finally, to that time and that failure. In those months of early 1945 which Herbert Feis, in his new book,[2] has

[1] Herbert Feis, *Churchill, Roosevelt, Stalin: The War They Waged and the Peace They Sought* (Princeton, N. J., 1957).
[2] *Between War and Peace: The Potsdam Conference* (Princeton, N. J., 1960).

called "between war and peace," the hard core of difference between East and West is to be found.

None of us can presume to discuss this question without anxiety or passion. One finds it peculiarly difficult to bring to bear on the problem of the cold war the intellectual discipline which, say, the Spanish-American or even the First World War can now readily call forth. The shrill and strained atmosphere, the partisan interpretations of war and quasi-war have been with us for an uninterrupted quarter of a century. We live, move, and have our intellectual being in a habitually clamorous climate of opinion.

Yet how precious would be the gift of seeing the cold war, now, with the kind of perspective which commonly comes only after the passage of much time. There are very few international crises which in the historian's retrospect altogether justify the ideology or behavior of any of the participants. We know today that the War of 1812 began days after, on the other side of the Atlantic, the English Orders in Council which occasioned it had been revoked. Today many of us would be ready to join Henry Thoreau in his Concord jail to protest the war against Mexico. Years after the Spanish-American War, experts examined the torn hull of the battleship *Maine* and concluded that the explosion had taken place not outside the boat but within. The blundering or hypocrisy or chicanery which brought on these wars seems to us today inadmissible. In short, if we could only approximate the historians' collective judgment, a generation hence, concerning the cold war, we might be helped in our understanding of the practical alternatives that are presently before us.

In search of objectivity the American student may attempt to balance the work of Westerners by consulting Soviet accounts. He will be disappointed. It is true that Soviet historians are far more familiar with English, French, and German sources than Westerners are with publications in Russian. For example, V. L. Israelyan's *Diplomatic History of the Great Patriotic War* (Moscow, 1959; in Russian) cites ten American collections of documents and over sixty memoirs and historical works in English. It is also true that the skeleton of events narrated by a work like Israelyan's is full and accurate. But time after time crucial interpretations are woodenly self-justificatory. . . .

One turns back, perforce, to Western scholarship. Here two first-class scholars have been at work: Feis, in the two books already cited, and William McNeill of the University of Chicago, in his brilliant earlier account, *America, Britain and Russia: Their Cooperation and*

Conflict, 1941–1946 (London, 1953). These works have a quasi-official character. Feis's books were, so he tells the reader, in part inspired by Averell Harriman, America's wartime ambassador to the Soviet Union. They draw both on unpublished papers of Harriman's and on the unpublished papers of the State Department (these have just been closed to scholars). McNeill's volume, similarly, was commissioned by the Royal Institute of International Affairs and scrutinized before publication "by a number of individuals familiar with the events narrated." Thus the works of Feis and McNeill are something more than individual interpretations. To a degree they represent the collective memory of British and American officialdom about their wartime alliance with Soviet Russia and how it broke down.

Perhaps because of their quasi-official character the Feis and McNeill books display the same defect as their Soviet counterparts. They narrate, but they do not really interpret. They do not face squarely the childlike and penetrating question, Why did the cold war start? Some of McNeill's sharpest observations are buried in footnotes. Feis concludes *Between War and Peace* with the moving sentence: "To choose life, the great nations must one and all live and act more maturely and trustfully than they did during the months that followed the end of the war against Germany." Moving, but also banal. Feis does not go beneath the surface of events in search of the specific men and motives that obstructed the choice for life, the inarticulate major premises which led each side to a point from which further retreat seemed inadmissible.

To go beneath the surface means, as I have said, going back. The climactic events of the six months after Yalta—the defeat of Germany, the San Francisco and Potsdam conferences, the testing and use of the atom bomb, all shadowed and confused by the death of Roosevelt and the political defeat of Churchill—brought into the open the conflict in objectives between England and America and the Soviet Union. But this conflict had existed in embryo from the first tentative discussions in 1941 to postwar aims among the three military partners. While the war lasted, each side, intensely needful of the other's military aid, tended to avoid direct confrontation of the latent political tensions. Even at Teheran (1943), perhaps the high point of Big Three harmony, McNeill comments that "Allied cooperation could be and was founded upon agreement on military strategy. Agreement on postwar issues was not genuinely achieved. All important decisions were left for the future after only vague exploration of the issues involved." Victory over Germany, together with the decision of the Truman cabinet that Soviet military assistance was not essential to the defeat of Japan, lifted the lid of a Pandora's box.

The characteristic, continuing objectives of each of the three powers had in fact become quite clear within a year of the German attack on the Soviet Union. When the Red Army, to the surprise of the highest military personnel in both England and America, survived into the winter of 1941–42, serious negotiation as to postwar goals began. Then as later Stalin underscored the fact that twice in thirty years Russia had been invaded through Poland, and insisted on a more westerly frontier (incorporation of the Baltic nations and the Curzon Line in Poland) and a friendly postwar Polish government. Then as later Churchill, also thinking in terms of his nation's security, showed himself ready to bargain with the Soviet Union on a *quid pro quo* basis but equally ready to invoke the threat of force if negotiation seemed inadequate; it was at this time that Churchill, having just signed the Atlantic Charter with its promise of democracy for "all the men in all the lands," told Parliament that the phrase was not meant to apply to the British Empire. In December 1941, Foreign Secretary Eden went to Moscow to seek an accommodation of Soviet and British diplomatic objectives.

Here American diplomacy intervened in a way which foreshadowed future Soviet-American tension. That December, and again in May 1942 when Molotov visited London and Washington, Secretary of State Hull brought strong pressure on the English government to avoid territorial commitments until a postwar peace conference. On the latter occasion, indeed, he threatened to issue a public statement dissociating the United States from any such agreement reached between Britain and the Soviet Union. The American objective, for Roosevelt and Hull as for Woodrow Wilson years before, was to prevent dictation to small nations so that they might determine their own destinies through democratic processes; and to substitute for the balance-of-power arrangements which seemed inevitable and natural to America's European partners, an international organization to keep the peace. Thus in the Second as in the First World War, American diplomacy sought nothing less than a diplomatic new deal, an altogether new start in the conduct of international relations.

Not only in objectives but in ways and means American diplomatic behavior in this first year of the war was symptomatic of much that was to follow. Avoiding hard bargaining on specific issues, America sought—in the words of a Hopkins memo—to "take the heat off" the Soviet territorial demands by pushing hard for a second front (as well as by talking of a postwar international organization in terms which were, as Feis says, "vaguely magnificent rather than sturdy"). The United States of course had other substantial reasons for desiring a second front. But both Feis and McNeill make it clear that the Americans found it a "happy coincidence" that the military strategy which they favored, a direct assault on Germany through France, was at the same time the form of assistance which the Soviet Union desired above all others. The American hope, Feis writes, was that "the Soviet government was to be lured away from one bone by a choicer one, away from its absorption in frontiers by the attraction of quick military relief."

By championing the second front and postponing to a later day the inherent conflict between the American concern for worldwide democracy and the Soviet preoccupation with the security of its borders, Roosevelt established himself, by the middle of 1942, as a mediator between Churchill and Stalin. As McNeill observes in a remarkable footnote, this relationship was a personal *tour de force* which rested on a peculiar and indeed artificial basis of fact:

> *The British public was perceptibly warmer in its feeling toward Russia than was the American public, among whom repugnance to socialism and consciousness of Russia's failure to join in the war against Japan were far greater than in Britain. On the other hand, the American Government in general assumed a more indulgent attitude towards Russia on current questions (for instance Lend-Lease), combined with a more rigid attitude on long-range issues (for instance, the question of the Baltic states) than did the British Government. The secret of this curious contradiction lay mainly in the fact that Churchill and Eden, thinking largely in terms of a balance of power, wanted to bargain with Stalin, whereas Roosevelt and Hull thought in terms of abstract principles to which they hoped Stalin could, if treated indulgently enough by his wartime allies, be committed.*

When in 1942 and again in 1943 Roosevelt failed to deliver on a second front, a foundation was laid for future ill-will.

Viewed in this way, Roosevelt's approach to the Soviet Union appears fundamentally similar to that of Wilson and to that of Eisenhower: personalities fall away, and the thread of a shared tradition stands forth. All three Presidents attempted to eschew diplomatic settlements based on a balance of power. Like Wilson at Versailles, and indeed in conscious recoil from Wilson's entanglement in secret wartime agreements, Roosevelt and Hull during World War II sought to brush aside concrete, immediate points of difference in order to establish agreement on general principles of world organization. Feis says of Hull in 1943:

> *Over each disjointed problem the interested and rival powers were poised—ready to contest, bargain and threaten. This had been the customary way in the past by which questions of frontiers, political affiliations and the like got settled. He wanted to bring it about that all such exercises of national power and diplomacy would in the future be subordinated to rules of principle. . . .*

Alike in placing too much reliance on the forms of international organization, Wilson, Roosevelt, and Eisenhower also have shared a tendency to evolve simplistic solutions to the internal problems of foreign nations. For all three men the sovereign nostrum for the domestic ills of other countries has been, "When in doubt, hold a free election." Roosevelt grasped the awakening of the colonial world but conceived it one-sidedly in formal political terms; less than Wendell Willkie did he perceive the universal challenge to the big house on the hill. Land reform, for example, was as germane to the emergence of democracy in Eastern Europe as were free elections. Indeed land reform was a principal bone of contention between the Soviet-sponsored Lublin government and the Polish government-in-exile. Yet the Big Three paid it scant attention in their interminable discussions of the Polish question.

One cannot avoid the suspicion that Roosevelt's intermittent demand for freedom in Eastern Europe did not altogether escape the tragicomic quality of Wilson's insistence that the revolutionary Huerta regime in Mexico conduct a plebiscite on its own legitimacy, or— *reductio ad absurdum*—President Eisenhower's recent proposal for a worldwide referendum on communism and democracy. In each of these instances, the American President expressed a sincere and idealistic concern, but a concern which did not really represent a practical alternative in the given situation. McNeill points out that "neither Roosevelt nor Churchill seems frankly to have faced the fact that, in Poland at least, genuinely free democratic elections would return governments unfriendly to Russia." Therefore, he continues,

> *the democratic process upon which so many eulogies were expended could not produce governments in Eastern Europe (or in many other*

parts of the world) that would further the harmony of the Great Powers and prove acceptable to all of them. Men were not so uniform, so rational, nor possessed of such good will, as the democratic theory presupposed; and in talking of Eastern European governments which would be both democratic and friendly to Russia the Western Powers were in large part deluding themselves.

George Kennan has written in much the same vein of the American Open Door policy in the Far East. "Our constant return to these ideas," Kennan says, "would not serve really to prevent the conflict of interests in China from living themselves out pretty much in accordance with their own strategic, political, and economic necessities." Just so the State Department policy toward Europe during World War II, according to Feis, "tried to arrest the march of armies, the clash of civil wars, the forays of diplomacy by repeated affirmations of the view that principle should govern European postwar settlements."

This syndrome of American attitudes—a syndrome which Walter Lippmann has called "Wilsonian" and E. H. Carr "Utopian," and which has been best characterized by Kennan—threw up significant obstacles to the making of a peace. . . . How similar to latter-day criticisms of American diplomacy's lack of "initiative" are these words of McNeill describing Roosevelt's passivity as the need for postwar decisions bore down on him:

From early in 1942 the American Government had repeatedly proclaimed the principle that no final decisions on matters of postwar frontiers or systems of government should be made until the end of the war. The theory that a political vacuum could be maintained in Europe was absurd on its face; but this principle helped to hide from American officials the daily necessity of making decisions.

American indecision in the closing years of the war diminished the chances for postwar settlements in both Poland and Germany. Long before Hungary, United States foreign policy was encouraging hopes in Eastern Europe which it had no concrete plans to support. Thus, early in 1944 Roosevelt refused to "back in an unambiguous manner" the proposals for Poland agreed on at Teheran, instead

contenting himself with amiable sentiments about "freely negotiated" and "friendly" settlement of the Soviet-Polish dispute. Clearly Roosevelt did not wish to grasp the nettle, hoping that Stalin and the Poles would come to terms of their own accord. But his attitude only confirmed the Poles in their obstinate disregard of the realities of their situation, and allowed them to cling to the belief that Roosevelt would come to their rescue.

"In this instance," McNeill continues, "and throughout the following year, Roosevelt tried to avoid the responsibilities of the new American power, and by not making himself clear to the Poles he stored up trouble for the future." Thus in October 1944, when Mikolajczyk went to Moscow to consult with Churchill and Stalin about Poland, he was astonished to learn that everyone but himself had thought that Roosevelt at Teheran essentially accepted the Curzon Line. At Yalta, Admiral Leahy warned Roosevelt that the vagueness of the accord reached on reorganizing the Polish government would permit the Russians to make their own interpretation: the President could only wearily reply, "I know, Bill, I know."

Of Germany, McNeill writes that "the American Government, because of its internal disputes and indecision, prevented even the discussion of a common Allied policy for Germany." Alarmed by the furor occasioned by the Morgenthau Plan, Roosevelt put a stop to all American efforts to make postwar plans for Germany from late 1944 until his death. "This ostrich attitude towards the future," says McNeill, "prevented whatever chance there may have been for arriving at Allied agreement upon policy towards Germany through the European Advisory Commission or in any other way, and left the subordinate American officials who were charged with the task completely at sea."

In default of an American initiative, what planning for peace took place in 1943–44 consisted chiefly of British and Soviet attempts to divide Europe between them into spheres of influence. The story of these attempts is an important one, for it suggests that the Soviets, like the West, felt in 1945 that past understandings between the Big Three concerning Eastern Europe were betrayed.

The pattern for postwar spheres of influence in the liberated European countries was established in Italy, however, not in Eastern Europe, and by England and America rather than by Russia. In theory the three military partners were committed to joint decision-making and to democratic self-determination within every European country, regardless of whose armies were occupying it. But in fact, the Big Three tacitly recognized and accepted spheres of influence all over the world. In China, Feis writes, "Stalin and Churchill seemed willing to have the American government take the lead in directing the political evolution of that country; and the American government was assuming it. Similarly, it was understood that Britain could be to the fore in dealing with Southeast Asia." And Churchill said of South America: "We follow the lead of the United States in South America as far as possible, as long as it is not a question of our beef and mutton." The habits twined about these long-standing arrangements proved too strong to be offset in meeting the challenge of liberated Europe when it first presented itself in Italy.

England took the lead. Churchill wanted to keep the monarchy in Italy, and deprecated any statement about self-determination. Russia's desire to take an active role through a tripartite military-political commission was deflected by the fact that Western commanders retained power, and when Russia established independent diplomatic relations with the Italian government, its move was strongly resented and protested by the West. The powers which Russia wanted, however, were the very ones which England and America were later to demand in Eastern Europe and which the Soviets denied, pointing persistently to Italian precedents. Some Westerners foresaw the result of the West's behavior in Italy; thus Ambassador Winant wrote in July 1943 that "when the tide turns and the Russian armies are able to advance we might well want to influence their terms of capitulation and occupancy in Allied and enemy territory." But this view did not prevail and the outcome was, in McNeill's words, that "in Italy, Russia had effectually been excluded from participation In Allied decision-making, and the Western Allies could hardly expect to be treated differently by the Russians in Rumania."

As German resistance began to crumble and the Allied armies poured into *Festung Europa,* the volume and pace of political decision-making in occupied territory necessarily increased. England began to make independent approaches to the Soviet Union looking toward an agreement on spheres of influence which would safeguard the Mediterranean lifeline and put some limit to the Red Army's advance. "Experience," Feis comments,

> was showing how hard it was to apply the rule of common consent in each of these unstable situations. And decision could not always wait. In brief, the diplomatic methods in use began to seem defective or unsuitable—awkward for war, ineffective for peace. Hence both diplomats

*and soldiers began to wonder whether an arrangement which made one
or the other Allies the dominant authority in each of these situations was
not the sensible way to end the discussion.*

Churchill, more tersely, stated that in each of the occupied countries
someone had to play the hand, and with this in mind he journeyed to
Moscow in October 1944 to make his division of Eastern Europe with
Stalin, and thus safeguard British predominance in Greece.

As in 1941–42, so in these negotiations of 1943–44 the United
States preferred to remain, in the words of the Monroe Doctrine, an
"anxious and interested spectator." Harry Hopkins intervened to
change the text of Roosevelt's cable to Churchill referring to the
latter's Moscow trip, so that the American President, rather than
empowering Churchill to speak for him, insisted on retaining "complete freedom of action." The reserved American veto imparted a
provisional character to the Churchill-Stalin agreement. Thus it was
that Western policy toward Eastern Europe in 1945 wavered because
England and America had not reached full agreement; but the Russians, as in the similar case of the second front, interpreted the
wavering as simple bad faith. Stalin protested that he had no idea
whether the governments of Belgium and France, created under
Western aegis, were democratic; he simply accepted them. Did not
the accord of October 1944, although expressly limited to provisional
arrangements until German surrender, give him by implication a similar free hand in Eastern Europe? . . .

In the absence of firm tripartite agreements, particularly about
Poland, the British government, hitherto the advocate of realistic
acceptance of a Soviet sphere of influence in Eastern Europe, at
war's end found itself imploring American military assistance to contain the expansion of Soviet power. The upshot was as paradoxical
as it was tragic. A sequence of events familiar in Anglo-American
diplomatic history then took place. As in the formulation of the
Monroe Doctrine, as in the formulation of the Open Door policy, the
British government suggested to America a joint declaration of policy
for reasons altogether in the realm of *Realpolitik*. As in the two
preceding instances, so in 1945–47 the United States government
proclaimed the policy as its own and lent it the panoply of a moral
crusade. Ten years later, in consequence, England was in the position of trying to restrain the partner which but yesterday it had to
prod.

Looking back, it is still difficult to assign responsibility with any sureness for this critical turn of events. America, which realized the importance of creating the United Nations before the bonds of war-time partnership were relaxed, failed to see the comparable impor-tance of more humble agreements about governments and frontiers, and this failure complicated the already inherent difficulty where two men so different in their points of view as Churchill and Stalin had to reach firm agreements. A number of prominent Americans, including Roosevelt and Hopkins, were deeply impressed by England's deter-mination to retain its empire: this made them slow to accept Chur-chill's growing fear of Russian expansion, just as it blinded them to the truth that, in actual hard fact, America had always depended on the English empire to shield it from potential aggressors. Had the Soviet leaders been less suspicious and dogmatic than they were, they might well have been confused in responding to an England which did not have the strength to enforce its realism, and an America which did not seem to realize that idealism must be sup-ported by something more than documents.

For the Soviets, such indecision on the part of the West must have encouraged the hope, championed by Trotsky after World War I, of carrying revolution westward on the bayonets of the Red Army. Ad-vocates of the Russian interpretation of these events have quoted the Forrestal diaries to show that military leaders in the West did not really fear Soviet attack: but these quotations begin no earlier than 1946, when the readiness to mobilize military force to deter such attack had already shown itself. Feis and McNeill reiterate that we possess very little material with which to interpret Soviet intentions in the spring of 1945. But there seems no good reason to doubt that the Russians were ready to carry their influence as far westward as they could safely go without risking the danger of war.

The inertia acquired by supposedly temporary military arrange-ments, their tendency then to turn into a political status quo unless deflected by new agreements for which, after Yalta, the Big Three alliance suddenly seemed no longer capable, posed for the West a genuinely "agonizing reappraisal." It seemed that to keep on a friendly footing with Russia it was necessary to betray (as it appeared to the West) the Polish people on whose behalf England had gone to war. Roosevelt and Truman were not as different in their reactions to this problem as extremists of both the right and the left would have one think: the President who sent the two most pro-Soviet men in

American governmental circles (Davies and Hopkins) as his first en-
voys to Churchill and Stalin cannot have been, initially, bitterly anti-
Soviet.

The course ultimately adopted was, of course, containment, and
its error lay, surely, in making such a "posture" the *whole* of one's
foreign policy. In itself, containment was simply the normal practice
of diplomacy which sought to maintain a balance of power, and
supported this effort with the threat of force; England has certainly
never practiced anything else, and when the United States has tried
to follow another course—as between 1801 and 1812 in our dealings
with England and France—it has altogether failed. Containment was
startling only in contrast with the Wilsonian idealism, today almost
hard to remember, which preceded it.

What was novel and alarming was the exaltation of containment
from one of many normal means to the entire substance of a policy.
There was nothing in the idea of containment itself which would have
precluded, for example, long-term credits for postwar reconstruction
to the Soviet Union. Even if this had seemed impossible for domestic
political reasons, such loans might have been offered to Eastern
Europe. When in the Marshall Plan proposals the offer was finally
made, the international atmosphere had become embittered, Communist parties had strengthened their hold throughout Eastern
Europe, and it was too late. In a sense, Eastern Europe was the first
underdeveloped area where we failed.

In its sudden, totalistic shift from a reliance on ideals alone to a
reliance only on the threat of war, American policy after 1945 exhib-
ited a characteristic tendency to go from one one-sided solution to
its opposite, equally one-sided. The Darlan and Badoglio deals, the
unconditional surrender formula, the dropping of the atom bomb,
also suggest an extremism of expediency and violence which all too
frequently was the sequel to the benevolent extremism of America's
first intentions.

George Kennan has shown how this tendency of American international behavior to oscillate between extremes of idealism and violence is magnified by our habitual self-righteousness.[3] "It does look,"
Kennan observes,

> *as though the real source of the emotional fervor which we Americans
> are able to put into a war lies less in any objective understanding of the*

[3] This quotation is from *American Diplomacy, 1900–1950* (Chicago, 1951).

wider issues involved than in a profound irritation over the fact that other people have finally provoked us to the point where we had no alternative but to take up arms. This lends to the democratic war effort a basically punitive note, rather than one of expediency. . . .

Instances of such behavior are legion. One recalls how the "peace without victory" position which Woodrow Wilson proclaimed in January 1917—which meant, if it meant anything, a negotiated peace—gave way in three short months to the complete conviction that autocratic governments could not be dealt with and must therefore be destroyed to "make the world safe for democracy." Again, McNeill has caught this quality in Roosevelt's attitude toward fascist Germany:

The conviction that Germany should be made to suffer for the wrongs done to the world by the Nazis was in a sense the obverse of Roosevelt's belief in the goodness and rationality of mankind at large. If a nation somehow failed to exhibit goodness and rationality, thus challenging Roosevelt's general belief about human nature, it endangered its claim to belong to humanity and deserved, Roosevelt came to feel, the severest sort of punishment.

It is as if, to sum up, the failure of reality to respond to innocent intentions (a lack of forethought as to means being itself considered a kind of innocence) calls forth a thirst for vengeance; then hope may give way to fear of an opaque reality which seems suddenly out of control; and reality be made to suffer for its intransigence.

This transition was the more inevitable after 1945 because English and American policy-makers had persistently underestimated Soviet strength, and the awakening to the real nature of the postwar balance of power came as something of a traumatic shock. One reason for the slow Anglo-American response to Soviet postwar demands in 1941 had been, as Churchill and Hull candidly confess in their memoirs, the conviction that Russia would grow weaker as the war went on. The colossal Red Army rolling east and west from Soviet borders in the spring and summer of 1945 caused latent anticommunism to come quickly to the surface of opinion and seem sensible policy.

Only then did many sincere and thoughtful persons in the West recall that the Soviet ideology, pressed on to the heroic defensive as it had been since 1941, nonetheless envisaged the transformation of capitalism to socialism throughout the world. Revolution from within

was the classical means toward this end; but Marx had never imagined a situation in which socialism and capitalism, represented by
different groups of countries, would duel for the allegiance of the
rest of the world; and it was a still more basic tenet in the Marxist
tradition that means were, in any case, secondary. This underlying
tension between opposing social systems facilitated the transformation of cautious cooperation into hostility at a time when public
opinion still basked in the glow of victory, and even the leaders of
the three victorious powers had far from lost hope in peaceful
negotiation. As McNeill puts it: "Each of the Big Three wanted peace
and security and recognized that only their continued cooperation
could secure these goals. But what seemed an elementary precaution
to safeguard the security of the Soviet Union to the one side seemed
Communist duplicity and aggression to the other."

If, then, we return to the question, Why did the cold war start? the
most fundamental answer might be: Because for the first time the
challenge of authoritarian socialism to democratic capitalism was
backed by sufficient power to be an ever-present political and military threat. It is a far more complicated and potent challenge than
that represented by Germany in 1914 or Japan in 1941; it is the kind
of challenge associated with the breakup of empires and the transformation of whole societies rather than with the ordinary jostling of
diplomatic intercourse. In this sense, those who now speak of
negotiation and disarmament as simple nostrums are being superficial, and those who invoke the American way of life are more nearly
correct.

Yet containment, while recognizing the seriousness of the problem, would appear to be an inadequate response. Even before the
possession of atomic weapons by both sides made reliance on military reprisal archaic, containment was a one-sidedly negative policy
which could lead only to slow defeat, and, by way of the frustration
and fear thereby engendered, to war. It involved and still involves an
identification of the United States with governments whose only qual-
ification for our friendship is their anticommunism, and which in
every other respect go against rather than with the grain of
worldwide aspiration. Only a narrow and superficial realism can look
to such alliances for strength in the long run.

Is there a moral to be drawn from this alternation between the
extremes of Wilsonian idealism and military "realism"? Ten years
after he formulated the containment policy, George Kennan saw a

moral clearly.[4] "I should like to raise today the question," Kennan stated in 1957,

> whether the positive goals of Western policy have really receded so far from the range of practical possibility as to be considered eclipsed by the military danger, whether we would not, in fact, be safer and better off today if we could put our military fixations aside and stake at least a part of our safety on the earnestness of our effort to do the constructive things, the things for which the conditions of our age cry out and for which the stage of our technological progress has fitted us.

"Surely everyone," Kennan continued,

> our adversary no less than ourselves, is tired of this blind and sterile competition in the ability to wreak indiscriminate destruction. The danger with which it confronts us is a common danger. The Russians breathe the same atmosphere as we do, they die in the same ways. . . . Their idea of peace is, of course, not the same as ours. . . . But I see no reason for believing that there are not, even in Moscow's interpretation of this ambiguous word, elements more helpful to us all than the implications of the weapons race in which we are now caught up. And I refuse to believe that there is no way in which we could combine a search for those elements with the pursuit of a reasonable degree of military security in a world where absolute security has become an outmoded and dangerous dream.

[4] These quotations are from *Russia, the Atom, and the West* (New York, 1957).

James B. Reston

NEGOTIATING WITH THE RUSSIANS

In this perceptive analysis of Soviet diplomacy, as demonstrated in the postwar conferences, James B. Reston, then the Washington reporter of the New York Times, posed the essential dilemma in Soviet-American relations as they existed in 1947. The U.S.S.R. was too big and too powerful to be disposed of by war at a price commensurate with the gain. At the same time Soviet tactics rendered agreement difficult, if not impossible. The failure of diplomacy from the closing months of the war through the Paris Conference of 1946 Reston attributes to mutual distrust and differences in diplomatic method. At times Soviet negotiators were permitted no flexibility at all; at other times they shifted position so completely that no obvious principle or body of reasoning could account for the change. In the continued absence of concrete settlements, the United States faced the necessity of learning to exist with the U.S.S.R. without the benefit of successful diplomacy. What mattered more than future diplomatic exchanges were the political and psychological techniques employed by the Kremlin to produce erosion in the unity and strength of the free world.

One of the stubborn facts of life, deplored by many but denied by none, is that the Russians are likely to be part of the world for quite a while. There are nearly 200 million of them and their birth rate is about 40 to the 1,000. It is never explained how the experts know about these things, but they say that this birth rate will continue and that the population of the Soviet Union will increase in the next two generations by 60 million. That is 12 million more than the total population of the British Isles.

As our more breathless colleagues intimate, it is extremely inconsiderate of the Soviet Union to have so many people (all potential Communists, too) and, as for the birth rate, it can be taken for granted that the House Committee on Un-American Activities takes a very dim view of that. Nevertheless, there you are; there is nothing in the United Nations charter about having a birth rate of 40 to the 1,000, so you have to adopt one of three courses about the Russians: you either have to fight them, which is not a very moral or practical policy; or you can ignore them, which is not likely to be very profitable; or you can try to negotiate some kind of settlement with them.

Reprinted by permission from James B. Reston, "Negotiating with the Russians," *Harper's Magazine* (August 1947), pp. 97–106.

That is what this piece is about: negotiating with the Russians, and it is addressed primarily to young men who are looking for a useful career, and to old men who think that if they could only have half an hour with Uncle Joe they could fix everything up.

Negotiating with the Russians is like playing tennis on a court without lines or umpire. If the indefatigable Mr. Molotov hits one into the net (as he often does) and cries "good," there is nothing you can do about it except argue. If you call in the French, the British, and the Chinese, and they all say, sorry, it went into the net, Mr. Molotov is not only adamant but angry. Did we not agree, he says, on "the rule of unanimity"? If he is in a bad mood, or if the Politburo feels that they need the point badly, Mr. Molotov will veto the others; if not, Mr. Molotov will "compromise": he will agree to play the point over.

This does not remove the need to negotiate some kind of live-and-let-live agreement with the Moscow government, but it complicates the process. The European Advisory Commission, which was established long before the end of the war to coordinate the postwar policies of the Big Three, met over 500 times and accomplished virtually nothing. The Council of Foreign Ministers, established at Potsdam in 1945, held 122 meetings over fifteen months before it reached the basis for agreement on the minor European peace treaties, and some of the most important aspects of these, such as the future of the Italian colonies and the governorship of Trieste, had to be set aside and are still unsettled. And, of course, the Japanese peace has not been tackled and six weeks of negotiation at Moscow on the German and Austrian treaties last March and April ended in stalemate.

The reasons for this are that we and the Russians start with different objectives and mentalities, are suspicious of the objectives of each other, and adopt totally different methods of negotiation. It is not, by any means, as some people say, a question of semantics alone (one wishes it were); it is not merely that we *define* "democracy" and "freedom" and "liberty" in different ways, but that each is determined to get a world in which his ideas of the individual and the state will prevail. It is not only that we negotiate in different ways, but that the entire role assigned to negotiation and diplomacy is more limited in Soviet strategy than in ours. (We think we can settle most things with talk and dollars; they use more diverse weapons; they are more effective in attaining their ends by political organization, infiltration, and bribery than diplomacy.) "The difference between us," former Secretary of State Byrnes told Molotov toward the end of the Paris peace conference in 1946, "is that we start with the facts and try, however falteringly and even selfishly, to reach true and fair conclusions, while you start with the conclusions you want and try to select and twist the facts to your own ends."

There is a good deal in this, but it is not alone that they select and twist the facts to suit themselves. The trouble in trying to define their methods is that their actions are so contradictory. They were willing to break up the first meeting of the Council of Foreign Ministers in London on the legal technicality that the Potsdam Declaration did not state that France should be represented in the council. One was impressed after that conference with the legalistic quality of their minds. But several months later, when the second meeting of the Council was held in Paris and they wanted to impress the French electorate with their friendliness to France, they insisted that France should participate in the discussions.

On the issue of conceding U.S. trusteeship over the Pacific islands, they opposed any discussion of the question for months, arguing that the whole thing should be left over until the Japanese peace conference; but just before the German and Austrian talks started in Moscow last March—where they wanted to argue that those who had contributed most to the military victory should get special concessions in the peace treaties—they switched their line completely and led the fight for our getting the islands on our own terms. As one diplomat put it recently: "You can't define their mentality; you can only report specific illustrations of how it works, and let the reader judge; they balance the books every day."

The most obvious fact about their negotiators is that they are held on a very tight rein by the Politburo. They do not attempt to conceal this. During the Greek border investigation last spring, Mark Ethridge, the U.S. delegate on the United Nations' commission, asked A. A. Lavrischev, the Soviet delegate, to look over a U.S. proposal. The Russian agreed. He read it and said it looked all right to him but added that, of course, he would have to send it to Moscow. Forty-eight hours later he came back to Mr. Ethridge and said: "I oppose every word of this. In fact I oppose it twice as violently as I ever thought I could."

The tight rein applies not only to junior officials like Lavrischev but to Molotov as well. When the latter agreed at Paris to hold a general peace conference last year, he was suddenly disciplined by Moscow and made to hold up the Big Four discussions for four days while Moscow argued about whether to go along with the public announcement that a general conference would be held.

Again, at the last Moscow conference, Molotov read a half-hour speech one day in reply to Secretary of State Marshall's proposal for a four-power treaty to keep Germany disarmed. Usually his remarks on subjects of this sort were printed in detail by *Pravda* next morning, but the following day nothing appeared. That afternoon, however, Molotov opened the meeting by saying he had a statement to make. He then proceeded to read almost precisely the same statement all over again: a half-hour's speech, followed by an hour's translation in French and English. Everybody was astonished, but next day the explanation was clear. He had omitted to make one point about keeping the question on the Council's agenda. He had evidently been instructed by the Politburo, therefore, to repeat the argument, to sharpen it up a bit and include the point he had overlooked. This he did without the slightest trace of embarrassment, and the following morning *Pravda* then printed his statement in detail.

Rigid instructions like these make the peace negotiations after this war much more severe and formal than in 1919. The Russian thrives on conflict, perhaps because conflict has been so inseparable a part of his political life. Thus, for example, Soviet negotiators never agree to anything the first time it is discussed. When in doubt, their answer is *"nyet!"* As a result, our negotiators have adopted the tedious procedure of running over the agenda as quickly as possible so that the Russians can demonstrate to the Politburo that they are in the proper disagreeable frame of mind. When that demonstration has been made, we can then begin to think about negotiations.

Unlike the British and ourselves, who find it useful and illuminating to discuss the question at issue informally and without commitments, they do not like to "explore" topics outside the council chamber. Occasionally, at critical points in the negotiations, they will discuss the crisis on the side, but in general they look on the habit of informal discussion before the conference opens as an Anglo-Saxon trick designed to outmaneuver them in the formal negotiations.

II

In the formal meetings, either at the Council of Foreign Ministers or in the United Nations, they are tireless. Both Molotov and Vishinsky are men of immense physical endurance. The New York meetings of the Council coincided last autumn with the sessions of the UN General Assembly. When he had finished with four or five hours of tense debate in the Waldorf Towers, former Secretary of State Byrnes was usually exhausted—but not the Soviet team. They shuttled back and forth between the meetings of the Council and the various sessions of the UN at Lake Success and Flushing and (unless it suited their tactics at the moment) were usually prepared to keep the discussions going long after everybody else was ready to quit.

This is perhaps not a matter of first importance in our negotiations with the Russians but it is worth noting. Negotiators who are working under rigid instructions do not tire as quickly as men who are given broad powers of discretion. The former can merely repeat their instructions over and over; the latter have authority to use discretion and must take responsibility for the concessions they propose. This imposes on the negotiators of the Western Powers much more responsibility and a great deal more tension.

This raises another interesting comparison between the negotiators of the East and West. In his book on the Paris Peace Conference of 1919, Harold Nicolson commented on the perils of weariness and friendliness in diplomatic negotiation. On the one hand, he noted that the negotiators then were tired from the Great War and that their ordeals of exhaustion at the council table encouraged an aptitude for the superficial rather than for the essential, for the expedient in preference to the awkward, and for the improvised as an escape from the carefully studied conclusion.

Also, he observed that one of the most persistent disadvantages of all diplomacy by conference was the human difficulty of remaining disagreeable to the same set of people for many days at a stretch. Thus, he concluded, many false decisions and misunderstandings grew out of hasty agreements which were, in turn, the result of weariness, and of such pleasant human qualities as shyness, consideration for others, affability, and ordinary good manners.

The observation is relevant now because it provides so many interesting parallels and contrasts with the negotiations after this war. Franklin Roosevelt was a friendly man. He had great confidence in his ability—as he often said to Harry Hopkins—to "deal with Stalin." But these very qualities of weariness and friendliness sometimes led the late President into the very imprecisions, improvisations, and impetuous judgments against which Nicolson had warned.

Late in the Yalta Conference, Marshal Stalin mentioned that he wished to raise, in connection with the organization of the new United Nations security organization, the special position of some of the Soviet states. Mr. Roosevelt was ready for this one.

He had heard rumors that Stalin might wish to give all the Soviet Republics a seat in the future council of nations. This rumor had been discussed by Mr. Roosevelt with some of his aides and they had all agreed that the entrance of these states into an association of sovereign nations would not only establish a Soviet voting bloc, but would enable the Soviet Union to manipulate the rules of the organization to suit itself.

When Stalin raised the question, therefore, Roosevelt immediately tried to head him off. He said that he hoped Marshal Stalin would not ask for separate representation, for If he did, the United States would feel obliged to ask for separate seats for all forty-eight states of the American federal union.

Stalin listened to the interpretation of this remark and then did something Roosevelt had never seen him do before. He rose from the table in obvious displeasure, walked all the way round it, came back to his seat and said, in effect, to Roosevelt: "You think that you in the West are the only ones who have internal difficulties. I assure you this is not true. I have serious difficulties in several of my own states, particularly those that have suffered grievously in the war. I am not asking for separate representation for all the Soviet Republics, but only for Byelo-Russia and the Ukraine."

The sympathetic nature of Roosevelt was touched by this admission; the politician in Roosevelt was moved. Here was the very symbol of authoritarian power admitting that all wasn't jake at home and that he had to find some way of doing with several of his states what Roosevelt had had to do so often with some of the American states: devise some way of appeasing them.

Well, said Roosevelt, that was different. He didn't realize Stalin had a problem like that, and since he did, he (Roosevelt) would instruct the American delegation at San Francisco to support the acceptance of the Ukraine and Byelo-Russia into the UN. The point is, unfortunately, that while what Stalin said was interesting, it did not really alter the essential point of principle: that the UN was an association of independent states, and the Ukraine and Byelo-Russia were no more independent in the formation of foreign policy than New York and Texas. But the President let it go out of friendliness;

and though Churchill demurred slightly, he too passed it by because it was difficult to oppose Roosevelt and Stalin.

As a result of this casual act, the United States had to go to San Francisco and make a deal with the Latin American states to bring Argentina into the UN so that we could make good our promise about Byelo-Russia and the Ukraine. And today we see the consequences: under the terms of the UN charter, the U.S.S.R. is deprived of the right of vote or veto in the early stages of a dispute to which it is a party. But all it has to do to evade this is to have the Ukraine start the dispute. Then the U.S.S.R. can retain its right of vote and veto on the fantastic assumption that the U.S.S.R. and the Ukraine are entirely sovereign and independent of each other. . . .

Like Franklin Roosevelt, Jimmy Byrnes is a friendly man. He went to the first meeting of the Council of Foreign Ministers convinced that he could reach an agreement fairly soon. On the way to London on the *Queen Mary* he remarked—quite accurately—that he had spent his life on Capitol Hill settling violent differences of principle and personality, and he concluded—quite inaccurately—that human beings were, after all, about the same everywhere.

He carried this idea into the London meeting, but he was soon disillusioned. At the start of the conference, all the ministers agreed that France and China should sit in on the peace treaty discussions without votes. Eleven days later, Molotov announced that the French and Chinese representatives would have to leave because, he said, their presence was a violation of the Potsdam agreement. Nobody else agreed with this interpretation, but Mr. Byrnes, to end the argument and get on with the questions of substance, finally agreed to their exclusion. He soon found, however, that friendliness did not beget friendliness and compromise did not beget compromise, as it usually had in Washington.

Nevertheless, he kept his patience: while Bevin reacted to Molotov's calm, maddening persistence on technical details with angry speeches (which led him often into embarrassing overstatements), Byrnes plodded on patiently, prefacing his remarks on Molotov with: "My good friend," "But my excellent friend," etc. The conference, however, concluded in stalemate. At the end, Cyrus L. Sulzberger, chief European correspondent of the *New York Times,* reported that Mr. Molotov addressed his colleagues as follows:

The previous meeting of the foreign ministers was a success, first, be-

*cause it was held in Moscow, and second, because Cordell Hull and
Anthony Eden were there.*

In spite of this sort of thing the Soviet negotiators are not personally
disagreeable. During negotiations, they do not hesitate to use any
tactic, including the provocative personal attack, to gain their ends or
even simply to make a point. As soon as the session ends, however,
they are generally courteous and even affable. They do not say one
thing in the council chamber and another outside, for except on rare
occasions they do not fraternize very much with their colleagues
except at formal functions. A session may end, however, in the most
bitter harangue, and while Bevin is stalking off, still angry at charges
made against him or his country, Molotov and Vishinsky will treat the
whole thing as a day's work done and immediately drop the manner
assumed before adjournment.

The Russian ideas on compromise and interpretation of agreements, however, are vastly different from our own. In the UN Commission on Conventional Armaments, the United States put forward a
proposal on the procedure to be followed in the discussions. Andrei
Gromyko, the Soviet delegate, countered with a different plan of
procedure. After studying his suggestions, the United States delegation thought it saw a way in which the two proposals could be
coordinated, so our representative later introduced a compromise,
combining the two plans. Mr. Gromyko's reaction to this was not that
we were trying to meet him half way in the interest of understanding.
He remarked that our compromise merely proved that we must not
have had much confidence in our original proposal, and therefore, he
concluded, since the Soviet delegation did have confidence in theirs,
why shouldn't it be accepted?

Even when the representatives of the West meet almost all the
points in a Soviet argument, the Moscow negotiators sometimes do
not go along with the final proposition. When Syria and Lebanon
appealed to the UN to get British and French troops out of their
territory, Vishinsky took up their argument and led the fight on their
behalf. One by one, the British and French met every major demand.
Finally the Syrians and Lebanese accepted the concessions and
agreed to an American resolution which contained them, but in the end
Vishinsky vetoed the resolution because it was not worded precisely
as he wanted it.

Sometimes concessions made by the West to meet the objections of the Soviet negotiators merely result in the weakening of international institutions, without winning the support of the Soviet Union. The protracted negotiations over the constitution of the International Refugee Organization were a case in point. The Russians took an active interest in these negotiations. The other powers weakened the constitution of that organization considerably in order to meet Soviet objections, but in the end the Soviet Union did not join. There is now in operation, consequently, an organization that not only does not have the membership of the Soviet Union but is much weaker than it would have been but for Moscow's amendments.

The Soviet Union has, of course, accepted many compromises in the postwar negotiations. The charter of the United Nations and the texts of the satellite peace treaties abound in them, but the actions of the Soviet Union in many cases suggest that, to them, compromise is not a terminal adjustment of differences but a halfway station to their original goal.

The best illustration is the case of Trieste. The United States, Britain, and France felt that this predominantly Italian city should remain under the Italian government. The Soviet Union argued that it should go to Yugoslavia. After months of contention, it was decided to reach a compromise. We recognized that there was something in the Soviet argument: the area outside Trieste proper was predominantly Yugoslav, and the port had been created originally as an outlet for the trade of the old Austro-Hungarian empire. The port, therefore, was important not only to Italy and Yugoslavia but to Austria, Czechoslovakia, and all the "succession states."

We proposed, consequently, the compromise of internationalizing the city. The Soviet Union accepted the compromise. As soon as it was accepted, we operated on the principle of compromise; we gave up trying to get the city for Italy, but the Russians defined the compromise not as an end but as a means to their original end. For additional months thereafter, they sought to twist the rules of the compromise in such a way that Yugoslavia would have the control of the city, if not the actual sovereignty over it. First they tried to stipulate that Yugoslavia should run its foreign affairs; then they proposed a customs union between the city and Yugoslavia; then a series of railroad arrangements; then an autonomous area in the port for Yugoslavia; and finally, a loose constitution open, like the old Danzig constitution, to endless manipulation. None of these succeeded, but the campaign continues.

Two or three other cases sustain the point. The Allies agreed at Yalta to "concert" their policies in the satellite states and to help establish representative governments in those areas. After Yalta, the United States and Britain did not think the Bulgarian government was representative and after much argument a separate agreement was reached to include members of the opposition parties in a coalition government. This agreement was carried out to the letter. The opposition nominees were sworn into the agreed cabinet posts; they were given their cabinet salaries and many of the superficial trappings of office, but they were given absolutely no power. They did not run the cabinet posts; they were not allowed to attend important cabinet meetings; they were not informed officially of the activities of the government; they were not even provided with personal staffs. They were left in their offices without any vestige of real power.

Stalin and Churchill had a specific agreement that Greece was to be left in the British sphere of influence, but not only did the Soviet Union concentrate the weight of its propaganda against the British there after the agreement, but U.S. official information shows a direct chain of command from Moscow to Yugoslavia to the direction, by a Yugoslav general, of the guerilla bands in Greece.

Even the specific letter of agreements among the major allies has been openly violated. The most famous case is the clear and direct Potsdam agreement: "Germany shall be treated as an economic unit." Another was Paragraph 6(c) of the statutes of the Allied Control Commission in Hungary. This stated that the United States and Britain, members of that commission, should have the right "to receive copies of all communications, reports, and other documents which may interest the governments of the United States and the United Kingdom." The Soviet authorities, however, arrested Bela Kovacs, a parliamentary deputy of the majority Smallholders party, denied his parliamentary immunity, held him incommunicado, elicited a report from him which was used as a pretext for overthrowing the majority government, and even denied the United States and Britain the right to see this and other documents on which these charges were made. We were clearly "interested" in these, asked for them, and were told in effect that it was none of our business.

The effect of this sort of thing has been disastrous. For the negotiators of the United States, the first reaction was one of dismay. When they observed the same tactics applied, not only to issues involving Eastern Europe but to issues in the UN—like the veto, the

creation of the security organization's military force, and so on—
dismay gradually developed into opposition, and finally into a kind of
resentment and frustration.

The sense that compromise is not a settlement but a way-station;
that diplomacy is not only a means of settling issues but a device for
preventing settlement so that other agencies of the Soviet Union can
attain national ends; and that even clearly stated written agreements
can be violated with cynical contempt—these have developed an
attitude of mind in which effective negotiation is extremely difficult.
The lack of agreement on basic things like the control and development of atomic energy, Germany, Austria and Japan is bad enough;
what is worse is the growing sense in Washington that even if all
these questions were wiped off the agenda tomorrow on our terms,
the agreements would mean very little. The circle of suspicion is now
complete.

III

What is the explanation of these disturbing incidents? What is the
strategy behind the Soviet tactics? And what, if anything, can we do
about it?

To explain the foreign policy of any country, it is usually necessary
to look at its philosophy and tactics at home. If we do this with the
Soviet Union and ourselves, the explanation of differences over the
council table is more apparent.

To begin with, the United States and the U.S.S.R. differ on the very
nature and purpose of intergovernmental negotiations. The process
of negotiation lies at the very heart of our national lives in this
country. We negotiate with each other on almost everything: workers
negotiate with their employers; employers negotiate with each other;
industries negotiate with agencies of the government; the legislature
negotiates with the executive; the executive "negotiates" with the
people every four years, etc., etc.

In these negotiations, the combative and acquisitive habits of man
being what they are, each side tries to achieve what is best for
himself, but that instinct is usually qualified by this principle: that
both sides must be reasonably satisfied with the final agreement if
there is to be a continuing and satisfactory relationship between the
parties concerned. . . .

Russian traditions and Russian life, however, are different. For all the propaganda out of Moscow about the "town meetings" of the peasants, and votes of the people, *life* in the Soviet Union does not mesh through the lubricating devices of negotiation. In the Politburo itself, there is undoubtedly an active exchange of ideas, but for the rest, the workers, the peasants, the managers, and even the artists are told by the state what to do. Even Molotov does not "negotiate" with Stalin.

In short, the principle that lies at the heart of what we, in *self*-government countries, call "negotiation" does not predominate in the Soviet Union: the Russians do not come to the council table with the idea that it is in everybody's interest for the other parties to be satisfied with the compromise too.

They appear to have started the postwar negotiations with their allies, not in a mood of compromise, but on the assumption that the experience of the war had changed nothing; that this was the same old United States and Britain which had opposed their revolution at the end of the First World War and sent expeditionary forces into the new Soviet Union to bring them down; that we were really out to encircle them and that Stalin's analysis of the situation (in *The Problems of Leninism*) was right: "The world," wrote Stalin, quoting Lenin, "has been severed into two camps, the imperialist camp and the anti-imperialist camp. . . . We are living, not merely in one state but in a system of states; and it is inconceivable that the Soviet Republic should continue to exist interminably side by side with the imperialist states. Ultimately, one or another must conquer. . . ."

From time to time, Stalin has expressed the view that the two systems could live peacefully together, but the attitude of his negotiators from the start of the peace negotiations was one of extreme suspicion. They appeared from the end of the war to accept the melancholy assumption that we were really out to create an anti-Soviet bloc for the purpose of destroying them; they seem to have based their diplomacy on that premise, and that was undoubtedly one of the greatest diplomatic blunders of our time.

It is not difficult to see how the blunder was made. We did intervene in their affairs after the First World War; we did send our troops into their country; we did try to bring them down; we did outlaw them and ridicule them and refuse to recognize them for a generation; and the men we ridiculed and vilified for nearly twenty years (this rabble from the gutters and ghettos of Eastern Europe, Churchill called them), these men who lived like hunted animals in their formative years and were forced to govern against a hostile world after they took power—these men (who had naturally developed a conspiratorial mentality in the process) were precisely the same men who were now negotiating for Russia in the settlement of a Second World War (which they did so much to win).

Though the blunder, therefore, is easy to explain, it is nonetheless real. For the central fact is that while the leaders of the Soviet Union were the same, the United States and Great Britain were not the same, as they assumed. It is, of course, a matter not of fact but of opinion, but can it seriously be argued that the United States and Britain ended the war in a mood to create an anti-Soviet bloc and encircle the Soviet Union?

I worked during much of the war in London, and the rest of it in Washington. From the end of 1941 until the latter months of the European War, the feeling in Britain for the Soviet Union was not only one of sympathy but of genuine friendship. Indeed, so profound was this British friendship for the Russians that, if it had not been squandered by Moscow's campaign of vilification of the British and its roughhouse diplomacy in Eastern Europe and the UN, no British government could have remained in office if it had opposed the Soviet Union's legitimate territorial and political ambitions.

In Washington, the feeling toward Moscow was much less friendly, but here again it can scarcely be denied that, despite all the shouting against the Soviet Union by many of our conservatives, the United States government and the American people were willing to collaborate generously with Moscow in rebuilding the world and preserving world security.

The Soviet government, however, apparently did not believe this. It overlooked the spectacle of a noisy, friendly, casual, generous, fair America coming, like itself, out of isolation, and fumbling toward a policy that would look forward instead of backward. It seems to have chosen instead to believe the barbaric yawps from the Tribune Tower and to believe, God help us, that these represented America.

Once this deeply pessimistic analysis of the United States and Britain was made, the pattern of their diplomacy developed with ruthless consistency: they seized at Dumbarton Oaks and San Francisco on the American proposal of the "veto"; they interpreted the "rule of unanimity" among the Big Five, not as an obligation to work out a compromise program of leadership for the security of all nations but as a device to achieve security for themselves; they defied their written agreements at Teheran, Yalta, and Potsdam and in the process created the very anti-Soviet coalition they feared the most.

Finally, that most disturbing prospect of all began to haunt the council tables: it began to settle in the minds of the negotiators on both sides that what they were really seeking were two different worlds of the mind and spirit. The East wanted a world in which the state was supreme; the West a world in which the individual was above the state; the East assumed the right of the big state to dictate to the small; the West fought for more equal responsibilities for the small; the West argued for the reconstruction of Europe; the East divided it, denied it the raw materials of reconstruction, and played politics with its misery.

IV

Negotiating with the Russians under these conditions is a new and delicate problem for the United States. These two countries are not only the two most powerful nations in the world, they are the two most different countries in terms of ideology and, what is equally unfortunate, they also happen to be the least experienced of the big states in the conduct of international negotiations.

Our inexperience has been aggravated in recent years by constant shifts at the top of the State Department. Our Secretary of State at the first Moscow Conference in 1943 was Cordell Hull; the Secretary of State at the Yalta Conference was Edward R. Stettinius, Jr.; James F. Byrnes was our chief negotiator at the third Russian conference in Moscow in December 1945; and General Marshall represented us at the last meeting in Moscow.

It would seem that in such an intricate and sensitive situation as this the United States will probably have to devise some way of getting a little more stability at the top, and may, indeed, have to build up an experienced team of young men to study and concentrate on the technique of negotiating with the Russians.

The point of this is not that our negotiators have been outwitted by the tactics of the Russians, or that they have been deceived by the amiable qualities of the human heart. The point is that this new diplomacy by open conference and by exhaustion is a unique problem, requiring exceptional and unusual powers of physical, intellectual, and moral endurance; that the problem will persist for many years; and that our capacity to deal with it will influence the fate of millions of people, the security of the Republic, and perhaps the peace of the world.

It is necessary, therefore, to define it accurately, to see where we have gone wrong in the past, to look to the future and prepare for it, and this cannot be done in a magazine article alone. The essential problem on both sides is lack of faith in the other. This lack of faith cannot be removed quickly, as Henry Wallace thinks, by some dramatic gesture like destroying all the atom bombs, or, as Molotov has intimated to Byrnes, by doublecrossing the British and dividing the world into two neat spheres of influence. It can, however, be minimized in these conferences by greater clarity on the part of our negotiators, and by the development, if possible, of a stable policy, supported by both political parties in the economic as well as the political field of foreign policy.

Also, it might be helped by direct negotiations between the President and Marshal Stalin. It is an astonishing fact, but nevertheless true, that the heads of these two states and their deputies have tried to make peace with everybody on the other side in the war but have never yet made a single attempt to run over the basic questions that keep them from making peace with each other.

Nevertheless, in conclusion, the limitations of diplomacy in this situation should be emphasized. There is no "solution" to the Russian problem, in the sense of there being some neat, quick way of getting rid of it. We are, as the diplomats say at the United Nations, "seized of the question," and will probably have to deal with it for the rest of our lives. It is akin to the "Negro problem" and the "labor-management problem" in that it cannot be removed by theory or dismissed by pure reason. Diplomats can *solve* some problems: they solved the Canadian Fisheries question and it took only 128 years (1783–1911) to do it. But problems like the Russian problem are different: you do not solve them; you devise ways of living with them.

One of these ways is diplomacy, but it is only one way. Diplomacy, as Mr. Nicolson defines it, is not an end but a means; not a purpose but a method. It seeks, by the use of reason, conciliation, and the exchange of interests, to prevent major conflicts arising between sovereign states. It is the agency through which nations seek to adjust their objectives, *by agreement,* rather than by war.

For the present, however, the process of adjusting objectives by agreement at the council table is not making progress. There has been very little reason or conciliation between Washington and Moscow in recent months. The real conflict, indeed, is taking place in an area between diplomacy and war; not in direct negotiations between the Russians and ourselves, but in a test of political and economic strength outside the council chamber in key areas in Europe and Asia.

It is in this area between diplomacy and war, the area of political and economic organization, that the Soviet Union is really effective. Diplomacy, as the Soviets wage it, is, as Joseph Alsop says, a process of erosion. But the vital thing is that while this incredibly tedious process is working in the various capitals, the more effective *political techniques* of the Soviet Union are changing the history of the world with incredible speed. By organizing the shop stewards in the labor unions in Germany; by controlling the supply of newsprint and food in Europe and doling it out to the weak and the faithful; by organizing and financing the Communist parties and destroying the center parties on the Continent; and by appealing to the dreams of hungry men, the Soviet Union has created a political technique that can take over a country in little more time than it takes to translate one of Mr. Gromyko's speeches.

It is definitely in this area that they have progressed rather than in the field of diplomacy. Indeed, if they are sincere in their protestations that what they are looking for is peace and understanding in the West, they are diplomats of dubious ability. But on the other hand, if they are seeking at the council table to create and sustain conditions in which the political technique of infiltration will work, then they have succeeded brilliantly.

II PERCEPTIONS OF THE SOVIET THREAT

Richard W. Van Alstyne

THE UNITED STATES AND RUSSIA

Tracing the evolution of Russian-American relations from the early nineteenth century, Richard W. Van Alstyne, Professor of History at the University of the Pacific, reveals that those relations prior to 1945 had been generally favorable. Russia's defiance of the Open Door principle in China early in the twentieth century and the American nonrecognition of the Bolshevik government prior to 1933 produced two comparatively brief periods of open tension. American diplomats, on the other hand, had always found Russia a strange, secretive, and forbidding country, and they often attributed such qualities to a Russian messianic consciousness that aimed at world domination. Like Staughton Lynd, Van Alstyne criticizes the Roosevelt leadership for making a partnership with Russia during World War II in order to triumph over Germany while ignoring "the terms of the partnership which Stalin, with reasonable candor, set forth." Herein, concludes Van Alstyne, lay the seeds of subsequent disagreement.

> *There are at present two great nations in the world, which seem to tend towards the same end, although they start from different points. I allude to the Russians and the Americans. . . . Their starting point is different and their courses are not the same, yet each of them appears to be marked by the will of heaven to sway the destinies of half the globe.*

Thus wrote Alexis de Tocqueville in his immortal book, *Democracy in America*, first published in Paris nearly one hundred and twenty years ago.

Throughout the past, American attitudes toward Russia, as reflected in presidential messages and in books, magazines and newspaper editorials, have fluctuated all the way from exuberant expressions of friendship and cordiality to violent manifestations of animosity and fear.

It is not yet 10 years since Wendell Willkie preached the gospel of eternal friendship between the two nations. Willkie's *One World*, which in 1944 carried conviction to millions of readers, now lies forgotten. Joseph E. Davies' *Mission to Moscow*, published at the time of Pearl Harbor, vanished into the same grave, happily escaping exhumation by the rude hands of Congressional inquisitors. And Edward R. Stettinius, wartime Lend-Lease administrator, in his book

Reprinted by permission from Richard W. Van Alstyne, "The United States and Russia," *Current History* 25 (August 1953): 107–12.

Lend-Lease: Weapon for Victory, painted a glowing picture of Soviet generosity and hospitality which does not square with the later accounts of Sir Winston Churchill, Admiral William H. Standley and others.

But World War II is by no means the only occasion when the cup has overflowed. Franklin Roosevelt heralded his act of recognition in 1933 with the assertion that "a deep love of peace is the common heritage of the people of both our countries." Woodrow Wilson, exulting over the downfall of the Romanoffs in March 1917, was characteristically ready with an appropriate phrase. "Here is a fit partner for a League of Honor," he declared, though he was soon to alter his opinion.

Farther back in history, during the American Civil War and after, Russia had also been welcomed as a boon companion, if not actually as a comrade in arms. In 1863, there arose a comforting story of Russian fleets arriving in New York and San Francisco harbors to serve as allies of the not-yet-victorious North. The story attained an all-time high in popularity in 1867 at the time of the Alaska Purchase and survived unchallenged until 1915.

History is a first cousin—or perhaps we should say a twin sister—of mythology, and the "Russian fleet myth," on which much ink has been spilled, is a small case in point. Historical scholarship exploded it in 1915, but unlike the famous case of Humpty the pieces were glued together again during World War II.

"The bear that walks like a man" picture of Russia is a very old conception, probably emanating from Britain during the Napoleonic wars, and he changed his physiognomy with the changing mood of the times. Sometimes he appears as a kindly, domesticated, almost cuddly type of creature, at other times he is a voracious animal with teeth bared and fangs dripping. At least once—in 1905 at the time of the defeats at the hands of Japan—"the bear" was held up to ridicule.

Nor is there anything new in our current impressions of the Kremlin. The letters of Theodore Roosevelt and John Hay abound with disparaging remarks on Russian mendacity and trickery. Neil S. Brown, the American minister to St. Petersburg in 1851–53, felt himself in a hostile land.

> *This is a hard climate, [he wrote] and an American finds many things to try his patience. . . . One of the most disagreeable features that he has to en-*

*counter is the secrecy with which everything is done . . . he may rely upon it,
that his own movements are closely observed, by eyes that he never sees. . . .
Nothing is more striking than the rigor of the police . . . there is a strong
anti-foreign party in Russia, whose policy would exclude all foreigners except
for mere purposes of transient commerce. . . . No courtesy or liberality whatever is shown . . . by this Government. But I do not believe that I have any
grievances on this subject, which are not common to other Legations. Secrecy
and mystery characterize everything. Nothing is made public that is worth
knowing. . . . A strange superstition prevails among the Russians that they
are destined to conquer the world. . . .*

In 1936, George F. Kennan, then secretary of the American Embassy in Moscow, dug Brown's dispatches from the files, and sent
them to the State Department over the name of William C. Bullitt,
President Roosevelt's first Ambassador to the Kremlin. Kennan said
he wanted the secretary of state to have an accurate picture of life in
Russia in 1936 but, he added dryly, the description was Brown's, not
his own. Still probably no more penetrating observation on Russia
has ever been made than Winston Churchill's epigrammatic "riddle
wrapped in a mystery inside an enigma" of 1939.

Collaboration

For the greater part of the nineteenth century Czarist Russia and
republican United States were in general cordial collaborators. Both
of them were "young giants," to borrow a thought from the editor of
the *New York Herald* in 1867. They were "engaged in the same
work—that of expansion and progression" and "must ever be
friendly." They have "neither territorial nor maritime jealousies to
excite the one against the other. The interests of both demand that
they should go hand in hand in their march to empire."

The *New York Herald* was consistently one of the most imperial-
minded of the American dailies, and the editor appears to have had a
sound grasp of the nature of international relations. The United
States was an ambitious republic seeking to annex to itself all of the
North American continent, to convert into an American lake the adjacent Caribbean Sea and bring the Central American isthmus under its
control, and to extend itself across the Pacific, absorbing Hawaii in
its path and bringing Japan, North China and Korea within its orbit.

Russia was an equally ambitious despotism seeking influence over the countries of Central Europe, extending its sway over the Christian peoples of the Balkans at the expense of "the unspeakable Turk," knocking at the gates of Constantinople itself, and taking a long look at distant Manchuria beyond the vast wasteland of Siberia.

The two countries had a slight brush in 1821–24 over rival claims to the Pacific Northwest, the Americans endeavoring to exploit the old Spanish claims to the coast as far north as the sixtieth parallel North Latitude, the Russians countering with an *ukase* which in effect extended the domain of Russian America southward to the fifty-first parallel. But the Russians, who earlier in the century had shown an interest in developing a North Pacific empire pivoting upon Sitka, Alaska, and upon the Hawaiian Islands, decided against contesting the point.

Russian adventurers and officials located in Alaska knew what riches would be theirs if only they could control the waters where the sea otter and the seal had their habitats. But the Russian-American Company, which held Alaska, lacked the capital and the business aggressiveness necessary for the execution of such designs, and the Americans already had a virtual monopoly on the carrying trade in sea otter skins from the Pacific Northwest to the markets of South China.

St. Petersburg, which appears never to have given the Russian-American Company strong backing, decided in favor of compromising with the United States at the line of fifty-four degrees and forty minutes, a step which foreshadowed the decision of 1867 to retreat altogether from the continent of North America. As a result the Russians were able to concentrate on the valley of the Amur and make a thrust in the direction of Manchuria and the warm waters to the south.

Meanwhile the United States, ignoring for the time being the Pacific Northwest, pursued its "manifest destiny" across the Pacific. Merchants, mariners, missionaries and naval commanders were busy extending a vast sphere of influence in their restless quest for making dollars and saving heathen souls. Chagrined at finding the British in the lead in the markets of South China, the United States at the halfway point of the century turned its attention more in the direction of Japan and the northwest Pacific, where it hoped to have a clear field unhampered by troublesome British or other foreign competition.

This was the meaning of the Perry expedition to force open Japan and of the lesser known, but equally important Ringgold-Rodgers expedition, whose job was to explore the waters from Formosa northwards to the vicinity of the Amur. Abetted by the government, American merchants hoped to capture the markets of North China, utilizing political advantages wrung from the Japanese or from the still more primitive rulers of the adjacent islands for the purpose of building in that region an American counterpart to the British controlled entrepôts at Singapore and Hong Kong. Besides charting the shores of the islands and the coasts of the mainland of Asia, Rodgers expected to survey two routes across the Pacific—one from Japan to San Francisco by way of Bering Sea and the Aleutian Islands, the other from San Francisco to Shanghai via Hawaii.

Prelude to Rivalry

Exultant over the head-start they had made on the British in this general area, both Perry and Rodgers nevertheless reacted nervously to the rumors that Russia was interested. Perry hastened to conclude, in March 1854, his celebrated "shipwreck convention" with the Japanese. Rodgers the very next year toyed with the idea of sailing with his squadron up the Amur because, in his judgment, that river was destined to serve as the great highway of commerce into the distant interior of Asia.

Here in the region of Japan and Northeast Asia just 100 years ago Perry, Rodgers and other American empire-builders were nailing down the first thin planks of the stage on which the great tragic drama of Russian-United States rivalry was later to begin. As today, so then Perry and Rodgers saw Japan as the pawn in the struggle, and they determined on gaining ascendancy over her. The play, which actually showed signs of starting in the 1850s, was delayed for 40 years.

The first act was begun in 1895, but by that time the lead role had been preempted by Japan, whose ambition became to push back both her American and Russian wooers the better to build in Northeast Asia an imperial stage of her own. For 50 years she acted out her role, only to see the original star performers return in 1945 and set the stage in the manner they had first planned it.

This sensitivity to impending rivalry between the United States and

Russia over the Far East, with Japan in the middle, began to register on the minds of American diplomats and other observers as they watched the changes wrought by the Sino-Japanese War of 1894. Russia cheated Japan out of her victory over China by forcing her to withdraw from Port Arthur and the Liaotung Peninsula. A subsequent Russian lease of this same territory, followed by the military occupation of Manchuria and the threat to the territorial integrity of Korea, brought on the Russo-Japanese War of 1904–1906.

In this oncoming clash one school of American thought sided with Russia, another sympathized with Japan. Thus Horace N. Allen, a Presbyterian missionary who had gained ascendancy over the Korean king and who had won valuable concessions in Korea for American business, pictured Japan as a dangerous rival of the United States and worked for the support of Russia. Allen ridiculed Great Britain for her traditional policy of containment:

> *It simply bottled her [Russia] up and made her phiz until she blew a vent hole for herself on the China Sea, just as she will surely blow another on the Persian Gulf if she is kept in on that side.*

But Roosevelt, Hay and their advisers encouraged Japan to stand firm and gave their private support to the Anglo-Japanese Alliance, first formed in 1902 to halt further Russian aggressions. Professor Paul Reinsch of the University of Wisconsin, who was later to be Wilson's minister to China, declared in 1905:

> *Japan is fighting our battle. . . . The very least that the Anglo-Saxon races can do for the representatives of their policy in the Orient is to counteract the diplomatic influence that would by roundabout means again deprive the Japanese of the fruits of their unexampled self-sacrifice.*

After the war, the United States gave the Japanese a free hand in Korea, but when the erstwhile foes combined to split Manchuria between them, as they did in 1907, American policy registered chagrin, if not resentment, at finding this new door of economic opportunity closed to it. Japan and Russia were henceforth paired off as evil geniuses thwarting American interests in Northeast Asia; but Japan, the nearer and the more dynamic of the two, loomed first in the American mind as the principal rival. Nevertheless, the play which had opened in 1895 was about to move into its second act.

The start of Act II is the Bolshevist Revolution of November 1917, and the curtain for the first time is drawn back to show all the world a stage. Communism stalked the Peace Conference at Paris in 1919, where fears were expressed that it would spread from Russia into Central Europe and Germany and from thence into France. With the Third Internationale formed in Moscow and calling upon the workers of the world to unite and overthrow their capitalist "masters," the United States reacted violently and, since it was now the leading capitalist nation, it showed no hesitation in waging ideological warfare for the defense of its economic and political system.

The Russian "Plot"

Internally this took the form of the "Great Red Scare" of 1919–20, fanned by reports that the Bolsheviks were sending infernal machines through the mails to the homes of prominent Americans.

Externally American hostility toward the Soviets under President Wilson took the form of collaboration with the Allies in seeking the overthrow of the Bolshevik government. Russian counter-revolutionaries, particularly General Denikin and Admiral Kolchak, were supported with arms and supplies, and American forces landed at Archangel and Vladivostok. In the words of one historian, these events gave birth to the policy of containment. The intervention at Vladivostok was particularly complicated because the Japanese too were interested. The dispatch of Japanese forces greatly superior in numbers to those of the Americans and the other Allies aroused the suspicion that Japan meant to annex Eastern Siberia, and so the American intervention was in part at least intended as a check upon Japan.

But there is some evidence that certain American interests intended to get control of the railways of Eastern Siberia and North Manchuria for the United States, thereby reviving the ambitious schemes of E. H. Harriman and the Taft administration. At any rate, there can be no doubt but that American policy under Wilson in 1919–20 was formulated on the hope and the expectation that the regime of Nicolai Lenin would collapse. When this eventuality failed to materialize, American diplomacy settled down during the 1920s to the pursuit of the fixed Wilsonian principle of not recognizing any government that did not conform to the American pattern of international morals.

Charles Evans Hughes, the executor of Wilsonian policies, proceeded at the Washington Conference of 1921 to erect an elaborate paper system of peace in the Far East based upon the theory that both Japan and Soviet Russia could be checked and China, under American tutelage, be built up as the strongest power of East Asia. For her part Japan in 1931 dealt a mortal blow at these fond illusions by expelling the Chinese from Manchuria and incorporating that region as a protectorate.

In the meantime, the Soviet government, having reached in 1920–21 the lowest point in its fortunes, began to gain in strength both at home and abroad. Friendly gestures in the direction of Germany, then the immediate object of Anglo-French hostility, resulted in 1922 in an important agreement with that country. The German move forced Britain and France to recognize the Soviet Union, thereby isolating the United States in its attitude of nonrecognition. Through more than a decade of stalemate the attitude persisted, although a number of large American corporations made contracts and entered into a profitable business with the Soviets.

The Roosevelt administration in 1933 tried a new tack: it decided upon recognition and establishment of diplomatic relations with the Soviets, but at the same time maintained the position of nonrecognition and moral disapproval that its predecessor, the Hoover administration, copying Wilson, had adopted toward Japan in Manchuria. This move bore the earmarks of a Soviet-American entente for the repression of Japanese ambitions—it was so interpreted in Japan.

But Mr. Roosevelt intended it only as a gesture, and the Japanese resumed their quest for Greater East Asia unchallenged, except for moral pinpricks, until the fateful collision of 1941. Furthermore, the optimism that had accompanied the rapprochement of 1933 with Moscow quickly turned sour.

Contrary to the understanding implicit in the recognition agreement, the Soviet government continued to foster the hidden Communist warfare against the West; anger and frustration dogged the footsteps of the diplomats both in Washington and in Moscow; and every American Ambassador from Bullitt to Steinhardt commented in their reports to the State Department on the impossibility of carrying on normal relations with the Soviets.

During this same period Moscow and Berlin carried on bitter ideological warfare against each other, bringing it to an abrupt conclusion, however, with the Nazi-Soviet Pact of August 23, 1939, the combination that precipitated World War II.

Russian Aims

During the two years that followed, the Roosevelt government was privileged to read the portent of Soviet ambitions. The Baltic states—Estonia, Latvia, Lithuania—vanished in the fall of 1939. The "dreadful rape of Finland"—Mr. Roosevelt's own characterization of the Russian attack on that country—came next. In December 1941, Stalin marked out for the benefit of Anthony Eden, the British foreign secretary, the line across Europe along which the Iron Curtain was fated to fall.

From the British Foreign Office Washington received full information, including the knowledge that Stalin wanted binding agreements with the Western powers relative to territorial changes after the downfall of Germany. Stalin's proposals to negotiate a postwar settlement while the war was in progress, presumably the better to avoid friction and misunderstanding later, were rebuffed, Roosevelt falling back on the familiar doctrinaire position of the United States that it could not make any secret agreements. (The secret agreement as a diplomatic device has been utilized by various American administrations commencing with Washington and including Wilson and both of the Roosevelts.)

Very little is known about these wartime exchanges between Moscow on the one hand and London and Washington on the other. But on the basis of the scanty information disclosed *by the principals themselves*, particularly Roosevelt, Harry Hopkins and Churchill, two conclusions can be drawn: (1) Roosevelt and his immediate associates had reasonably full information regarding Soviet postwar intentions; (2) Roosevelt even on past the Yalta Conference crusaded both at home and abroad in behalf of the United Nations, he and other Americans deluding themselves into thinking they were winning over the Russians to the American dream of a world legal and moral order.

Equipped with factual information at least as early as December 1941, Roosevelt, like Wilson in World War I, embarked on a romantic adventure in the vague general direction of "world peace," pinning his faith on a partnership with Stalin without paying heed to the terms of the partnership which Stalin, with reasonable candor, set forth.

Not long after the Yalta Conference—when the Russians forced a Communist government on Rumania—the few Americans on the inside began to awaken to the unpleasant truth, but it was not until the Council of Foreign Ministers began its meetings in London in the following September that they really roused themselves from their dreams. The "open disagreements openly arrived at" of this body in turn brought disillusionment.

It soon became the accepted thesis, now widely believed, that the Russians had treacherously broken their wartime agreements, but the record is plain that no real agreements were ever reached. There were only formulas, generalized pledges and vague declarations of intentions. These were what the United States wanted, and these were what it got. On their part the Russians wanted some agreements—to insure them hegemony in Central and Eastern Europe at least.

But, supposing for the sake of argument that Mr. Roosevelt had consented to negotiate over the satellite states, it is more than doubtful whether any proposal forthcoming from Moscow for the disposition of Germany could have been acceptable to either British or American diplomacy. It is not on record that Mr. Stalin himself had reached a firm conviction on this knotty subject.

And so the curtain came down in 1945 on Act II, with the opening scenes of Act III following the plot of a Greek tragedy. More than ever the world was the stage, with the players shifting the scenes madly about. Moderate statesmanship is trying to establish a balance between the two great contestants, and looks to Western Europe to develop enough strength and unity to discourage the extremists on either side. . . .

William Appleman Williams

OPEN DOOR POLICY AND
THE COLD WAR

*One important element in the emerging cold war after victory in Europe was
the Soviet-American conflict over the political and economic orientation of
Slavic Europe. American motives in resisting the Soviet encroachment
(which had the support of Russia's occupying armies) were complex. Still,
for New Left historians the explanation lay overwhelmingly in economic
factors—the determination of Washington officials to gain access to the opportunities of trade and investment in Eastern Europe. Inasmuch as the
region was of little strategic and economic importance to the United States
when contrasted to Soviet interests and concerns, and inasmuch as the
United States could under no circumstances gain free access to the region
except as the price of an unwanted war, American policy appeared to be
unnecessarily aggressive and futile. It was, according to this revisionist interpretation, responsible for the disruption of the wartime alliance. Some
revisionists saw the problem in the necessities of American capitalism, some
in the mistaken ambitions of American leaders. William Appleman Williams of
Oregon State University, always a key exponent of the revisionist school,
placed responsibility for the cold war on both of these factors in the following selection, which was published in 1959.*

Stalin's effort to solve Russia's problem of security and recovery
short of widespread conflict with the United States was not matched
by American leaders who acceded to power upon the death of
Roosevelt. The President bequeathed them little, if anything, beyond
the traditional outlook of open-door expansion. They proceeded
rapidly and with a minimum of debate to translate that conception of
America and the world into a series of actions and policies which
closed the door to any result but the cold war.

   The various themes which went into America's conception of the
freedom and the necessity of open-door expansion, from the doctrine
of the elect to the frontier thesis, had been synthesized into an
ideology before Roosevelt's death. Once it was frozen into ideology,
it became very difficult—and perhaps artificial, even then—to assign
priorities to its various facets. Even a single man, let alone a group,

From *The Tragedy of American Diplomacy*, by William Appleman Williams, pp. 229–43.
Copyright © 1962, 1959 by World Publishing Company. Used by permission of Thomas
Y. Crowell Company, Inc.

emphasized different themes at various times. Yet the open-door outlook was based on an economic definition of the world, and this explanation of reality was persistently stressed by America's corporate leadership as it developed its policy toward the Soviet Union and other nations. It was not the possession of the atomic bomb which prompted American leaders to get tough with Russia but rather their open-door outlook which interpreted the bomb as the final guarantee that they could go further faster down that path to world predominance.

Long before anyone knew that the bomb would work, most American leaders were operating on the basis of three assumptions or ideas which defined the world in terms of a cold war. The first specified Russia as being evil but weak. This attitude, predominant among American leaders from the first days of the Bolshevik Revolution in 1917, was reinforced and deepened by the nonaggression pact signed by Russia with Nazi Germany in 1939. There is little evidence to support the oft-asserted claim that Americans changed their basic attitude toward the Soviet Union during the war. Most of them welcomed Russian help against Germany, and some of them mitigated their antagonisms and suspicions, but several careful studies make it clear that large and crucial segments of the American public remained "dubious about the prospects of building the peace together with Russia."

Even before the end of the war in Europe, many Americans were again comparing Stalin with Hitler and stressing the importance of avoiding any repetition of the appeasement of Nazi Germany. Others, like John Foster Dulles, who had sought persistently and until a very late date to reach a broad compromise with Hitler and Japan, changed their approach when it came to dealing with Russia. They made no such efforts to reach an understanding with Stalin. And by the time of the San Francisco Conference on the United Nations, such leaders as Averell Harriman were publicly expressing their view that there was an "irreconcilable difference" between Russia and the Western powers.

At the same time, however, very few—if any—American leaders thought that Russia would launch a war. Policy-makers were quite aware of the "pitiful" conditions in western Russia, of the nation's staggering losses and its general exhaustion, of its "simply enormous" need for outside help "to repair the devastation of war," and of Stalin's stress on firm economic and political agreements with the

United States to provide the basis for that reconstruction. In their own discussions, American decision-makers drew an astute and crucial distinction between Soviet actions to establish a security perimeter in eastern Europe and an all-out aggressive move against the entire capitalist world. They were right in their estimate that Russia was concerned with the first objective. They were also correct in concluding that the Soviet Union—unlike Nazi Germany—"is not essentially constructed as a dynamic expansionist state."[1]

Far from emphasizing the imminence of a Russian attack, American leaders stressed the importance of denying any and all Soviet requests or overtures of a revised strategic agreement in the Middle East, and at the same time concentrated on reasserting American influence in Eastern Europe while pushing the Russians back to their traditional borders. The first such American action came in the spring and summer of 1945 in the form of protests over Soviet influence that developed as the Red Army moved westward in pursuit of the Nazis. These protests were not prompted by the fear that Russia was about to overwhelm Europe or the world in general, but rather by the traditional outlook of the open door and the specific desire to keep the Soviets from establishing any long-range influence in Eastern Europe.

Another basic attitude held by American leaders defined the United States as the symbol and the agent of positive good as opposed to Soviet evil and assumed that the combination of American strength and Russian weakness made it possible to determine the future of the world in accordance with that judgment. One important congressional leader, for example, remarked in 1943 that Lend-Lease provided the United States with a "wonderful opportunity" to bring the United States to "a greater degree of determining authority" in the world. He was quite aware that his view was "shared by some of the members of the President's Cabinet" and that important State Department officials were "fully in accord" with the same outlook. Another key congressman was thinking in terms of the "United States seeking world power as a trustee for civilization."[2] Following the even earlier lead of publisher Henry R. Luce, who had announced in 1941 that it was high noon of the American Century, various

---

[1] See, as a typical report of such discussions within the American policy-making community, the story in the *New York Times*, September 27, 1945 (p. 4), from which the quotation is taken.
[2] See, as typical of such remarks, the comments of Karl E. Mundt, A. A. Berle, Jr., John M. Vorys, and Charles A. Eaton, in *Extension of Lend-Lease Act: Hearings Before the Committee on Foreign Affairs, House of Representatives* (78th Cong., 1st Sess., 1943).

business spokesmen began stressing the need to become "missionaries of capitalism and democracy." Shortly thereafter, a leading oil-industry leader asserted that America "must set the pace and assume the responsibility of the majority stockholder in this corporation known as the world." Such remarks were not unique; they merely represented the increasing verbalization of one aspect of America's traditional policy.

The third essential aspect of the open-door outlook, which also made its appearance before the end of the war, was the fear that America's economic system would suffer a serious depression if it did not continue to expand overseas. Stressing the fact that there remained roughly nine million unemployed in 1940, one leading New Deal senator warned in 1943 that the danger of another depression could not be overemphasized. A government economic expert promptly supported this view with his own report that "it unfortunately is a fact that for the majority of the people in the United States the thing we have liked to refer to as the American standard of living is only possible in situations where two people in the family are working."

The reason for this concern, and the extent to which government participation in the financing of such expansion was crucial, is nicely revealed by two sets of statistics. The first figures concern direct exports. In 1928, when the United States enjoyed a net export surplus with every region of the world except some areas in the tropics, the nation sold 17.1 percent of the world's exports. Ten years later, during the depression, that share had dropped, despite government loans and subsidies to exporters, to 14.9 percent. The proportion in 1953, 21.3 percent, seems at first glance to indicate a dramatic recovery and further gain. But 5.6 percent of that total was paid for by government loans and grants financed by the American taxpayer. Hence the net share of world exports was only 15.6 percent. Not until 1956, when it reached 17.9 percent, did the net figure surpass the American export position of 1928.

The second kind of data concerns the extent to which various American corporations depend upon overseas operations. Total foreign sales, including those of directly owned overseas branches and subsidiaries as well as exports from parent American companies, amounted in 1956 to $58 billion. When classified according to the percentage of total sales accounted for by all foreign operations, the pattern is indicated by the following examples: 75 percent—Standard

Oil of New Jersey; more than 70 percent—H. J. Heinz and Colgate-Palmolive; over 40 percent—American Radiator, International Harvester, F. W. Woolworth, Gillette Razor, and National Cash Register; better than 30 percent—Parke Davis Drugs, Sterling Drugs, and Otis Elevators; and between 15 and 30 percent—Johnson and Johnson, Corn Products Refining, Firestone, Goodyear, International Business Machines, Coca Cola, and Eastman Kodak.[3]

The drive to achieve those postwar results began in earnest while the war was still being fought. For his part, Secretary Hull never eased off on the pace he had established in 1933. "The primary object," he reiterated in 1940, "is both to reopen the old and seek new outlets for our surplus production." One of his principal concerns was to break into the British trading system, a campaign in which he was vigorously encouraged and supported by American exporters. Hull's weapons included Lend-Lease, and Britain's growing need for a major recovery loan. The United States made its aid conditional upon the acceptance by England of the open-door principle.[4]

One of the most vigorous proponents of this assault upon the British imperial market was William L. Clayton, a self-made man who became head of the world's largest cotton export business and then moved into the Roosevelt Administration as a policy-maker. His underlying attitude was very similar to Hull's: "The international economic policies of nations," Clayton remarked in 1943, "have more to do with creating conditions which lead to war than any other single factor." He was committed, as one might expect, to the Open Door Policy as the way to expand exports. Clayton was unusual, however, in that he was considerably more candid than most American leaders when speaking about the nature of that overseas economic expansion. He admitted, for example, that the United States often tried to close the door to competition once it had gone through and established its own position. "As a matter of fact, if we want to be honest with ourselves, we will find that many of the sins that we freely criticize other countries for practicing have their counterpart in the United States."

---

[3] A convenient, though merely surface, survey is: C. E. Silberman and L. A. Mayer, "The Migration of U.S. Capital," *Fortune* (1958). On investments, see the authoritative *U.S. Business Investments in Foreign Countries* (Washington: Department of Commerce, 1960).

[4] Here see R. N. Gardner, *Sterling-Dollar Diplomacy* (Oxford: Oxford University Press, 1956).

Clayton's comment is particularly relevant to America's insistence that former Axis colonies, and other trustee territories, should be handled in such a way that the United States would be assured of unrestricted economic access. As Assistant Secretary Sayre explained the policy, it was centered on establishing "sound economic foundations." "Here again," he noted, "another distinctively American ideal, expressed at various times as the Open Door Policy, is made a binding obligation in all trust territories." The remarks of Sayre and Clayton serve to clarify and dramatize one of the issues that plagued American-Soviet relations after 1943. The United States interpreted Russian resistance to the Open Door Policy in Eastern Europe as an unfriendly act, even though Stalin acquiesced in the principle throughout the Pacific and elsewhere in the world.

Another policy-maker dramatized this ever-increasing concern with overseas economic expansion by comparing the American system with the old British empire. America, he explained, was "a great island" dependent upon a "greater volume of exports" than even the British had needed in the nineteenth and early twentieth centuries. But what was very probably the clearest and most direct statement and explanation of the American approach to the postwar world was provided in November 1944—five full months before the death of Roosevelt—by Assistant Secretary of State Dean Acheson. Testifying before a special congressional committee on Post-war Economic Policy and Planning, Acheson analyzed the situation in a remarkable and almost unique outburst of blunt candor. His remarks cast such a dazzling light on American foreign policy ever since that date that they warrant extensive quotation.[5]

Along with almost every other American leader, Acheson was gravely concerned lest the economy slide back into the depression of the 1930s or collapse in a new debacle at the end of the war. That was the danger, and Acheson repeatedly emphasized it during his entire career in the Department of State.[6] If that happened, he began his testimony in 1944, "it seems clear that we are in for a very bad time, so far as the economic and social position of the country is

---

[5] All of the testimony during these hearings, however, is very pertinent. *Post-War Economic Policy and Planning: Hearings Before the Special Subcommittee on Post-War Economic Policy and Planning, House of Representatives* (78th Cong., 2nd Sess., 1944).
[6] When compared with their subsequent political and historical rhetoric about the success of the New Deal itself, the candid and sworn testimony of New Deal leaders after 1943 offers a valuable corrective. More historians should examine it.

concerned. We cannot go through another ten years like the ten years at the end of the twenties and the beginning of the thirties, without having the most far-reaching consequences upon our economic and social system."

"When we look at that problem," he continued, "we may say it is a problem of markets. You don't have a problem of production. The United States has unlimited creative energy. The important thing is markets. We have got to see that what the country produces is used and is sold under financial arrangements which make its production possible." The solution, Acheson explained to the Congressmen, was not in doubt. "You must look to foreign markets.". . .

As the policy developed, however, American leaders did come to rely rather extensively on the threat of force implied by their short-lived monopoly of the atom bomb. That attitude, and the tension it produced in relations with Russia, ultimately provoked strong protests from Secretary of War Stimson and Secretary of Commerce Henry A. Wallace. Prior to their changes, however, both men supported the orthodox line of policy. Deeply concerned about the problem of preventing a depression, Wallace persistently talked between 1943 and 1947 about overseas economic expansion as the new frontier. "Private enterprise in the United States can survive only if it expands and grows," he argued, and pointed out that he was only trying to help the businessmen do what they themselves advocated. "The old frontiers must be rebuilt," as he put it, and pointed to American economic expansion into the poor, underdeveloped countries as "this unlimited new frontier of opportunities." Wallace of course wanted to reform and improve conditions abroad as part of that extension of American enterprise, and was in many respects the epitome of the New Deal version of Woodrow Wilson's reforming expansionism.

But it is very revealing that Wallace himself spoke favorably of Hoover's similar desire to improve the lot of the overseas poor as an integral part of extending American business operations. "I have considerable sympathy," Wallace remarked as he took over the same cabinet post in 1945, "with Herbert Hoover's problem as Secretary of Commerce." The one obvious difference in their outlooks was Wallace's willingness to provide the private entrepreneurs with public capital. "It is vital," he asserted, "that Government cooperate with the export trade . . . to put on an aggressive sales campaign abroad."

Wallace's version of the expansionist outlook won him sharp criticism from Senator Robert A. Taft. Along with his repeated warnings that American policy might well provoke the Soviets into ever more militant retaliation, and perhaps even war, Taft's attack on Wallace serves to illustrate the misleading nature of the popular stereotype of the Senator. Taft immediately spotted the contradiction between the rhetoric of the New Deal and the reality of its policies. "Dollar diplomacy is derided," he commented very pointedly in 1945, "although it is exactly the policy of Government aid to our exporters which Mr. Wallace himself advocates to develop foreign trade, except that it did not [in its earlier forms] involve our lending abroad the money to pay for all our exports."

Despite the perception of his analysis, Taft stood virtually alone. Congressman Clarence Murdock of Arizona offered what was perhaps the most striking summary of the majority view: "The proper foreign outlet is our safety valve." Milo Perkins, a New Deal businessman who for a time headed the Board of Economic Warfare, offered a pungent statement of the familiar either-or thesis that had originated in the 1890s. "We must sell great quantities of machinery and transport equipment and machine tools abroad if we are to avoid large-scale factory shutdowns here at home." Labor and farm leaders joined corporation executives and government officials in supporting that analysis. "We cannot possibly maintain full production and full employment," the United Auto Workers announced in 1945, "unless we have a world pool of free and prosperous consumers." "Foreign trade," the union explained, "can be the margin between a drop into economic chaos and a steadily expanding economy." Edward O'Neal, President of the American Farm Bureau Federation, was equally vehement. Agricultural surpluses "will wreck our economy unless we can find sufficient outlets in foreign markets to help sustain the volume of production." In his view, the "finest" policy proposal involved Wilson's old idea of extending the Monroe Doctrine to the world at large. "Let us spread it all over," O'Neal suggested to the congressional committee on postwar planning; "let us run it into China, if necessary, and run it around into Russia."

As it moved quickly to take over government affairs after the death of Roosevelt, the Truman administration made it clear that it would sustain all these aspects of the traditional approach to foreign policy. "The United States cannot reach and maintain the high level of employment we have set as our goal," Secretary of State James F.

Byrnes reiterated, "unless the outlets for our production are larger than they've ever been before in peacetime." Byrnes had neither time nor interest for the idea of working out some agreement with the Russians that involved the recovery loan they had requested. He even sidetracked the basic memorandum dealing with the issue. "I had it placed in the 'Forgotten File,' " he later revealed, "as I felt sure that Fred Vinson, the new Secretary of the Treasury, would not press it."

President Harry S. Truman was for his part an enthusiastic and militant advocate of America's supremacy in the world. He seemed, indeed, to react, think, and act as an almost classic personification of the entire Open Door Policy. From a very early date, moreover, he led the rapid revival of the analogy between Nazi Germany and the Soviet Union (and Hitler and Stalin) which became one of the fundamental clichés of America's analysis of the postwar world. Given that analogy, which was very rapidly and very generally accepted, American policy can without much exaggeration be described as an effort to establish the Open Door Policy once and for all by avoiding what were judged—on the basis of the analogy—to have been the errors of appeasement made during the 1930s.

There were two central fallacies involved in that estimate of the world. Soviet Russia and Nazi Germany were significantly different in crucial aspects of domestic and foreign policy; and, unlike the situation in the 1930s, the United States was neither weak nor disarmed. Indeed, it enjoyed a great absolute as well as relative advantage in both economic and military power. As the United States Government candidly admitted even as late as 1962, the United States had been the strongest power in the world ever since 1944. For that matter, it was the existence and the knowledge of that strength that encouraged Truman and other leaders after 1945 to think that they could force the Soviets to accept American proposals without recourse to war.

It is no doubt wrong and inaccurate to conclude that the effort to establish the false analogy between Soviet Russia and Nazi Germany was the product of conscious distortion by America's private and official leaders. Many of them adopted and used that argument in complete sincerity. They simply accepted it without serious thought or critical evaluation. However mistaken in fact and logic, such men were not hypocrites. But it also is true that there were a good many men who shared the attitude of Senator Arthur K. Vandenberg. He thought it was necessary "to scare hell out of the American people" in order to win their active approval and support for the kind of vigorous anti-Soviet policy he wanted. Those men did consciously employ exaggeration and oversimplification to accomplish their objectives. Senator Taft would seem to have offered a sound judgment on that conduct. He remarked during congressional consideration of the European Recovery Program that he was more than a bit tired of having the Russian menace invoked as a reason for doing any- and everything that might or might not be desirable or necessary on its own merits.

Truman not only thought about Russia in terms of Nazi Germany, but he made it clear very soon after he took the oath as President that he intended to reform the world on American terms. He casually told one early visitor "that the Russians would soon be put in their places; and that the United States would then take the lead in running the world in the way that the world ought to be run." Then, on April 23, 1945, he told the Cabinet "that he felt our agreements with the Soviet Union so far had been a one-way street and that he could not continue; it was now or never. He intended to go on with the plans for [the] San Francisco [Conference] and if the Russians did not wish to join us they could go to hell." Senator Vandenberg, soon to become (along with John Foster Dulles) the Republican leader of that bipartisan approach to the Soviet Union, caught the spirit—and reflected the absurd exaggeration—of the outlook of his diary entry of the following day: "FDR's appeasement of Russia is over."

As one insider remarked, "the strong view prevailed" from the very beginning, though it did not take on the form and tone of a great crusade against the Soviet Union and international communism until the end of 1946. Thus, for example, additional Lend-Lease allocations and shipments to Russia were canceled in May 1945. The full story of the cancellation has never been revealed. In the narrow sense, the action can be interpreted as a blunder. Truman later referred to it as "my greatest mistake," and claimed that, given a second chance, he would have handled it differently. Nevertheless, all Lend-Lease to the Soviets was closed off promptly once the Japanese surrendered. It is also clear that, on a comparative basis, Russia was treated far less considerately than England and France during the process of termination. In those respects, therefore, the action was repeated.[7]

---

[7] This reconstruction of the affair is based in the main upon the following sources: *Memoirs by Harry S. Truman*. Volume One: *The Year of Decisions* (New York: Double-

But in the first instance, and as Truman later explained, the authority to act had been sought by Leo Crowley, the Foreign Economic Administrator, who proceeded to interpret it very broadly and to use it very vigorously. Truman's oblique comment that the whole affair was "clearly a case of policy-making on the part of Crowley and Grew" implies an explanation that can be substantiated by other evidence. Crowley's push for the power was supported by Admiral William D. Leahy, Assistant Secretary of State Joseph Grew, and Harriman. All those men wanted to use American economic power to coerce the Soviets on policy issues. This is established beyond any question in a Grew memorandum of his phone conversation with Crowley on May 12, 1945, as they were working to obtain a grant of authority from Truman. The document makes it absolutely clear that Crowley and Grew had Russia in the very forefront of their minds as they pressured the President. For his own part, Crowley refused to consider the Russian request for a loan as coming under the Lend-Lease law, even though he did negotiate such an arrangement involving $9 million with France. Crowley's general outlook was revealed when congressmen questioned him about loans in general. "If you did not like the government," he was asked, "you would not have to make them a loan at all?" "That is right," Crowley replied. "If you create good governments in foreign countries, automatically you will have better markets for ourselves."

Whatever further details may ultimately be added to the story of the termination, there is no doubt that the action seriously antagonized the Russians. Stalin interpreted it as a move to put pressure on him to accept American policies, and bluntly called it "disturbing." Then, in a very revealing series of comments, Stalin told Harry Hopkins in May 1945 that such an approach would not produce Soviet acquiescence.[8]

---

day and Co., 1955); William D. Leahy, Manuscript Diaries, 1941–1945, State Historical Society of the State of Wisconsin, Madison; Foreign Relations: The Conference at Malta and Yalta (Washington: Government Printing Office, 1958); Extension of the Lend Lease Act: Hearings Before the Committee on Foreign Affairs, House of Representatives (79th Cong., 1st Sess.); Export-Import Bank of 1945: Hearings Before the Committee on Banking and Currency, House of Representatives (79th Cong., 1st Sess.); Export-Import Bank: Hearings Before the Senate Committee on Banking and Currency (79th Cong., 1st Sess.); and materials from the Manuscript Papers of Henry L. Stimson and Joseph Grew, Harvard University Library.
[8] The following quotations come from a stenographic record of the conversations reproduced in R. E. Sherwood, Roosevelt and Hopkins: An Intimate History (New York: Harper and Bros., 1948), pp. 893–94.

Stalin first provided an insight into the differences within the Soviet hierarchy. The Russian leader said that "he would not attempt to use Soviet public opinion as a screen but would speak of the feeling that had been created in Soviet governmental circles as a result of recent moves on the part of the United States Government." "These circles felt a certain alarm," he explained, "in regard to the attitude of the United States Government. It was their impression that the American attitude towards the Soviet Union had perceptibly cooled once it became obvious that Germany was defeated, and that it was as though the Americans were saying that the Russians were no longer needed."

To be specific, Stalin continued, the way Lend-Lease had been cancelled "had been unfortunate and even brutal . . . [and] had caused concern to the Soviet Government. If the refusal to continue Lend-Lease was designed as pressure on the Russians in order to soften them up, then it was a fundamental mistake."

In this episode involving Lend-Lease, as well as in additional examples reported by Truman, Byrnes, and other American leaders, Molotov emerges as the leader and spokesman of the militant wing of the Soviet hierarchy. It should be remembered in this connection that Molotov caught the full impact of Truman's vehement anti-Soviet attitude in a face-to-face meeting on April 23, 1945, that followed the crucial discussion of that policy among American leaders on the same day. There is considerable and convincing evidence, furthermore, that Molotov often took and persisted in a very tough line with the United States until Stalin intervened to modify and soften the Russian position. This interpretation of the disagreements among Soviet leaders is further and dramatically reinforced by events after Stalin's death, and particularly by the continued agitation by Molotov against Premier Nikita S. Khrushchev's efforts to establish the policy of co-existence and peaceful transition to socialism and communism.

In 1945, as in later situations of a similar nature, the position of Molotov and his supporters was unquestionably strengthened by the actions of the United States. Stalin was broadly justified in his fears expressed to Hopkins about the developing American attitude concerning the importance of Russia after the defeat of Germany. Truman and his advisors did not immediately and drastically downgrade Russian help. They continued to seek Soviet assistance against the Japanese until they learned that the atom bomb was a success. At that point, their attitude changed drastically: they clearly wanted to defeat Japan before the Russians entered the war. Even before that, however, at the end of April 1945, the change had begun to occur. Following the meeting of April 23, for example, the United States stopped pressing for air bases in Siberia, and ceased worrying about clearing the North Pacific shipping lanes to Russia's Far Eastern ports. In a similar way, American position papers prepared for the forthcoming meeting with Stalin at Potsdam revealed a determination to push for the open door in Eastern Europe.

George F. Kennan
THE SOURCES OF SOVIET CONDUCT

This article, published by a leading Soviet expert in 1947 when the national leadership was searching for some persistent and long-range meaning in Soviet behavior, has an historic significance that transcends the quality of its argumentation. It served as an important rationale for the subsequent containment policies of the Truman administration. Mr. Kennan, who published the essay as Mr. "X," attributed Soviet policy partially to the Marxist assumption of the ultimate collapse of capitalism, partially to the search of Kremlin leaders for security at home and abroad. Ideology served to rationalize the totalitarian nature of the Soviet system by creating the myth of an implacable foe beyond the nation's borders. To Kennan Soviet foreign policy was an expression of an internal power structure. The conviction that capitalism would collapse from its own inconsistencies rendered destruction of the enemy through force unnecessary. It permitted flexibility in diplomacy without conceding the goal of creating a Communist world. Kennan anticipated years of stalemate with some gradual change, perhaps for the better, rather than any complete Western triumph over the Soviet Union.

The political personality of Soviet power as we know it today is the product of ideology and circumstances: ideology inherited by the present Soviet leaders from the movement in which they had their political origin, and circumstances of the power which they now have exercised for nearly three decades in Russia. There can be few tasks

Reprinted by permission from George F. Kennan, "The Sources of Soviet Conduct," *Foreign Affairs* 25 (July 1947): 566–69, 571–82. Copyright 1947 by the Council on Foreign Relations, Inc., New York.

of psychological analysis more difficult than to try to trace the interaction of these two forces and the relative role of each in the determination of official Soviet conduct. Yet the attempt must be made if that conduct is to be understood and effectively countered.

It is difficult to summarize the set of ideological concepts with which the Soviet leaders came into power. Marxian ideology, in its Russian-Communist projection, has always been in process of subtle evolution. The materials on which it bases itself are extensive and complex. But the outstanding features of Communist thought as it existed in 1916 may perhaps be summarized as follows: (a) that the central factor in the life of man, the fact which determines the character of public life and the "physiognomy of society," is the system by which material goods are produced and exchanged; (b) that the capitalist system of production is a nefarious one which inevitably leads to the exploitation of the working class by the capital-owning class and is incapable of developing adequately the economic resources of society or of distributing fairly the material goods produced by human labor; (c) that capitalism contains the seeds of its own destruction and must, in view of the inability of the capital-owning class to adjust itself to economic change, result eventually and inescapably in a revolutionary transfer of power to the working class; and (d) that imperialism, the final phase of capitalism, leads directly to war and revolution.

The rest may be outlined in Lenin's own words: "Unevenness of economic and political development is the inflexible law of capitalism. It follows from this that the victory of Socialism may come originally in a few capitalist countries or even in a single capitalist country. The victorious proletariat of that country, having expropriated the capitalists and having organized Socialist production at home, would rise against the remaining capitalist world, drawing to itself in the process the oppressed classes of other countries." It must be noted that there was no assumption that capitalism would perish without proletarian revolution. A final push was needed from a revolutionary proletariat movement in order to tip over the tottering structure. But it was regarded as inevitable that sooner or later that push would be given.

For fifty years prior to the outbreak of the Revolution, this pattern of thought had exercised great fascination for the members of the Russian revolutionary movement. Frustrated, discontented, hopeless of finding self-expression—or too impatient to seek it—in the confining limits of the Tsarist political system, yet lacking wide popular support for their choice of bloody revolution as a means of social betterment, these revolutionists found in Marxist theory a highly convenient rationalization for their own instinctive desires. It afforded pseudoscientific justification for their impatience, for their categoric denial of all value in the Tsarist system, for their yearning for power and revenge, and for their inclination to cut corners in the pursuit of it. It is therefore no wonder that they had come to believe implicitly in the truth and soundness of the Marxian-Leninist teachings, so congenial to their own impulses and emotions. . . .

The circumstances of the immediate post-Revolution period—the existence in Russia of civil war and foreign intervention, together with the obvious fact that the Communists represented only a tiny minority of the Russian people—made the establishment of dictatorial power a necessity. The experiment with "war Communism" and the abrupt attempt to eliminate private production and trade had unfortunate economic consequences and caused further bitterness against the new revolutionary regime. While the temporary relaxation of the effort to communize Russia, represented by the New Economic Policy, alleviated some of this economic distress and thereby served its purpose, it also made it evident that the "capitalistic sector of society" was still prepared to profit at once from any relaxation of governmental pressure, and would, if permitted to continue to exist, always constitute a powerful opposing element to the Soviet regime and a serious rival for influence in the country. Somewhat the same situation prevailed with respect to the individual peasant who, in his own small way, was also a private producer.

Lenin, had he lived, might have proved a great enough man to reconcile these conflicting forces to the ultimate benefit of Russian society, though this is questionable. But be that as it may, Stalin, and those whom he led in the struggle for succession to Lenin's position of leadership, were not the men to tolerate rival political forces in the sphere of power which they coveted. Their sense of insecurity was too great. Their particular brand of fanaticism, unmodified by any of the Anglo-Saxon traditions of compromise, was too fierce and too jealous to envisage any permanent sharing of power. From the Russian-Asiatic world out of which they had emerged they carried with them a skepticism as to the possibilities of permanent and peaceful coexistence of rival forces. Easily persuaded of their own doctrinaire "rightness," they insisted on the submission or destruction of all competing power. Outside of the Communist Party, Russian society was to have no rigidity. There were to be no forms of collective human activity or association which would not be dominated by the Party. No other force in Russian society was to be permitted to achieve vitality or integrity. Only the Party was to have structure. All else was to be an amorphous mass.

And within the Party the same principle was to apply. The mass of Party members might go through the motions of election, deliberation, decision and action; but in these motions they were to be animated not by their own individual wills but by the awesome breath of the Party leadership and the overbrooding presence of "the word."

Let it be stressed again that subjectively these men probably did not seek absolutism for its own sake. They doubtless believed—and found it easy to believe—that they alone knew what was good for society and that they would accomplish that good once their power was secure and unchallengeable. But in seeking that security of their own rule they were prepared to recognize no restrictions, either of God or man, on the character of their methods. And until such time as that security might be achieved, they placed far down on their scale of operational priorities the comforts and happiness of the peoples entrusted to their care.

Now the outstanding circumstance concerning the Soviet regime is that down to the present day this process of political consolidation has never been completed and the men in the Kremlin have continued to be predominantly absorbed with the struggle to secure and make absolute the power which they seized in November 1917. They have endeavored to secure it primarily against forces at home, within Soviet society itself. But they have also endeavored to secure it against the outside world. For ideology, as we have seen, taught them that the outside world was hostile and that it was their duty eventually to overthrow the political forces beyond their borders. The powerful hands of Russian history and tradition reached up to sustain them in this feeling. . . .

Now the maintenance of this pattern of Soviet power, namely, the pursuit of unlimited authority domestically, accompanied by the cultivation of the semi-myth of implacable foreign hostility, has gone far to shape the actual machinery of Soviet power as we know it today. Internal organs of administration which did not serve this purpose withered on the vine. Organs which did serve this purpose became vastly swollen. The security of Soviet power came to rest on the iron discipline of the Party, on the severity and ubiquity of the secret police, and on the uncompromising economic monopolism of the state. The "organs of suppression," in which the Soviet leaders had sought security from rival forces, became in large measure the masters of those whom they were designed to serve. Today the major part of the structure of Soviet power is committed to the perfection of the dictatorship and to the maintenance of the concept of Russia as in a state of siege, with the enemy lowering beyond the walls. And the millions of human beings who form that part of the structure of power must defend at all costs this concept of Russia's position, for without it they are themselves superfluous.

As things stand today, the rulers can no longer dream of parting with these organs of suppression. The quest for absolute power, pursued now for nearly three decades with a ruthlessness unparalleled (in scope at least) in modern times, has again produced internally, as it did externally, its own reaction. The excesses of the police apparatus have fanned the potential opposition to the regime into something far greater and more dangerous than it could have been before those excesses began.

But least of all can the rulers dispense with the fiction by which the maintenance of dictatorial power has been defended. For this fiction has been canonized in Soviet philosophy by the excesses already committed in its name; and it is now anchored in the Soviet structure of thought by bonds far greater than those of mere ideology.

II

So much for the historical background. What does it spell in terms of the political personality of Soviet power as we know it today?

Of the original ideology, nothing has been officially junked. Belief is maintained in the basic badness of capitalism, in the inevitability of its destruction, in the obligation of the proletariat to assist in that destruction and to take power into its own hands. But stress has come to be laid primarily on those concepts which relate most specifically to the Soviet regime itself: to its position as the sole truly Socialist regime in a dark and misguided world, and to the relationships of power within it.

The first of these concepts is that of the innate antagonism between capitalism and socialism. We have seen how deeply that concept has become imbedded in foundations of Soviet power. It has profound implications for Russia's conduct as a member of international society. It means that there can never be on Moscow's side any sincere assumption of a community of aims between the Soviet Union and powers which are regarded as capitalist. It must invariably be assumed in Moscow that the aims of the capitalist world are antagonistic to the Soviet regime and, therefore, to the interests of the peoples it controls. If the Soviet Government occasionally sets its signature to documents which would indicate the contrary, this is to be regarded as a tactical maneuver permissible in dealing with the enemy (who is without honor) and should be taken in the spirit of *caveat emptor*. Basically, the antagonism remains. It is postulated. And from it flow many of the phenomena which we find disturbing in the Kremlin's conduct of foreign policy: the secretiveness, the lack of frankness, the duplicity, the wary suspiciousness, and the basic unfriendliness of purpose. These phenomena are there to stay, for the foreseeable future. There can be variations of degree and emphasis. When there is something the Russians want from us, one or the other of these features of their policy may be thrust temporarily into the background; and when that happens there will always be Americans who will leap forward with gleeful announcements that "the Russians have changed," and some who will even try to take credit for having brought about such "changes." But we should not be misled by tactical maneuvers. These characteristics of Soviet policy, like the postulate from which they flow, are basic to the internal nature of Soviet power, and will be with us, whether in the foreground or the background, until the internal nature of Soviet power is changed.

This means that we are going to continue for a long time to find the Russians difficult to deal with. It does not mean that they should be considered as embarked upon a do-or-die program to overthrow our society by a given date. The theory of the inevitability of the eventual fall of capitalism has the fortunate connotation that there is no hurry about it. The forces of progress can take their time in preparing the final *coup de grâce*. Meanwhile, what is vital is that the "Socialist fatherland"—that oasis of power which has been already won for Socialism in the person of the Soviet Union—should be cherished and defended by all good Communists at home and abroad, its fortunes promoted, its enemies badgered and confounded. The promotion of premature, "adventuristic" revolutionary projects abroad which might embarrass Soviet power in any way would be an inexcusable, even a counterrevolutionary, act. The cause of Socialism is the support and promotion of Soviet power, as defined in Moscow.

This brings us to the second of the concepts important to contemporary Soviet outlook. That is the infallibility of the Kremlin. The Soviet concept of power, which permits no focal points of organization outside the Party itself, requires that the Party leadership remain in theory the sole repository of truth. For if truth were to be found elsewhere, there would be justification for its expression in organized activity. But it is precisely that which the Kremlin cannot and will not permit.

The leadership of the Communist Party is therefore always right, and has been always right ever since in 1929 Stalin formalized his personal power by announcing that decisions of the Politburo were being taken unanimously.

On the principle of infallibility there rests the iron discipline of the Communist Party. In fact, the two concepts are mutually self-supporting. Perfect discipline requires recognition of infallibility. Infallibility requires the observance of discipline. And the two together go far to determine the behaviorism of the entire Soviet apparatus of power. But their effect cannot be understood unless a third factor be taken into account: namely, the fact that the leadership is at liberty to put forward for tactical purposes any particular thesis which it finds useful to the cause at any particular moment and to require the faithful and unquestioning acceptance of that thesis by the members of the movement as a whole. This means that truth is not a constant but is actually created, for all intents and purposes, by the Soviet leaders themselves. It may vary from week to week, from month to month. It is nothing absolute and immutable—nothing which flows from objective reality. It is only the most recent manifestation of the wisdom of those in whom the ultimate wisdom is supposed to reside, because they represent the logic of history. The accumulative effect of these factors is to give to the whole subordinate apparatus of Soviet power an unshakable stubbornness and steadfastness in its orientation. This orientation can be changed at will by the Kremlin but by no other power. Once a given party line has been laid down on a given issue of current policy, the whole Soviet governmental machine, including the mechanism of diplomacy, moves inexorably along the prescribed path, like a persistent toy automobile wound up and headed in a given direction, stopping only when it meets with some unanswerable force. The individuals who are the components of this machine are unamenable to argument or reason which comes to them from outside sources. Their whole training has taught them to mistrust and discount the glib persuasiveness of the outside world. Like the white dog before the phonograph, they hear only the "master's voice." And if they are to be called off from the purposes last dictated to them, it is the master who must call them off. Thus the foreign representative cannot hope that his words will make any impression on them. The most that he can hope is that they will be transmitted to those at the top, who are capable of changing the party line. But even those are not likely to be swayed by any normal logic in the words of the bourgeois representative. Since there can be no appeal to common purposes, there can be no appeal to common mental approaches. For this reason, facts speak louder than words to the ears of the Kremlin; and words carry the greatest weight when they have the ring of reflecting, or being backed up by, facts of unchallengeable validity.

But we have seen that the Kremlin is under no ideological compulsion to accomplish its purposes in a hurry. Like the Church, it is dealing in ideological concepts which are of long-term validity, and it can afford to be patient. It has no right to risk the existing achievements of the revolution for the sake of vain baubles of the future. The very teachings of Lenin himself require great caution and flexibility in the pursuit of Communist purposes. Again, these precepts are fortified by the lessons of Russian history: of centuries of obscure battles between nomadic forces over the stretches of a vast unfortified plain. Here caution, circumspection, flexibility and deception are the valuable qualities; and their value finds natural appreciation in the Russian or the Oriental mind. Thus the Kremlin has no compunction about retreating in the face of superior force. And being under the compulsion of no timetable, it does not get panicky under the necessity for such retreat. Its political action is a fluid stream which moves constantly, wherever it is permitted to move, toward a given goal. Its main concern is to make sure that it has filled every nook and cranny available to it in the basin of world power. But if it finds unassailable barriers in its path, it accepts these philosophically and accommodates itself to them. The main thing is that there should always be pressure, increasing constant pressure, toward the desired goal. There is no trace of any feeling in Soviet psychology that that goal must be reached at any given time.

These considerations make Soviet Diplomacy at once easier and more difficult to deal with than the diplomacy of individual aggressive leaders like Napoleon and Hitler. On the one hand, it is more sensitive to contrary force, more ready to yield on individual sectors of the diplomatic front when that force is felt to be too strong, and thus more rational in the logic and rhetoric of power. On the other hand, it cannot be easily defeated or discouraged by a single victory on the part of its opponents. And the patient persistence by which it is animated means that it can be effectively countered not by sporadic acts which represent the momentary whims of democratic opinion but only by intelligent long-range policies on the part of Russia's adversaries—policies no less steady in their purpose, and no less variegated and resourceful in their application, than those of the Soviet Union itself.

In these circumstances it is clear that the main element of any United States policy toward the Soviet Union must be that of a long-term, patient but firm and vigilant containment of Russian expansive tendencies. It is important to note, however, that such a policy has nothing to do with outward histrionics: with threats or blustering or superfluous gestures of outward "toughness." While the Kremlin is basically flexible in its reaction to political realities, it is by no means unamenable to considerations of prestige. Like almost any other government, it can be placed by tactless and threatening gestures in a position where it cannot afford to yield even though this might be dictated by its sense of realism. The Russian leaders are keen judges of human psychology, and as such they are highly conscious that loss of temper and of self-control is never a source of strength in political affairs. They are quick to exploit such evidences of weakness. For these reasons, it is a *sine qua non* of successful dealing with Russia that the foreign government in question should remain at all times cool and collected and that its demands on Russian policy should be put forward in such a manner as to leave the way open for a compliance not too detrimental to Russian prestige.

III

In the light of the above, it will be clearly seen that the Soviet pressure against the free institutions of the Western world is something that can be contained by the adroit and vigilant application of counterforce at a series of constantly shifting geographical and political points, corresponding to the shifts and maneuvers of Soviet policy, but which cannot be charmed or talked out of existence. The Russians look forward to a duel of infinite duration, and they see that already they have scored great successes. It must be borne in mind that there was a time when the Communist Party represented far more of a minority in the sphere of Russian national life than Soviet power today represents in the world community.

But if ideology convinces the rulers of Russia that truth is on their side and that they can therefore afford to wait, those of us on whom that ideology has no claim are free to examine objectively the validity of that premise. The Soviet thesis not only implies complete lack of control by the West over its own economic destiny; it likewise assumes Russian unity, discipline and patience over an infinite period. Let us bring this apocalyptic vision down to earth, and suppose that the Western world finds the strength and resourcefulness to contain Soviet power over a period of ten to fifteen years. What does that spell for Russia itself?

The Soviet leaders, taking advantage of the contributions of modern technique to the arts of despotism, have solved the question of obedience within the confines of their power. Few challenge their authority; and even those who do are unable to make that challenge valid as against the organs of suppression of the state.

The Kremlin has also proved able to accomplish its purpose of building up in Russia, regardless of the interests of the inhabitants, an industrial foundation of heavy metallurgy, which is, to be sure, not yet complete but which is nevertheless continuing to grow and is approaching those of the other major industrial countries. All of this, however, both the maintenance of internal political security and the building of heavy industry, has been carried out at a terrible cost in human life and in human hopes and energies. It has necessitated the use of forced labor on a scale unprecedented in modern times under conditions of peace. It has involved the neglect or abuse of other phases of Soviet economic life, particularly agriculture, consumers' goods production, housing and transportation.

To all that, the war has added its tremendous toll of destruction, death and human exhaustion. In consequence of this, we have in Russia today a population which is physically and spiritually tired. The mass of the people are disillusioned, skeptical and no longer as accessible as they once were to the magical attraction which Soviet power still radiates to its followers abroad. The avidity with which people seized upon the slight respite accorded to the Church for tactical reasons during the war was eloquent testimony to the fact that their capacity for faith and devotion found little expression in the purposes of the regime.

In these circumstances, there are limits to the physical and nervous strength of people themselves. These limits are absolute ones, and are binding even for the cruelest dictatorship, because beyond them people cannot be driven. The forced labor camps and the other agencies of constraint provide temporary means of compelling people to work longer hours than their own volition or mere economic pressure would dictate; but if people survive them at all they become old before their time and must be considered as human casualties to the demands of dictatorship. In either case their best powers are no longer available to society and can no longer be enlisted in the service of the state.

Here only the younger generation, despite all vicissitudes and sufferings, is numerous and vigorous; and the Russians are a talented people. But it still remains to be seen what will be the effects on mature performance of the abnormal emotional strains of childhood which Soviet dictatorship created and which were enormously increased by the war. Such things as normal security and placidity of home environment have practically ceased to exist in the Soviet Union outside of the most remote farms and villages. And observers are not yet sure whether that is not going to leave its mark on the overall capacity of the generation now coming into maturity.

In addition to this, we have the fact that Soviet economic development, while it can list certain formidable achievements, has been precariously spotty and uneven. Russian Communists who speak of the "uneven development of capitalism" should blush at the contemplation of their own national economy. Here certain branches of economic life, such as the metallurgical and machine industries, have been pushed out of all proportion to other sectors of economy. Here is a nation striving to become in a short period one of the great industrial nations of the world while it still has no highway network worthy of the name and only a relatively primitive network of railways. Much has been done to increase efficiency of labor and to teach primitive peasants something about the operation of machines. But maintenance is still a crying deficiency of all Soviet economy.

Construction is hasty and poor in quality. Depreciation must be enormous. And in vast sectors of economic life it has not yet been possible to instill into labor anything like that general culture of production and technical self-respect which characterizes the skilled worker of the West.

It is difficult to see how these deficiencies can be corrected at an early date by a tired and dispirited population working largely under the shadow of fear and compulsion. And as long as they are not overcome, Russia will remain economically a vulnerable, and in a certain sense an impotent, nation, capable of exporting its enthusiasms and of radiating the strange charm of its primitive political vitality but unable to back up those articles of export by real evidences of material power and prosperity.

Meanwhile, a great uncertainty hangs over the political life of the Soviet Union. That is the uncertainty involved in the transfer of power from one individual or group of individuals to others.

This is, of course, outstandingly the problem of the personal position of Stalin. We must remember that his succession to Lenin's pinnacle of preeminence in the Communist movement was the only such transfer of individual authority which the Soviet Union has experienced. That transfer took twelve years to consolidate. It cost the lives of millions of people and shook the state to its foundations; the attendant tremors were felt all through the international revolutionary movement, to the disadvantage of the Kremlin itself.

It is always possible that another transfer of preeminent power may take place quietly and inconspicuously, with no repercussions anywhere. But again, it is possible that the questions involved may unleash, to use some of Lenin's words, one of those "incredibly swift transitions" from "delicate deceit" to "wild violence" which characterize Russian history, and may shake Soviet power to its foundations. . . .

It must be surmised from this that even within so highly disciplined an organization as the Communist Party there must be a growing divergence in age, outlook and interest between the great mass of Party members, only so recently recruited into the movement, and the little self-perpetuating clique of men at the top, whom most of these Party members have never met, with whom they have never conversed, and with whom they can have no political intimacy.

Who can say whether, in these circumstances, the eventual rejuvenation of the higher spheres of authority (which can only be a matter of time) can take place smoothly and peacefully, or whether rivals in the quest for higher power will not eventually reach down into these politically immature and inexperienced masses in order to find support for their respective claims. If this were ever to happen, strange consequences could flow for the Communist Party: for the membership at large has been exercised only in the practices of iron discipline and obedience and not in the arts of compromise and accommodation. And if disunity were ever to seize and paralyze the Party, the chaos and weakness of Russian society would be revealed in forms beyond description. For we have seen that Soviet power is only a crust concealing an amorphous mass of human beings among whom no independent organizational structure is tolerated. In Russia there is not even such a thing as local government. The present generation of Russians have never known spontaneity of collective action. If, consequently, anything were ever to occur to disrupt the unity and efficacy of the Party as a political instrument, Soviet Russia might be changed overnight from one of the strongest to one of the weakest and most pitiable of national societies.

Thus the future of Soviet power may not be by any means as secure as Russian capacity for self-delusion would make it appear to the men in the Kremlin. That they can keep power themselves, they have demonstrated. That they can quietly and easily turn it over to others remains to be proved. Meanwhile, the hardships of their rule and the vicissitudes of international life have taken a heavy toll of the strength and hopes of the great people on whom their power rests. It is curious to note that the ideological power of Soviet authority is strongest today in areas beyond the frontiers of Russia, beyond the reach of its police power. This phenomenon brings to mind a comparison used by Thomas Mann in his great novel *Buddenbrooks*. Observing that human institutions often show the greatest outward brilliance at a moment when inner decay is in reality farthest advanced, he compared the Buddenbrook family, in the days of its greatest glamor, to one of those stars whose light shines most brightly on this world when in reality it has long since ceased to exist. And who can say with assurance that the strong light still cast by the Kremlin on the dissatisfied peoples of the Western world is not the powerful afterglow of a constellation which is in actuality on the wane? This cannot be proved. And it cannot be disproved. But the possibility remains (and in the opinion of this writer it is a strong one) that Soviet power, like the capitalist world of its conception, bears within it the seeds of its own decay, and that the sprouting of these seeds is well advanced.

IV

It is clear that the United States cannot expect in the foreseeable future to enjoy political intimacy with the Soviet regime. It must continue to regard the Soviet Union as a rival, not a partner, in the political arena. It must continue to expect that Soviet policies will reflect no abstract love of peace and stability, no real faith in the possibility of a permanent happy coexistence of the Socialist and capitalist worlds, but rather a cautious, persistent pressure toward the disruption and weakening of all rival influence and rival power.

Balanced against this are the facts that Russia, as opposed to the Western world in general, is still by far the weaker party, that Soviet policy is highly flexible, and that Soviet society may well contain deficiencies which will eventually weaken its own total potential. This would of itself warrant the United States' entering with reasonable confidence upon a policy of firm containment, designed to confront the Russians with unalterable counterforce at every point where they show signs of encroaching upon the interests of a peaceful and stable world.

But in actuality the possibilities for American policy are by no means limited to holding the line and hoping for the best. It is entirely possible for the United States to influence by its actions the internal developments, both within Russia and throughout the international Communist movement, by which Russian policy is largely determined. This is not only a question of the modest measure of informational activity which this government can conduct in the Soviet Union and elsewhere, although that, too, is important. It is rather a question of the degree to which the United States can create among the peoples of the world generally the impression of a country which knows what it wants, which is coping successfully with the problems of its internal life and with the responsibilities of a World Power, and which has a spiritual vitality capable of holding its own among the major ideological currents of the time. To the extent that such an impression can be created and maintained, the aims of Russian communism must appear sterile and quixotic, the hopes and enthusiasm of Moscow's supporters must wane, and added strain must be imposed on the Kremlin's foreign policies. For the palsied decrepitude of the capitalist world is the keystone of Communist philosophy. Even the failure of the United States to experience the early economic depression which the ravens of the Red Square have been predicting with such complacent confidence since hostilities ceased would have deep and important repercussions throughout the Communist world.

By the same token, exhibitions of indecision, disunity and internal disintegration within this country have an exhilarating effect on the whole Communist movement. At each evidence of these tendencies, a thrill of hope and excitement goes through the Communist world; a new jauntiness can be noted in the Moscow tread; new groups of foreign supporters climb on to what they can only view as the band wagon of international politics; and Russian pressure increases all along the line in international affairs.

It would be an exaggeration to say that American behavior unassisted and alone could exercise a power of life and death over the Communist movement and bring about the early fall of Soviet power in Russia. But the United States has it in its power to increase enormously the strains under which Soviet policy must operate, to force upon the Kremlin a far greater degree of moderation and circumspection than it has had to observe in recent years, and in this way to promote tendencies which must eventually find their outlet in either the break-up or the gradual mellowing of Soviet power. For no mystical, Messianic movement—and particularly not that of the Kremlin—can face frustration indefinitely without eventually adjusting itself in one way or another to the logic of that state of affairs.

Thus the decision will really fall in large measure in this country itself. The issue of Soviet-American relations is in essence a test of the over-all worth of the United States as a nation among nations. To avoid destruction the United States need only measure up to its own best traditions and prove itself worthy of preservation as a great nation.

Surely, there was never a fairer test of national quality than this. In the light of these circumstances, the thoughtful observer of Russian-American relations will find no cause for complaint in the Kremlin's challenge to American society. He will rather experience a certain gratitude to a Providence which, by providing the American people with this implacable challenge, has made their entire security as a nation dependent on their pulling themselves together and accepting the responsibilities of moral and political leadership that history plainly intended them to bear.

III IDEOLOGY, POWER, AND INTEREST

Zbigniew Brzezinski

COMMUNIST IDEOLOGY: KEY TO SOVIET POLICY

In this scholarly examination of Soviet ideology, Professor Brzezinski of Columbia University is concerned both with the shaping of that dogma by the Russian experience of the half century to 1960 and with the amplification of its significance because of that experience. "It is precisely because the ideology is both a set of conscious assumptions and purposes and part of the total historical, social, and personal background of the Soviet leaders," he writes, "that it is so pervading and so important." The Kremlin, he believes, is too committed to the Marxist-Leninist ideology to modify measures designed to achieve the ultimate triumph of that ideology. The pressures emanating from changing world conditions, the diversity of outlook in the Communist camp, and the weapons of mass destruction are countered, Brzezinski concludes, by influences which reassert and revitalize the ideology. The challenge of diversity merely confirms the broad commitment of the Soviet ruling elite to the Marxist-Leninist dogma, the chief source of its power and authority.

The persisting and important role of ideological assumptions in the thinking and actions of Soviet leaders . . . can be appreciated only if it is seen in a perspective which takes into consideration the various factors which go into the shaping of an ideology. The triumphant assertions that the Soviet leaders are abandoning their Marxism or communism, voiced in the West with such monotonous regularity and persistent ignorance, might possibly be dismissed more quickly if the usual image of an abstract and arid Marxist dogma were to give way to a better appreciation of the inextricably close linkage between the Soviet social environment and the Soviet ideology. It is precisely because the ideology is both a set of conscious assumptions and purposes and part of the total historical, social, and personal background of the Soviet leaders that it is so pervading and so important.

Without undertaking a comprehensive review of the development and substance of Soviet Communist ideology, it may be useful to recall in "capsule" form some of the factors that have gone into

Reprinted by permission from Zbigniew Brzezinski, "Communist Ideology and International Affairs," *Journal of Conflict Resolution* 4 (September 1960): 266–90.

molding it (or perverting it, as the purists would claim), thereby making it much more a part of the Russian reality and infusing it with genuine social vitality. Such variables as the general historical context, the role of personalities, the manner in which a foreign doctrine was understood and absorbed, the emergence of the party and its special organizational experience, and, finally, the process of shaping a new society—all interacted dynamically to give the ideology its particular flavor and emphasis. No one of these factors alone can be said to have determined the character of the Soviet ideology; taken together they do help to understand how it emerged and developed. In summary form the following assumptions and principles may be said to be part of the ideological framework with which the Soviet leaders evaluate and organize their perception of the outside world: Marxist doctrine is the basic source of their commitment to economic and dialectical determinism in history, and of their persistent conviction that the vehicle of history is the class struggle. . . . Closely related to this "scientific" conception of history is the apocalyptic image of the future and the belief in the inevitable triumph for their form of social organization. . . .

The experience of the Bolshevik leaders in pre- and post-revolutionary Russia resulted in the emergence of a series of further basic postulates, which jointly with the above categories constitute the Soviet ideological framework. Probably the most important of these is the Soviet conviction that the construction of "socialism" anywhere requires that power be wielded solely by the Communist party. This belief, in part rooted in the Russian experience and in part reflecting the institutionalized vested interest of the ruling elite, has become a fundamental thesis of the Soviet leaders. Its impact on their vision of the world should not be underestimated, for it colors particularly their appreciation of changes occurring in the underdeveloped parts of the world. Similarly, the Leninist concepts of the seizure of power, with their emphasis on violent revolution, went far in the direction of establishing the supremacy of "consciousness" over "spontaneity" in historical processes, in turn consolidating the importance of the organized and conscious agent of history. The Soviet commitment to monolithic dictatorship and intensified class struggle as necessary attributes of the "socialist construction" thus again reflects the combination of doctrine and practice becoming ideology. Similarly, Lenin's discussion of the nature of imperialism reflected his pragmatic awareness that theory must always be related to a given reality; in the case of his historical era it was to provide a meaningful insight into the inner dynamics of the underdeveloped and restless part of the world. The Marxist approach was the basis for the Leninist theory of imperialism and gave Lenin his point of departure as well as his basic analytical tools. However, the combination of Marxist doctrine, Russian revolutionary experience, social-economic backwardness, and the vested interest of the ruling Bolshevik party resulted in the development of the notion that social developments throughout the world operate on the basis of a sharply definable dichotomy—a dichotomy which is proof per se of an unbridgeable hostility between the emerging "socialist" state (later a system of socialist states) and the rest of the world. A paranoiac image of the world conspiring against "socialism" easily followed.

All these conceptual and analytical factors combined serve to organize the Soviet vision of international affairs, to define goals, and to evaluate reality. These aspects should not be confused with the utopian elements of the ideology, which are necessary as part of a long-range vision and which perform essentially a rationalizing and legitimizing function. Confusing these two, or failing to distinguish between Marxist theory and the ideology, can lead to the simplistic conclusion that Soviet ideology is merely a cynical sham, consciously manipulated by the Soviet leaders. Similarly, it can result in the opposite and extreme conclusion that the Soviet approach to reality can be understood merely by consulting a Marxist handbook. In the preceding paragraphs we have tried to show that the Soviet Communist ideology must be viewed as combining certain doctrinal assumptions with principles derived from the theory but closely reflecting the specific reality of those who subscribe to the ideology. It then becomes part of the reality and an autonomously existing factor, conditioning behavior through the selection of the various policy alternatives that may exist at any particular moment.

Role and Impact in International Affairs

How, then, does the Soviet Communist ideology affect the Soviet approach to international affairs? Here a distinction must be drawn between short-range and long-range prospects. The former are naturally much more often determined by the imperatives of the moment. For example, on the matter of choice of international friends, Soviet freedom of action was severely circumscribed in June

1941, quite unlike the situation in the summer of 1939. In the latter case the essentially ideologically determined conclusion that the objective of the West was to embroil the USSR in a war with Germany dictated a policy of creating the conditions for conflict among the capitalist powers, that is, giving the Germans the freedom of action which they felt necessary for the commencement of hostilities. However, Soviet short-range moves are only in part a function of the situation as created by outside forces. They are also the consequence of certain long-range commitments made by the Soviet Union itself, and in that sense they are the product of the factors that shape the nature of that long-range commitment. From that standpoint they do feel the impact of ideology on Soviet external behavior and policy.

The general Soviet approach to international affairs is strongly affected by the fundamental Soviet assumption that all material reality changes continuously through the clash of antagonistic contradictions. This conflict is said to be the basic law of social development until such time as "socialism" becomes a world system. As a result, the Soviet approach to international affairs is characterized by an intense preoccupation with change. This awareness of continuing change, and the conviction that the inner nature of that change is only understood by them, creates the basis for the faith of the Soviet leaders that they have unraveled the internal logic of history and that their policies are not merely an aspiration but a "scientific" calculation. . . .

The preoccupation with change, the willingness to adjust to the particular "historical" phase, and the quest for understanding the inner dynamics of other societies has not, however, prevented the ideology from infusing Soviet foreign policy with a sense of continuity in purpose. This sense of continuity is derived from their militant conception of relations, in which reality is viewed as being a continuing conflict. In the Soviet view, occasional equilibriums result in international détentes; they do not, however, halt the fundamental process of change and therefore cannot create enduring conditions of stability. This means that any political arrangement is binding only until it ceases to interpret accurately that reality. For this reason, no long-range commitments to the status quo can be contemplated except in terms of communicating with those who are accustomed to thinking in terms of the present and who regard the changing reality as part of a vaguely definable, free-flowing, and gradual historical process. Given that, the overall purpose of Soviet foreign policy is to remain associated with, and to stimulate, the evolution of these processes of change in the direction of ultimate consummation. The ideological commitment inherent in this attitude permits the Soviet leaders to remain persistent in their tasks, transcending reversals and failures which inevitably occur and despite shifts in their own policies. . . .

In addition, despite the shifts and turns in Soviet foreign policy in the last several decades, a persisting attribute of its long perspective is the sense of compulsive obligation to assist the spread of communism throughout the world. This universality of goal makes the Soviet foreign policy something altogether different from tsarist foreign policy or, for that matter, from the relatively vague and rather generalized American desire to see a "free" but otherwise undefined world. (However, there are some striking parallels between the Soviet view and the traditional American image of America as an active symbol of certain universal norms.) Admittedly, Soviet foreign policy, especially in its short-term aspects, is concerned with national security, frontiers, national power, etc.—factors which inherently introduce similarities with Russia's traditional concerns. Quite unlike its predecessors, however, the Soviet leaders view these issues in terms of certain long-range perspectives and not as ends in themselves. Indeed, the Soviet conception of their own security is inherently offensive; as long as alternative political systems exist, there is continued need to be preoccupied with security issues. Because they see themselves as part of a historical process toward a defined end, the Soviet leaders are compelled to view any effort to "stabilize" or to "normalize" the international situation as a hostile design.

The universality of goals aspect of Soviet foreign policy also makes it clear that, while the concept of "national interest" may not be irrelevant to an understanding of Communist foreign policy, to be useful, it must be linked to the ultimate ideological objective. As far as Communist leaders are concerned, Soviet national interest is that which increases the power and the capability of the USSR to promote communism. Communist ideology, therefore, does not raise the dilemma of national versus international objectives—at least, not until such time as a series of other Communist states come into being (see below). Dovetailing of national and international interests is hence another important ideological element and permits the Soviet leaders to strengthen their power without power becoming the sheer end of their actions. Ideology which makes power both a tool and an end allows the Soviet leaders to be continuously concerned with the maximization of their power but without that power becoming an impediment to the fulfillment of ideological values.

For instance, even if the reason for enforcing dramatic and, indeed, revolutionary changes in East Europe were merely the desire to strengthen Soviet power over the area and not to construct communism per se, the mere fact that the method of strengthening that power was conceived in terms of large-scale social and economic changes showed the underlying ideological bias. One can certainly argue that a more moderate program would have created much less resistance and hence would have favorably affected the Communist power situation. The standard Communist answer—communism is not safe without creating a social upheaval that uproots the existing interest groups—in itself reveals an approach to problems of political power that is strongly tinged with ideological assumptions. Similarly, in economics the issue of collectivization is a case in point. In addition, insofar as the international Communist movement is concerned, ideology permits the Soviet Union to enjoy an additional operational advantage without always having the actual power to control the behavior of the various Communist parties throughout the world. Ideology, as a binding system of belief, thereby translates itself into a factor of power.

Admittedly, the ideological factor can and often does create difficulties. It can lead to excessively dogmatic evaluation of the situation, stimulate premature optimism, or simply mislead. Furthermore, insofar as the Soviet leaders are consciously aware of the ideology's role as a unifying bond for international communism, it may tend to limit their freedom of action lest this unity be strained. This consideration was less important during Stalin's days than before and after the dictator's rule.

However, on balance, the various roles of the ideology cannot be viewed merely as a liability. There is a tendency in the West to view ideology as something irrational and to counterpoise it against pragmatism and empiricism. From what has already been said, it would appear that ideology is not incompatible with rational behavior, once the basic assumptions are granted. While these assumptions may or may not be rational, they are at least so far removed from immediate concerns that they do not produce a conflict between the ideology and a rational approach to reality. The goal of an ultimate worldwide Communist society, allegedly determined by history, may be irrational, but it does not necessarily impose irrational conduct.

Second, and more significantly perhaps, some of the concepts of the ideology do offer meaningful insights into international affairs. The preoccupation with the nature of the domestic dynamics of other societies and the realization that economic processes create political problems which are international can result in a more meaningful appreciation of reality than arguments about "traditional national goals," or moralistic pontifications to the effect that democracies are inherently peaceful and more powerful, while dictatorships are war-like and ultimately doomed. For all its limitations (see above), Soviet ideology at least seems to point to some of the inner mechanisms of international affairs. The approach of Western statesmen still is often derived from an image of international affairs shaped by the emergence of nation-states. As long as these states operate in an environment in which mass emotionalism, particularly nationalism, was not politically determinant, international politics could operate relatively stably on the basis of certain commonly accepted rules. The intervention of mass public opinion, rallying around, first, nationalist symbols, and, second, ideological ones (democratic or totalitarian), necessarily transforms interstate political conflicts into national ones, with profound social-economic overtones. The differences between the Vienna Congress of 1815 and the Versailles Treaty of 1919 are symptomatic.

The Soviet Communist ideology has made an Important contribution toward the transformation of international politics from a "game" with certain commonly accepted rules into a profoundly intense conflict, insoluble without a major social transformation either of some of the participating societies or at least of the outlook of some of their elites. . . .

International Affairs and Prospects of Ideological Erosion

There is a difference between ideological change and ideological erosion, although the two are closely related. Change has to take place if ideology is to continue to respond to social needs. However, when the ideology begins to lose its social vitality, either by becoming so dogmatic that it no longer corresponds to reality or because reality has so changed that even the widest stretching of the ideology can no longer encompass it, the change develops into erosion. The ideology becomes merely declamatory or simply fades away. These verbal dialectics can perhaps be made meaningful by a discussion of the impact on the ideological framework which shapes the Soviet foreign policy of the following three sets of factors: (1) the interaction of Communist objectives and domestic change; (2) the emergence of the Communist bloc; and (3) the impact of international affairs. . . .

The development of the Soviet ideology has been closely linked with the various phases of the activity of the political movement which embodies the ideology and, beyond that, with the various men who have stood at the helm of that movement. A recent and perceptive analysis of these stages characterized them as that of transplantation, adaptation, and implementation. To the extent that it is possible to compartmentalize social development into neat phases, the first two may be said to have been closely associated with the name of Lenin; the third, with Stalin. Each of these phases was dominated by some central objective which necessarily magnified or minimized some of the ideological principles to which the movement subscribed. For instance, the emergence of the party as the central, indispensable agent of history has been a crucial ideological ingredient of the entire span of Soviet development, a necessity interdependent with the changing central objective. On the other hand, the stage of transplantation permitted or maybe even required a measure of internal dialogue which gradually became incompatible with the subsequent stages of adaptation and implementation and with the character of the movement which such a dialogue bred. Increasingly, the antiauthoritarian and democratic elements of the doctrine gave way to ideologically supported discipline, ending finally with the physical liquidation of all those who by their mere presence reminded the party or its leader of the movement's former diversity. Similarly, the essentially antistate orientation of the early revolutionaries gradually gave way to the acceptance and then to the enshrinement of the state as a central and positive factor in effecting the desired socioeconomic change. The building of a new industrial society also meant that the principle of egalitarianism had to be abandoned and be replaced by a highly stratified social system. The emphasis on a mounting class struggle during the difficult phase of implementation again reflected both the dynamics of the central objective and the impatient disposition of the party leadership which came to power in that particular phase. Finally, even after the seizure of power the party continued to view itself as a conspiratorial movement, and this too helped to define the character of its relations with the society subject to it and with the world at large.

The process of shaping new principles or changing old ones is not without its tensions. One could almost say that there is a kind of "dialectical" relationship between an ideologically oriented party and reality. The ideological party attempts to change reality and, in this way, is a revolutionary force; the new changed reality for a while corresponds to the ideology even while gradually changing itself; in time, the ideology may become a conservative force; a new adjustment is eventually forced, and the ideology may then again become a revolutionary force. The varying stages of Soviet Communist ideology—Leninism, Stalinism, Khrushchevism—and the relatively violent transitions from one to the other can be seen as part of this dialectical relationship between ideology and reality. Yet, it is exactly this adaptability that permits the ideology to exercise a continuing influence and prevents it from becoming sterile and irrelevant, thereby allowing it to retain a certain identity of its own.

However, in the present period two factors threaten to translate this process of change into erosion. The raising of the banner of Communist construction, proclaimed by the Twenty-first CPSU Congress in an effort to revitalize the ideological sense of purpose, will produce much sooner than hitherto might have been expected a confrontation between reality and ideology. This confrontation might threaten the role of the party as the agent of history and undermine the validity of the ideology. As long as the party was actively shaping Soviet society and as long as that society was mere putty in the hands of the leaders of the party, the position of the party could not be contested. But a highly industrialized Soviet society, increasingly conscious of its achievements, could cease to be a passive object and could begin to exert pressures even on the party. These pressures now seem to be most timid, but so are the initial stirrings of life. Even most restrained social pressures, as, for instance, those in favor of a higher rate of consumption or more freedom in the literary arts, would argue a changing relationship and, as a result, a somewhat changing conception of the ideology. Some alert Communists, more alert perhaps than Khrushchev, have already signaled warnings that excessive emphasis on industrial indexes and on material well-being as the expression of the achievement of socialism-communism could result in the "unconscious" acceptance of many "bourgeois" values by the Communists themselves. . . .

In the initial phase of the existence of the Communist bloc, the bloc served to strengthen the ideological conviction that history is on the side of communism (or vice versa). The expansion of communism to include one-third of the globe, effected by force of arms or by revolution, seemed to recapture some of the old revolutionary fervor which had been denied the Russian Communists since the twenties. History was again in its dynamic phase. To this day the Soviet leaders glory in the size and population of the camp and frequently cite these as proof that "the east wind is now blowing over the west wind." Furthermore, as long as Stalin lived, the expansion of the camp did not raise insurmountable ideological difficulties. Even the old theory of capitalist encirclement was still maintained, to be attacked, finally, only as late as 1958. This dismissal of capitalist encirclement, however, did not include an important ideological consideration; rather it was a matter of reassessing the relationship of forces on the international arena and reaching a more optimistic (and as it happens, a more correct) conclusion.

Insofar as new Communist-ruled states were concerned, after a brief transition period they adopted an essentially Stalinist pattern of domestic restructuring and conceptions. The Soviet experience in "construction of socialism" was adjudged to have universal validity and, consequently, a complex of methods and beliefs, which formed the Soviet ideology and reflected the Soviet adaptation of Marxism, was grafted onto all the ruling Communist elites, whatever their intellectual and political heritage. Stalin's death soon revealed the inadequacy and the fundamental instability of this application. And the subsequent search for new forms of ideological and political unity within the camp underscored the full complexity of the problem of applying Soviet ideology, with its universal aspirations, to varied national conditions.

Without retracing the involved series of attempted solutions and without discussing their relative merits, it can be observed that the efforts to develop common ideological prescriptions for the post-Stalin Soviet bloc came face to face with two obvious and related difficulties: the matter of different social contexts within which an ideology matures and the problem of varying stages of "socialist" development. The first of these could be ignored as long as Stalinist power and Stalinist prestige were available and could be applied so as to universalize the Soviet outlook. Furthermore, the early stage of Communist rule in the newly subject nations meant that the main thrust of Communist efforts was directed at consolidating their power and at destroying the old society. These essentially negative tasks did not raise ideological problems as acute as the later one of building new social institutions.

However, Stalin's death and the dissipation of Stalinism took place when the attention of the Communist leaders was increasingly turning to the latter objective. Within the context of relative relaxation and faced with domestic problems peculiar to their own societies, some of them increasingly eschewed Soviet solutions and step by step began to feel the full weight of their own social traditions and their own "apperception" of the ideology. A general consequence of this was the emerging ideological diversity which characterized the bloc in 1956–57 and which potentially exists even today, despite conscious and essentially expedient-motivated efforts by the ruling elites to reestablish ideological uniformity.

Moreover, the varying stages of social-economic development of the various countries within the Soviet bloc inherently produced different problems requiring different solutions. China, going through an economic and social revolution at a pace even more rapid than the Soviet Union did in the most violent Stalinist phase, could not escape drawing primarily on those aspects of the ideology which justified the application of violence, which maximized the power of the party, which simplified international issues into simple relations of hostile dichotomy, and which viewed with profound suspicion any voices of moderation. The Soviet Union, on the brink if not of a Communist fulfillment then at least of reaping a partial harvest of several decades of social sacrifice, was becoming increasingly concerned with rationalizing the operations both of its own society and of the bloc. Many Communists in Poland, Hungary, and Rumania, countries suffering the pangs of transition from a rural society to an industrial one and lacking the indigenous support which both the Russian and Chinese Communists enjoyed, were increasingly coming under the influence of "revisionism"; that is, abandoning the simplifications of the Soviet ideological outlook, increasingly viewing the problems of social transformation as organic worldwide processes, requiring also a gradual and continuous transformation of social consciousness. On the other hand, the leaders of the industrially advanced East Germany and Czechoslovakia, not faced by social-economic tribulations, were increasingly sympathetic to the Chinese outlook, since it provided the political justification for their politically unstable regimes. Striking evidence of this was provided by the Chinese tenth-anniversary celebration in Peking in October 1959: on foreign policy issues and on Chinese domestic policies, including the "Great Leap Forward" and the communes, the East Germans and the Czechs adopted the most enthusiastic line, quite in contrast to the Poles and the Russians.

The consequence of this differentiated ideological conditioning, of the different stages of development of the respective "socialist" states, as well as of different interests of the ruling elites, has been an occasional diversity of outlook on a variety of important issues. In the case of China and the Soviet Union, this diversity seems to involve an issue not new to the Soviet Communists: To what extent can a Marxist revolutionary cooperate with the existing social forces and merge himself with the observable trends in the direction of the inevitable victory? To what degree must he remain alienated from the world, rejected, and strive to alter it by first destroying it? Perhaps it would not be too gross an oversimplification to say that the crux of the problem was whether peaceful coexistence with the enemy was transitionally possible. . . .

Quite a different challenge to ideological unity is raised by some of the East European Communist states. The most extensive statement of contemporary East European revisionism is contained in the program adopted by the Yugoslav Communist party in April 1959. The general response of the camp to it has been to anathematize the Yugoslavs. Nonetheless, within all the ruling European Communist parties such views are entertained by many members, particularly among the intellectuals, and provide the underpinning for potential ideological disunity. The reason for this is simply that the Soviet ideology will not meaningfully reflect or shape reality in the Eastern European context unless Soviet force is available to back it. Anyone familiar with the ideological traditions of Polish left-wing socialism, with the cultural climate of the country, and its "political style," or with the role played by the populist writers in Hungary in the shaping of Hungarian radicalism would agree that forceful measures would be necessary to prevent the dilution and revision of Marxism-Leninism when that ideology comes to be embodied by large mass movements within these countries. Such forceful measures were undertaken by the small, dedicated Marxist-Leninist minorities which exist in these countries, but even they found it difficult to remain immune to their environment. Much the same could be said for some of the other Communist-ruled states.

It was this environmental influence which was at the root of the 1956 crisis, and the same consideration has recently forced the Soviet leaders to equivocate on the old issue of the class struggle after the seizure of power. In response to the needs of Soviet society and attempting to explain the "aberrations of Stalinism," Khrushchev negated and condemned the principle of the mounting class struggle as a Stalinist distortion of Marxism-Leninism. In 1959, however, faced in East Europe with the dilemma of social opposition to "socialist construction" and fearful that his abandonment of this Stalinist principle might strengthen the hands of the revisionists in Eastern Europe, he modified it "dialectically":

> The Twentieth Congress of our Party rightly criticized Joseph Stalin's mistaken proposition that the class struggle grows sharper with progress in socialist construction. But criticism of this proposition certainly does not mean that we can deny the inevitability of class struggle in the period of socialist construction. . . . This development does not proceed along a straight line. Class struggle in the epoch of building socialism can intensify at certain periods in connection with some of the changes in the internal and external situation and assume an extremely sharp form, up to and including the armed clash, as was the case in Hungary in 1956.

Khrushchev's efforts were symbolic of the growing necessity to adjust the ideology to varying national conditions. In spite of his efforts, however, the radically different conditions which the ruling Communist elites encountered in Eastern Europe as compared to Russia in 1917 or to China in 1949 pose a continuing dilemma to the unity of Communist practice and, therefore, to the unity of the ideology.

Despite Soviet efforts to maintain an ideological equilibrium, the consequence of this growing diversity, and the Soviet elasticity in response to it, is to *relativize* the meaning of the ideology. For forty years the Soviet leaders have been accustomed to reject those who talk a different "language" than they and to eject those who use the same language to disagree. Now, for the first time they have to tolerate fellow Communists who use similar concepts to reach different conclusions. Even today one should increasingly speak not of Communist ideology but of Soviet Communist ideology, Chinese Communist ideology, Yugoslav Communist ideology, etc. And, since it was the Marxist-Leninist ideology's claim to universality which originally stimulated such intense Soviet involvement not only in the domination of its neighbors but particularly in directing the character of their domestic transformation, the increasing diversity in ideological emphases threatens the universal validity of even the Soviet ideology itself and thereby undermines one of the factors which shape the Soviet approach to the world. It also threatens the domestic legitimacy of this Soviet ideology by denying its central claim, that is, its universal validity, which is used as a justification for its domestic application. Efforts to reassert unity in response to this threat can further divorce the ideology from reality, while the toleration and resulting extension of such diversity threatens to introduce elements of relativism dangerous to the cohesion of the ideology. . . .

After the seizure of power, the Soviet leaders had to adjust to an international reality which did not quite fit their earlier expectations. The adjustment was not easy and involved a series of conflicts between reality and ideology, e.g., the controversy generated by the Brest-Litovsk negotiations with Germany. Even after their power had been consolidated, the spread of the revolution was both expected and artificially stimulated by Moscow. Gradually and painfully, however, ideology began to correspond to reality, and the principle of "socialism in one country" emerged. It took a long time for this principle to lapse, and many Soviet actions after the war with respect to their new Communist neighbors were rooted in this principle lagging behind the new political situation.

Insofar as Soviet conduct on the international arena was concerned, given the weakness of the new Soviet state, ideology could not exercise a wide latitude in action. The number of policy alternatives open to the Soviet Union was relatively limited, if one excludes political suicide as an alternative; and Communist ideology, unlike the Nazi one, lays the greatest emphasis on self-preservation. Faced with international politics which operated essentially on the balance-of-power principle, the Soviet Union, in order to pursue its ideological objectives, had no choice but to attempt "to play the game," employing the openings which the game provided to its best advantage. . . .

The situation has changed with growing Soviet power and with the even more rapidly growing Soviet sense of confidence. For the first time since the 1920s, the Soviet leaders seem to feel again that the day of their victory is not far away. However, balancing this are also several factors related to international affairs which eventually could serve to modify this Soviet sense of ideological fulfillment. These may be treated under three headings: stability in Western society; patterns of development in the underdeveloped societies; the nature of modern weapons systems. With respect to the first, it would appear that in 1947 the Soviet leadership still entertained some hopes that revolutionary upheavals might take place in France, Italy, and/or Greece, and they were counting on the expansion of communism into Western Europe. Failure of these attempts followed by a remarkable Western European recovery seems to have convinced the Soviet leaders that in the foreseeable future they cannot count on the duplication of either the Leninist type (seizure of power) or the Stalinist form (military occupation) of Communist development. Beyond that, they increasingly appear to be willing to concede that in such stable, prosperous, and democratic societies an altogether different form of transition from the bourgeois stage to the socialist stage must be contemplated. Khrushchev finally articulated this when he stated at the Twentieth Party Congress of the CPSU that, Lenin to the contrary, a peaceful takeover by the Communist party was possible and that parliamentary devices could be used to that end. Such a conception comes dangerously close to an abandonment of Leninism, and the Soviet leaders were not unaware of it. Therefore they refrained from taking the next step (taken by the Yugoslavs), namely, that of conceding that socialism may be built by social-democratic parties; and they continued to insist that only the Communist party can effect such a true transition. Nonetheless, the importance of the change should not be underestimated. The change does involve an important modification of their outlook. . . .

The new and still underdeveloped states . . . pose the challenge of claiming by and large to be building societies of a socialist type and of actually doing it through democratic political means and highly pragmatic and certainly not Soviet (nor capitalist) economic methods. If they should succeed, and they possibly might with both Soviet ("socialist") and American ("capitalist") aid, the consequence will have to be a major redefinition of the processes of social-economic change, whatever the Soviet ideologues may choose to call the new society. Such a development would strike not only at the ideology and its dichotomic image of social change but even at its doctrinal foundations. It would pose a threat to the entire historical structure of the ideology and would strengthen the appeal of "revisionism" within the Communist ranks.

The third and probably the most important aspect of international affairs which could promote the erosion of ideology pertains to the weapons systems. The Soviet Union has always considered its strength to be an important determinant of its policy dictating caution or warranting action. Insofar as military strategy is concerned, the Soviet leaders, particularly Stalin, have considered their society to be especially well equipped for lengthy wars of attrition, given its size, morale, endurance, and discipline. That remained the prevailing Soviet doctrine even after World War II, which was not surprising, given the nature of the Soviet experience in it. After Stalin's death, however, following a period of internal strategic debate, the primacy of nuclear weapons in Soviet military thinking was established, with the consequent emphasis on striking power and the element of surprise. As this conception gained the upper hand in Soviet thinking, it was only a matter of time before the converse came to be recognized, namely, that similar strategies might be equally decisive if used by the opponent.

This had immediate bearing on the Soviet thinking concerning the inevitability of war. For a long time the basic Soviet conception has been that wars are inevitable as long as capitalism, and particularly imperialism, creates the economic basis for war. Stalin restated this principle as late as 1952. However, if such a war should occur and if the Soviet Union were drawn into it, there could be only one result: the end of capitalism. Gradually, with the mounting possibility of mutual destruction, the Soviet leaders were forced to conclude that war was no longer, as Khrushchev put it at the Twentieth Party Congress, "a fatalistic inevitability." The further extension of this shift has involved an increasing willingness to concede that war would be mutually destructive and that it would not benefit either side. The formal explanation for this change in position was that the strength of the "Socialist Bloc," and of the Soviet Union in particular, has become, so to speak, a sufficiently powerful political-military superstructure balancing the economic necessity for war.

Of course, it could be argued that this change reflects increased Soviet confidence that history's scales have finally been tipped in favor of communism and that rash action, therefore, is to be avoided.

In other words, the adjustment is not merely the product of necessity but also of Soviet interest. Furthermore, there can be little doubt that if the military situation were to become one-sidedly favorable to the U.S.S.R., making it invulnerable, the Soviet viewpoint might change again. However, the important point is that, under the impact of the concrete factor of admittedly decisive importance, namely, the problem of survival, the Soviet ideology had to gradually adjust again, modifying a hitherto important ideological assumption. Peaceful coexistence as an alternative to mutual destruction cannot easily be squared with some of the historical inevitabilities inherent in the ideology, even if such peaceful coexistence is defined as competition. By implication, at least, it does seem to elevate nuclear weapons into a force capable of interfering with history. It would be naive, of course, to assume that Soviet commitment to such "peaceful coexistence" involves an irreversible commitment; but given a general fear of war, the Soviet leaders would have to think twice before restoring "the inevitability of war" principle. However, a necessary precondition for the maintenance of the new formulation is the perpetuation by the West of its destructive capability. Without it, the "objective" reason for peaceful coexistence will have disappeared.

The cumulative effect of the various processes discussed in the preceding pages could be the gradual erosion of certain ideological aspects of the Soviet perspective on international affairs. The ideological syndrome, containing an oversimplified conception of an antagonistic confrontation between two social systems and of historical change in general, the commitment to conflict, the universality of goals, the sense of self-righteousness, and the belief in the imminence of victory—all could be threatened by the combined impact of domestic change, the emergence of ideological relativism due to the spread of communism, and the stark threat of nuclear extinction. A growing willingness to accept some common and overt rules of behavior could follow, buttressing the existing informal and undefined restraints on violence that both sides have tacitly recognized. But this process of erosion is at the present time balanced by certain pressures in the opposite direction, which reassert and even revitalize the ideology. The final outcome of these clashing tendencies depends on too many variables to be safely predicted, but uncertainty about the outcome should not obscure the certainty about conflicting pressures. . . .

In the Soviet Union several established commitments act as powerful counterforces and protect the ideology from erosion. The most important of these is the institutional commitment in the form of the ruling party. Not much needs to be said about this most important factor. If the ideology were to fade, particularly among the membership, the power of the party would be threatened, even though ritualization could delay the disintegration. The upper echelons of the party are very conscious of this. The steps taken by Khrushchev to reestablish the role of the party in Soviet society and the recent measures adopted to invigorate the ideological indoctrination of the population at large suggest that the party is determined to maintain ideological consciousness in its ranks. In the foreseeable future there is little reason to doubt its capacity to do so.

The institutional commitment to ideology is backed by a personal commitment. To individuals like Khrushchev, the ideology is the source of their insight into reality, a conscious treasure to be guarded against pollution (unless by themselves, which is a different problem), the basic source of their education (*Rabfak,* in Khrushchev's case), and the emotional source for their personal sense of life. . . .

Broad social commitment is another "defensive" element. As values become socially ingrained, they resist new values. The reconstruction of Soviet society on the basis of the ideology and the indoctrination of many decades has created a social residue which will resist the intrusion of new ideas, even though the intellectually alert elements may be drawn by them. The influence of the latter can be effective only if they either penetrate the party or succeed in infusing the society with new notions. Given the nature of the Soviet society, the task for the carriers of new ideas is not easy, unless a major crisis should shake its stability. In some ways it can even be argued that urbanization and industrialization, achieved within an ideological context and by an ideologically motivated movement, will tend to perpetuate the role of ideology. First, they institutionalize an environment which is based on the ideological aspirations and which in time begins to act as a buffer for that ideology; second, through a very tangible sense of achievement, they create a widespread acceptance of the ideology, which, even if lacking its original revolutionary zeal, becomes gradually more pervading; third, the nature of a modern industrial society, which is based on social ownership and has severely limited individual initiative, requires a continuous articulation of societal goals to help preserve the broadly accepted purpose. These factors together are inimical to a rapid erosion of the ideology. Finally, action commitment revitalizes the ideology. Action provokes reaction and breeds hostility and conflict and thereby intensifies belief, steeled by trial. Action crowned by success strengthens the ideology even more. Insofar as the masses are concerned, the Soviet leadership has been making strenuous efforts to identify its successes in launching Sputniks or achieving a higher rate of growth with its ideology. Indeed, it might be one of the ironies of the Soviet version of communism that Soviet military preponderance might become an element which retrenches and intensifies ideological belief.

To the party membership, Soviet international achievements are increasingly becoming the "ersatz" method of establishing the correctness of the ideology, thereby preserving the inner sense of ideological purpose without which the party could decay. This ersatz method of revitalizing the ideology is not entirely a matter of conscious design. Having become a great power, at a rate certainly not expected in the West and possibly not even by the Kremlin either, the Soviet Union has a degree of involvement in the rapidly changing world which by itself tends to create conflicts with other powers. Such conflicts can easily be translated into ideological terms, especially as some of the competing units do differ in values and social systems.

In a sense, therefore, the very act of involvement on a massive scale, an involvement which in part is also a function of size and power and which would continue to generate conflicts between the U.S.S.R. and the United States even if no ideology were involved, tends to revitalize the ideology and to translate even simple issues into broader conflicts. For instance, one could see the Berlin problem as a proper matter of international dispute between several parties, comparable to the Saar. However, quite unlike the Saar problem, the disputing parties differ sharply in political and socioeconomic conceptions, and any change in the status of Berlin has immediate implications for the stability of some of the disputing parties. Beyond that, the presence of other Communist states, some possibly more ideologically radical than the Soviet Union, as well as the Soviet interest in maintaining unity in the Communist bloc, is likely to intensify the action commitment of the ideology. The Soviet leaders have recently been making strenuous and generally successful efforts to reestablish ideological ties throughout the bloc.

It is these forces which impede the erosion of the ideology and inhibit the Soviet leadership from accepting international affairs as "a game" with a series of rules; instead, these forces make them insist on treating international affairs as a conflict with only one solution. For the moment, possibly the least hazardous conclusion would be to suggest that, while the pressures for the erosion of ideology are gradually building up, the "conservative" forces of the ideology are still well entrenched and have not lost their capacity to exert influence. In the near future an international "conflict resolution" is unlikely.

Robert V. Daniels

WHAT THE RUSSIANS MEAN

In this perceptive article, Professor Daniels, historian at the University of Vermont, reverses the relationship between ideology and action as developed in the previous reading by Zbigniew Brzezinski. Daniels attributes an entirely different role to ideology when he writes, "Theory is utilized by the Communist leadership to justify their power and policies, and its meaning is periodically reinterpreted to this end. Theory, in communism, does not determine the nature of action; action determines the meaning of theory." Leaders of the Russian Revolution required an ideology to rationalize their seizure and employment of power. They could have revived the nineteenth-century national sense of mission, but decided that Marxism was the more useful dogma. Marx provided the Soviet leaders with a store of quotations by which they could explain and defend policies determined by immediate necessity. Stalin, motivated by political and economic reality, declares Professor Daniels, modified Marxist doctrine almost beyond recognition. To maintain his gains of World War II Stalin simply had to seal Russia off from the West. Theory, designed to support a wide range of national policies, means what the leaders want it to mean at any given moment.

The prevailing image of the Soviet Union and its aims among American publicists and politicians is that of a single-minded international conspiracy, guided step-by-step by the writings of Marx and Lenin and determined to establish by force a worldwide revolutionary Communist dictatorship. This image is fundamentally wrong and a

Reprinted by permission from Robert V. Daniels, "What the Russians Mean," *Commentary* 34 (October 1962): 314–23. Copyright 1962 by the American Jewish Committee.

danger to intelligent policy-making. Its source, of course, is understandable: the profoundly misleading self-portrait expressed in Communist doctrine.

By contrast, a good many of the more sophisticated observers tend to the opposite extreme. They are aware of the falsity of the Communist ideology, and they therefore assume that the Communist leaders themselves do not believe in it, but only use it cynically for propaganda or camouflage while pursuing their Machiavellian goals of power and national expansion. Though more realistic, such a view still cannot account for the pervasive presence of ideology in Soviet life and Soviet official thinking. Moreover, the often-proposed in-between interpretation, that communism operates with short-run tactical flexibility but within the guidelines of strategy and objectives firmly laid down by Marxist-Leninist doctrine, is also inadequate when considered against the background of Soviet history. What has been generally overlooked, in all such thinking about the Soviet Union, is the fact of substantial change in the meaning and role of the Marxist doctrine itself. Marxisim is manifested in everything the Communists say and do, but it does not enter into policy except in the short run. Theory is utilized by the Communist leadership to justify their power and policies, and its meaning is periodically reinterpreted to this end. Theory, in communism, does not determine the nature of action; action determines the meaning of theory.

It is not surprising that the American public harbors so distorted a view of what Marxist doctrine actually means: The Communist movement itself has a deep vested interest in spreading such distortion. The writings of Marx and Engels offer no plan or timetable of revolution. They represent an analysis of history that purports to show where and when revolution of a certain type is likely or natural. On the role that leadership and aggressive planning might play, Marx and Engels were ambiguous; they urged action, but were also sure that economic conditions would impel the working class, willy-nilly, to revolution. They envisaged democratic as well as violent paths to socialism and more than once warned against the working class becoming the victim of its own leaders. The aspirations expressed by Marxism have been widely influential in recent decades, but as a system of social theory Marxism does not really explain much of recent history or the nature of Soviet communism.

Aside from occasional expressions of hope in the "workers of the world, unite" vein, Marx wrote very little on international revolution.

The notion of a sweeping, coordinated world revolution was invented much later by Lenin and Trotsky, in their attempt to rationalize Russia's place in the general Marxist scheme. Their problem, familiar to all students of Marxism, was that Russia, in the 1900s still in the early stages of industrialization, was regarded as too backward for a proletarian revolution. But the impatient Russian Marxists who rallied around Lenin would not consider languishing under capitalism until the West had led the way toward socialism. They contrived the argument that a workers' uprising in Russia would set off what Trotsky called the "permanent revolution," sweeping the whole of Europe into advanced proletarian socialism.

This was not Marxism: it was a revival of the peculiar faith in the Russian national mission which in the nineteenth century had gripped both revolutionaries and Czarists. The famous Russian agrarian socialist Alexander Herzen had been the foremost proponent of the belief that Russia's spirit of total revolution and uncorrupted "communal principle" would show Europe the path to socialism. And Dostoevsky spoke for the conservative nationalists when he wrote in his diary:

> *Our great Russia, at the head of the united Slavs, will utter to the world her new . . . and as yet unheard word. That word will be uttered for the good and genuine unification of mankind as a whole in a new, brotherly, universal union whose inception is derived from the Slavic genius. . . .*

The question can well be raised why the Russian revolutionaries subscribed to Marxism instead of some of the older direct-action messianic Russian philosophies. The answer seems to lie in the psychological appeal which Marxism had as a pseudo-science of inevitable revolution. As Adam Ulam has brilliantly shown in *The Unfinished Revolution,* Marxism's strongest emotional impact is characteristically found not in the advanced industrial countries to which the theory primarily applies, but rather in areas which are just beginning to experience the upsets of industrialization and Westernization. And here its main support is not the industrial workers but the intellectuals and the "intellectual proletariat" of uprooted Westernized students and ex-students. So it was in Russia of the 1900s.

It is vital to understand this: that at the very outset Soviet communism had a relation to Marxist doctrine that was emotional rather than logical. As a quasi-religion rather than a scientific program, the real nature of the movement was neither expressed nor determined by the Marxist doctrine. There is, in fact, no reason to regard the Russian Revolution as the one predicted by Marx, or to accept the Soviet regime as a representative of the future he had in mind. Marxism was of little value to the Russian Communists in consummating their revolution or in deciding practical questions of either foreign or domestic policy afterward. It has served them solely as a fount of righteousness and a store of quotations which could make hastily improvised policies look like doctrinal obligations.

II

The parting of the ways between Communist theory and practice began early in 1918 with the question of either making peace with Germany or proclaiming a revolutionary war. The hotheads maintained that anything less than an antibourgeois crusade was a betrayal of the international revolution; but Lenin, in order to buy time and spare the Soviet government, insisted on giving in to the German terms at Brest-Litovsk. He expected world revolution from one month to the next, but would take no steps involving an immediate risk to the Soviet regime. As Alfred Meyer shows in his penetrating study, *Leninism,* this established the basic Soviet strategic doctrine which has remained in effect ever since—Russia is the "heart" or citadel of world revolution; no revolution independent of Russia is worthy of the name; If Russia falls, the revolution is lost; as long as Russia stands, the revolution has a chance in the future; therefore take no risks with Russia's security; use revolution when it strengthens Russia; sacrifice extensions of the revolution in the short run if they jeopardize Russia's immediate security. Stalin said in 1927, "The USSR is the base of the world revolutionary movement, and to defend, to advance this revolutionary movement is impossible without defending the USSR."

Since 1917, Russian communism has undergone a profound internal evolution—not surprising in the light of our knowledge of the history of revolutions and the impact of modern industrial life on backward societies. What we observe in Soviet Russia is the simultaneous development of post-revolutionary despotism (like that of Bonaparte and Hitler) and the accelerated industrial revolution. The two processes have interacted and mutually accentuated each other, with Stalin serving as the unique personal catalyst.

The fact of a major historical change in the nature and purposes of the Communist system has of course been constantly obscured by the Communist use of fixed ideological terms to describe the system. Communism uses Marxism as "ideology" in the invidious sense which Marx himself gave the word—a system of "illusions" or "false consciousness" that serves to give the appearance of absolute truth and justice to a particular form of class domination and exploitation. Who dominates and who exploits in the Communist system that we know? Marxism is much too narrow to give a meaningful answer about this, but a good deal of truth is contained in such neo-Marxist views as James Burnham's theory of the "Managerial Revolution" and Milovan Djilas's indictment of the "New Class." Both of these writers, expanding on Trotsky's earlier argument (in *The Revolution Betrayed* of 1936), see the Communist system as one in which a new class of managers or party officials has supplanted the bourgeoisie and goes on exploiting the masses through its monopoly of administrative or political power.

This historical development was personified by Stalin, though quite unintentionally. Stalin will long be the subject of speculation by the psychoanalysts of history. He evidently coupled an intense drive for power and personal vindication with heavy dependence on justification by higher authority, together with complete tactical unscrupulousness. These qualifications made him useful to Lenin in the Communist party organization. In 1922 he was made General Secretary of the party, and was then well on his road to power.

When Lenin died in 1924 Stalin's path to power was still blocked by a galaxy of Communist stars who shone more brightly than he, especially in their grasp of theory and their reputations in the worldwide Communist movement. Stalin joined the alliance against Trotsky, whose brillance threatened most of his colleagues. During the bitter controversy between the leadership and the Trotskyist opposition that went on until 1927, the Trotskyists tried to use Marxist doctrine to prove that Stalin & Co. were leading the country down an unsocialist path. It was clear that the Russian "spark" had failed to ignite immediate world revolution. Since Russia was backward and could not be socialist without the support of the world revolution—so the argument went—what was Soviet Russia actually becoming now?

Stalin's reply was a clever though casuistical twist of doctrine—his famous "Theory of Socialism in One Country." He searched back in Lenin's collected works and discovered one quotation which, taken out of context, could be intrepreted to mean that Russia might achieve socialism first and independently of the more advanced countries. Though all the rest of Lenin was permeated with the assumption that Russian socialism depended on world revolution, Stalin and his associates demanded acceptance of the new view as established doctrine. They denounced all objectors for "lack of faith."

This issue was not, as is so often thought, whether to push the international revolution actively. Neither of the Russian factions had any compunctions about this, though in practice both were cautious. The controversy revolved around the use of theory as a weapon in factional politics and the Stalinists' patent fabrication of a new theoretical line to suit their immediate political purposes.

Stalin's stance implied the necessity for strict thought control within the Communist party, as well as outside it. And this requirement still prevails in the Communist system: a Communist has no more freedom in discussing Marxism than a nonparty Soviet citizen has to attack it. Secondly, Stalin's technique of manipulating theory meant that the fixity of doctrine was destroyed, since the line on what the theory originally meant was changed to fit each new political situation.

Stalin's personal dictatorship became a reality in 1928 and 1929, when, after expelling Trotsky's Left Opposition from the Communist party, he turned against Nikolai Bukharin and the Right Opposition and defeated them as well. At the same time he initiated some of the basic policies which have characterized the Communist system ever since: the intensive industrialization drives of the Five Year Plans; the complete nationalization of industry and trade; the collectivization of the peasants; the extension of totalitarian controls from politics to all areas of thought and culture.

To understand Stalin it is important to know how he arrived at most of these policies—not through theory, nor through objective analysis of the problems he faced, but mainly through political feel. His immediate concern was to defeat Bukharin, and this made him interested in proposals that would provoke the Bukharin group into open opposition where they could be defeated. To this end Stalin repeatedly intensified the industrialization and collectivization drive to the point where the Bukharinists shuddered in fear and protested his "military-feudal exploitation" of the country. The result was a period of turmoil, privation, and famine. Yet in all this Stalin had stumbled upon the formula which in later decades was to give communism its great relevance to the countries of Eastern Europe and Asia: the planned and disciplined drive to convert backward peasant societies into modern industrial lands by the combined methods of socialism and Oriental despotism.

As Stalin's industrialization drive went into full swing, he was led to measures of tighter control and further policy revision, which he probably had not himself anticipated. The most striking feature of this period was Stalin's repudiation of most of the social experiments and cultural innovations that had stirred so much worldwide interest in the Soviet regime during its first decade. Equal wages, progressive education, free love, modern art, and the economic interpretation of history, among other things, were all officially condemned between 1931 and 1936. Confusingly, they were condemned on the grounds of being "petty-bourgeois," while the conservative standards which Stalin now demanded were represented as the true Marxist line. Whatever his merits in the abstract, the point is that Stalin was radically revising everything communism actually stood for in the way of ultimate goals and values, while he retained the literal Marxist faith—and intensified his totalitarian methods. As for the "dictatorship of the proletariat," it became pure myth when all political favoritism toward genuine proletarians was finally abandoned, and Soviet society settled down under a permanent hierarchy of officials and technicians.

III

Stalin's policies toward the outside world evidenced almost as great a change in the 1930s as his domestic policy. By 1933 he was justifiably alarmed over the German and Japanese threat to his regime, and in 1934–35 he enunciated a complete about-face. Instead of defying the capitalist world he would seek alliances, and the Communist parties everywhere would suspend their propaganda of revolution in order to enter into political alliances with any "anti-Fascist" forces. These, of course, were the celebrated lines of "Collective Security" and the "Popular Front," which represented nearly the final step in subordinating international proletarian revolution to the requirements of Soviet diplomacy.

In 1936, Roy Howard, the newspaperman, asked Stalin, "Has the Soviet Union to any degree abandoned its plans or intentions for bringing about a world revolution?" and Stalin replied, "We never had such plans and intentions." Since the Popular Front, communism has never returned to the old frank call for the dictatorship of the proletariat. The appeals are devious—to reformism, nationalism, antifascism—all to the end not of a working-class ideal but of Soviet power. For internal consumption, Stalin revived the virtues of nationalism, banned any antinationalist treatment of Russian history, and gave the go-ahead to the cultural Russification of the national minorities.

In view of the vastness of the policy changes which he felt compelled to make, Stalin was hard put to sustain belief in either his practical wisdom or his theoretical correctness. Covert opposition grew, even among his own party officials, and Stalin's suspicion mounted to the point of outright paranoia. The upshot was the Great Purge of 1936–38, in which hundreds of thousands of party leaders and government officials lost their lives or were deported to forced-labor camps.

With such methods of direct totalitarian repression Stalin was able to destroy every challenge to his power inside Russia. In the Communist movement outside Russia, he could not impose his authority so easily, but he could take steps—particularly in Spain—to see that Communists with personal prestige and theoretical sophistication did not achieve independent power in regions beyond his direct control. The Communist refugees from other countries living in Russia almost disappeared in the Great Purge. It is plausible to believe, as George Kennan writes in *Russia and the West,* that

> *unless other states were very small, and contiguous to Russia's borders, so that there were good prospects for controlling them by the same concealed police methods he employed in Russia, Stalin did not want other states to be Communist. . . . He was, in his own eyes, the enemy of all the world.*

Stalin's maintenance of a rigid theoretical rationale accounts for the peculiar responses of many Communist sympathizers throughout the world during the thirties and forties. They had believed that Marxist doctrine showed the only road to the good society, and that everything done in the Soviet Union necessarily followed from Marxist doctrine. Such belief in the good society therefore required a total defense or justification of Stalin's policies in Russia; the crimes he committed had to be either justified as the unfortunate breaking of eggs without which the omelet couldn't be made, or denied altogether as the fictions of right-wing propaganda.

Sooner or later, reality was likely to undermine these defenses. This happened conspicuously on the occasions of the Moscow Trials and the Molotov-Ribbentrop Pact (and more recently, the Hungarian repression of 1956). However, in response to such climactic demonstrations of the primacy of Soviet power interests over revolutionary principles, the sympathizer was more often than not inclined to throw the Marxist baby out with the Stalinist bath—former Communists or sympathizers took to blaming belief in the good society itself for the evils which the Soviets perpetrated in its name. Here, no doubt, is the root of the intellectual phenomenon so common in America and England in the forties and fifties, of ex-radicals repudiating the whole Enlightenment tradition of rational social progress, and going all the way over to a fideistic conservatism.

IV

The period of World War II offers the ironic spectacle of rising Western hopes for firm cooperation with the Soviet Union, just when the most insane antiforeignism had taken hold in post-purge Moscow. It was in 1939, between the dismissal of Litvinov and the pact with Germany, that the Soviet foreign office was subjected to a sweeping purge of all Western-oriented individuals and influences. As a number of the contributors show in Ivo Lederer's fascinating new book, *Russian Foreign Policy,* the truly Byzantine deviousness of Soviet diplomacy, and the severance of all genuine personal communication with the outside world, date from that time. In due course, some of Stalin's policy changes—his nationalism and his social conservatism—were perceived in the West, but these steps were given the wholly erroneous interpretation that they meant a more reasonable Russia in the postwar world.

Most people's illusions were quickly dispelled by Stalin's postwar intransigence and the resumption of violently anti-Western Marxist talk. But this gave rise to the converse error that Soviet Russia had never changed at all but was still committed to the propagation of the proletarian revolution. Stalin's actual achievement, in foreign as well as domestic affairs, was a synthesis of modern techniques and Muscovite ends with doctrinaire Marxist language. Dialectical materialism affected Stalin about as much and as little as the doctrine of Christian charity affected Ivan the Terrible.

To be sure, the achievements of communism between 1945 and

1950 gave the appearance that a Marxist-Leninist master plan of world revolution was dusted off and put in high gear. To the cursory observer, unacquainted with the changes and contradictions in communism which have been outlined here, there seems no reason to doubt that the series of Communist advances starting in Eastern Europe in 1945 and climaxing in China in 1949 and Korea in 1950 were planned and deliberate steps toward implanting the Marxist utopia all over the world. But the close study of Soviet history shows that Stalin had identified communism with his power in Russia, and his power in Russia with a policy pattern of conservative totalitarianism under Marxist labels.

There is reason to suspect that the successes of communism between 1945 and 1949 surprised Stalin as much as they did the West, and that they were not an unmixed blessing from the standpoint of his rather precarious ideological authority. In 1945, everywhere except Poland and Iran, Stalin was using his tactics of the Spanish Civil War, of worming into positions of influence but holding back on revolution so as not to scare the capitalist powers. He was obsessed about a repetition of Hitler's 1941 invasion (much like America's Pearl Harbor complex), and his remedy was simply to push the Russian border as far west as possible. His determination to take over eastern Poland, no matter what political difficulties this caused with Poland, Germany, and the West, suggests that he had no firm expectations of finally controlling all Poland as a satellite. Typically it was the immediate security advantage to the Russian citadel that governed Soviet policy.

Stalin soon discovered the possibility of taking over the whole of Eastern Europe by military pressure and police revolutions, but he had no intention of letting the native Communists pursue the Marxist ideal as they saw it, or even enjoy full revolutionary status. For the new satellites Stalin invented the novel theoretical category of second-class communism or "People's Democracy," lest anyone venture to suggest full-fledged alternatives to his own Soviet version of the one true path. The final step, successful everywhere save Yugoslavia, was to purge all the native Communists whose notions of communism, humanity, or national independence stood in the way of Stalin's determination to dominate them.

In the Far East, Stalin's immediate concern in 1945 was the recovery of the possessions Japan had taken in 1904–1905 or before—Southern Sakhalin Island, the Kuriles, Port Arthur, and the Manchurian sphere of influence. His V-J Day Speech—coming from an Old Bolshevik who had presumably welcomed the defeat of the Czarist government by the Japanese—reveals how the nationalist tradition had been assimilated into Soviet thinking:

> *The defeat of the Russian troops in 1904 during the Russo-Japanese war left bitter memories in the minds of our people. It lay like a black stain upon our country. Our people believed in and waited for the day when Japan would be defeated and the stain would be wiped out. We of the older generation waited for this day for forty years, and now this day has arrived.*

Stalin evidently did not expect the victory of communism in China. (This is one of the few instances, if we can credit Vladimir Dedijer's testimony in his biography of Tito, when the Soviet dictator admitted an error in foresight.) He was able to persuade even Chiang Kai-shek that he was not interested in supporting the Chinese Communists: for this we have the word of Ambassador Patrick Hurley. Indeed, Stalin's prolonged dealings with the Nationalists, and his meager aid to the Communists, raise the question how much he was willing or desirous of gambling on the Chinese Communist victory—though he appeared to welcome it when it finally came.

The fact is that Chinese Communism, from the standpoint of Sovietology, only makes sense as an independent phenomenon—a revolution taken over by an independent group of revolutionaries who subscribed to Marxist doctrine in the same dogmatic, illogical way as the Russian Communists, but made their own self-interested interpretation of it. Theoretical manipulation was carried even further in China: there the proletariat was entirely absent from the stage of active revolutionary events—but the revolution nevertheless had to be described as "proletarian." Stalin had feared an independent communism and it had become a reality in China. Now in the Khrushchev era the Chinese have ventured into major acts of autonomy in doctrine. It is becoming clear that within this Communist world of contrived ideological manipulation, theory serves not as a bond of unity between the present two centers of power, but as a source of discord and perhaps schism.

V

Communist Doctrine of itself did not and could not create the post-World War II enmity between the Soviet bloc and the Western powers.

As we have seen, by the 1940s doctrine was entirely subordinated to the whims of the Soviet dictator and the exigencies of practical politics. Fundamentally, the cold war between communism and the democracies must be accounted for by two factors: the unprecedented situation of "bi-polarity"—a world dominated by two superpowers, the United States and the U.S.S.R.; and the traditional Russian aspects of the dictatorship of Stalin, who could see no way to secure his position and his ideological pretensions save in the old game of power politics and in sealing his country off from the West.

To be sure, Communist doctrine does play a major supporting role in the drama of Soviet-Western conflict. It serves to define the contending sides in terms of black-and-white morality—although the terms can be shifted to include any given country either among the angels or the devils, as convenience dictates. The United States and Great Britain, for example, were theoretically classified among the "progressive" forces for purposes of World War II, while Tito's Yugoslavia was overnight reclassified from "socialist" to "fascist" in 1948 because it refused to accept Soviet domination. The U.S.S.R. and Albania presently characterize each other as enemies of the working class, and it is conceivable that Sino-Soviet tensions could lead to a similar exchange of ideological anathemas.

Doctrine, by its direct influence and by the hostile reactions it evokes, sets up a state nearly approximating that of religious war, where the stakes are not material interests but rival myths or theological loyalties. Such a state of irrationally grounded international tension seems almost indispensable to any totalitarian regime, and particularly to the Soviet Union. International tension lends some reality to the doctrine, and a sense of the doctrine's reality is indispensable to the Communist party apparatus to justify its power, its discipline, its function of control and repression—in fact its very existence. Finally, doctrine and the atmosphere of religious war harness a worldwide army of emotional revolutionaries in the service of Soviet power interests.

De-Stalinization has not altered the fact that the whole corps of officials in the Communist states has a vested interest in maintaining the ideological mythology which both justifies and requires their power of control. In this way international tension is built into the structure of Communist society. Free exchange of opinion cannot of course be tolerated in this power system built around a shaky core of ideological pretenses. Genuine international understanding is the last thing Communists want; nothing offends them more than to be understood for what they really are. It goes without saying that such a regime will go to any lengths to prevent the free circulation of foreign ideas and individuals within its boundaries. This fact alone makes the Western insistence on a system of unfettered international inspection of military preparations an almost utopian goal.

Between Stalin and Khrushchev the changes with respect to the fundamentals of ideology and power have not been so great as often imagined in the West (in contrast to the great changes during Stalin's rule which are usually neglected or minimized). Stalin's death did open the door to manifold tactical innovations in both foreign and domestic policy, usually toward concession and the soft sell. The police and the labor camps were curtailed, consumer living standards raised, artistic controls relaxed, allies sought and neutrals wooed beyond the sphere of abject Communist puppets. But the party leadership took every one of these steps deliberately, and can reverse them at will. There has been no major change in the system of power and controls, nor in the habit of contriving eternal doctrinal justification for each opportune policy shift.

Khrushchev has, to be sure, introduced interesting new twists into the ideology, in his apparent desire to go down in history in the Marxist line of apostolic succession. He has proclaimed that "the transition from socialism to communism" has begun in Soviet society, and Soviet theoreticians now have to write as though a momentous historical change were actually taking place from the "dictatorship of the proletariat" to the "state of all the people." It is all done with words; we are witnessing a mythological transition—from one social myth to another, all equally irrelevant to the real Soviet society and its gradual evolution into a moderately affluent managerial technocracy.

Present Soviet foreign policy is no freer of ideological mythology than the domestic realm, and no more genuinely Marxist. Khrushchev, like Stalin, feels compelled to represent his expediency as the application of an unchanging Marxist-Leninist principle. When the menace of thermonuclear war becomes sufficiently apparent to him, he conveniently finds that war was never inevitable according to the theory, and that "Soviet foreign policy . . . has always been, and will be Lenin's policy of peaceful coexistence." Compare this with such a typical remark as Lenin's statement in 1920, "As long as capitalism and socialism exist, we cannot live in peace; in the end one or the other will triumph." In fact, theoretical limitations do not bind the Communist policy-maker either for good or for evil. The theory is simply made to mean what the leader wants it to mean at the moment.

VI

In the light of this history, why does the American public still hold fast to a conception of the Communist movement in terms of strict doctrinal intent?

Popular American impressions of Russia have been based mainly on two occasions of traumatic awareness—the initial impact of the Bolshevik Revolution in 1917–19, and the breakdown of the World War II alliance in 1945–47. The assumptions about international revolutionary conspiracy established in these moments of alarm were often wrong, always unreflecting and exaggerated, and rarely subject to later modifications. America's post-World War II reaction to Soviet Russia was particularly emotional because it coincided with this country's unsought responsibilities of great-power status and the uneasy circumstances of the bi-polar world where Soviet hostility was inevitable. All the old anti-Communist emotion of the earlier period, with its deep fears for the sanctity of religion and property, returned; and apparently much of the anti-Hitler feeling generated in the war was now transferred to the Communists.

Americans, used to assuming a certain correspondence between ideas and action, find it difficult to understand the true relation of Marxist ideology to Communist strategic planning. The American attitude, perhaps stemming from a fusion of the Calvinist and utilitarian traditions, is that people freely decide what is right or to their interest; express an intention to pursue such right or interest; and then take action according to some rational plan that is calculated to achieve these goals. This may or may not actually be the way Americans behave, but it is the way they think people in general behave. In this view there is no room for a theory of social determinism such as Marx's, according to which mass responses are bound to lead to certain revolutionary results regardless of any individual's intent.

An American hearing the Marxian *prediction* can only understand it as a statement of *intent,* of intent, furthermore, that is going to be acted upon. The American outlook cannot allow for any discrepancy between statement and action, between theory and practice. It cannot grasp the possibility of certain ideas becoming mere doctrinal comforters which do not guide action to any significant degree. Americans themselves, like practically everyone else, may be guilty on this score: stock phrases like "freedom" and "democracy" sustain the sense of American self-righteousness but may be conveniently overlooked when practical business or foreign decisions have to be made. Though in a vastly less bureaucratic and oppressive way than the Communists, we too are rationalizers and we cannot look too deeply into the psychological processes of ideological rationalization. To keep one's own ideology intact, it is easier to believe in the consistency of the other side's as well.

Only some such analysis, it seems to me, can explain why, when Khrushchev prophesies the Red Flag over America, much of the American press and public fly into a panic. They take his prediction as an intent: the intent as literal and the prediction as infallible. Americans cannot seem to work with a mode of analysis that would make possible a corrected prediction of their own. They can see only a future of clashing intent, unless the millennium should arrive when the Communists "repudiate their doctrine of world domination."

Any student of Soviet affairs knows that the last thing that could happen would be a Communist repudiation of Marxist-Leninist doctrine. On the other hand, a historical understanding of the meaning and role of doctrine would make it clear that such a repudiation is not necessary and would not be meaningful. Soviet hostility and intransigence could continue under another doctrinal cover, or—a more likely possibility—Soviet accommodations with the West could be reached under the ideological cover of an appropriately commanded reinterpretation of doctrine. Even now, literal doctrine determines very little that most Americans assume it is responsible for. Doctrine does not prescribe aggression by a Marxist state in order to expand the revolution by force. All the Communist talk of inevitable war has revolved around the question of a counterrevolutionary attack on the Marxist state by the so-called "imperialists." But here again Americans read prediction or warning as intent to fight, and they fail to understand the ways and means of bringing their own desires to bear on the formation of Communist policy.

The ultimate question—doctrines and intentions aside—is whether Communist policy decisions and actions in the short run can be so influenced by resistance, inducement, or pressure from the United States and the Western alliance, that the long-run pattern of Communist behavior and political development will take a direction consistent with our own fundamental desire for peace with security and freedom in the Western world. The lesson of history as this writer reads it is that nothing in Communist doctrine will prevent such an approach. As long as the Soviet Union is made to realize that its security interests are best promoted by respecting the fundamental interests of the Western world, the dictates of doctrine can always be suitably adjusted.

The *sine qua non* for such an approach on the part of the United States is a recognition that Marxist doctrine is not fixed in its practical meaning and does not rigidly guide Soviet policy in a predetermined course. It is equally necessary to recognize that the literal doctrine which the Soviet officialdom feels compelled to enforce and reiterate does not give a true picture of Soviet policy or intentions. We cannot wait for the Soviet Union to announce that it will change; we must recognize that it has changed (though not always for the better), and that it will continue to change, partly in response to America's own policies.

We must at the same time realize that none of these changes are going to be stated for what they actually are by the official Communist ideologists. We must anticipate continuing harassments and doctrinal fulminations, and at the same time be able to recognize the underlying reality of tacit concessions and agreements that bit-by-bit bring Soviet policy into line with our own requirements. Recent developments of this sort include the acceptance of cultural exchanges, the reluctant status quo in Berlin and Germany, the remarkable three-year informal moratorium on nuclear testing, and the Soviet refusal to back an aggressive Chinese Communist policy.

The Soviet Union, as is so often said, must indeed be judged by its actions, not by its words. This holds true even when welcome actions are accompanied by offensive words. Communist dogmatism is such that hostility must be maintained on the verbal level even when it has been abandoned in practice. Straightforward communication between governments and peoples is the very last thing that will be achieved in relations between the United States and the U.S.S.R. We will never achieve any agreements if we depend on prior understanding. The security of mutual understanding and world order can only be envisioned as the remote outcome of continually careful and sophisticated diplomacy.

Samuel L. Sharp

NATIONAL INTEREST: KEY TO SOVIET POLITICS

Samuel L. Sharp, Professor of International Relations at American University, in assigning to Soviet foreign policy the traditional goal of serving the Russian national interest, regards Marxist-Leninist ideology as quite irrelevant to any analysis of the day-to-day response to world politics. So persistently have Soviet policies adjusted to political and military realities that, in the words of Barrington Moore, Jr., they have "caused the means to eat up the ends." Ends become meaningless, declares Professor Sharp, unless they are pursued by actual policies. Means comprise the real substance of foreign policy. The habitual listing of quotations from the writings of the Communist philosophers to prove the acceptance by the U.S.S.R. of the goal of world domination he believes quite fruitless, for such phrases have been eliminated from the world of policy by power factors outside the Soviet Union which the Kremlin leaders are too rational to ignore.

An enormous body of Western research and analysis focuses on Marxist-Leninist ideology as a clue to understanding Kremlin policy. This extensive and intensive preoccupation with matters doctrinal is, at least in part, the result of a rather widely circulated belief that the democratic world was guilty of neglect when it refused to take seriously the "theoretical" writings and pronouncements of Adolf Hitler. It has been alleged that these writings later guided Hitler's actions and that a ready key to his conduct was thus overlooked.

When, at the end of World War II, the Soviet Union appeared on the international scene as a power—and a menace—of the first order, led by a group consistently claiming its adherence to a body of doctrine as a guide to action, legions of experts began to dissect that body in a search for a key to Soviet behavior, current and future. The material at hand was certainly more promising than the intellectually scrawny homunculus of Nazi or Fascist "ideology." After all, Marxism has its not entirely disreputable roots in legitimate Western thought. Even in terms of sheer bulk there was more to operate on, what with Lenin's and Stalin's additions to and modifications of the original scriptures and the voluminous exegetic output of a generation of Soviet propangandists.

Reprinted by permission from Samuel L. Sharp, "National Interest: Key to Soviet Politics," *Problems of Communism* 7 (March–April 1958): 15–21.

The massive study of Communist ideology has had one happy result in that some serious scholarly output has been provided to counterbalance party-line apologias, thereby destroying a number of primitive notions concerning the Soviet system and what makes it tick. At the same time, in this writer's view, preoccupation with the search for a formula of interpretive and predictive value has produced its own distortions. These distortions seem to be the composite result of cold-war anxieties, faulty logic and disregard of some of the elementary principles and practices of international relations. To these causes must be added the human tendency to look beyond the simple and obvious for the complicated and mysterious in attempting to explain any condition which is exasperating and which is therefore perceived as strange and unique. Baffled by the Soviet phenomenon, millions in the Western world have found a negative consolation of sorts in the famous statement by Winston Churchill that Russian policy is "a riddle wrapped in a mystery inside an enigma." But how many have bothered to read the qualifying words which followed? Having disclaimed ability to forecast Soviet actions, Churchill added: *"But perhaps there is a key. That key is Russian national interest."*[1]

Clearly implied in this observation was the logical supposition that the policy-makers of the Soviet Union act in what they believe to be the best interest of the state over whose destinies they are presiding. In this sense the Soviet Union is to be looked upon as an actor, a protagonist, on the stage of international politics; and in this writer's view, its actions can be interpreted most fruitfully in terms of behavior politics. Without denying the possible pitfalls of this approach, the writer proposes to argue its usefulness as a key to understanding a phenomenon which the non-Communist world can ill afford to envelop in a fog of self-generated misinterpretation.

The Doubtful Art of Quotation

Whenever the suggestion is made that the concept of national interest be applied as an explanation of Soviet behavior on the international scene, objections are raised in many quarters. The most vigorous protests come, of course, from Soviet sources. It is a standard claim of Soviet spokesmen that their state is by definition something "different" (or "higher") and that the foreign policy of this entity is

[1] Radio broadcast of October 1, 1939, reprinted in Churchill, *The Gathering Storm* (Boston, 1948), p. 449. Author's italics.

different in principle *(printsipialno otlichna)* from that of other states because the latter are capitalist and the former is socialist.[2] It would seem that only uncritical adherents of communism could take such statements seriously. Yet non-Communists very often cite them as a convenient *ipse dixit* in support of their own claim that the Soviet Union is indeed "different," though not in the way Soviet propaganda wants one to believe. The claim is that the Soviet Union is, at best, "a conspiracy disguised as a state" and cannot be viewed as a "normal" member of the world community of nations. There is no attempt to explain on what basis some Soviet statements are to be taken as reliable indices of regime motivations, while other statements, no less abundantly scattered throughout the Marxist-Leninist scriptures, are rejected as lie and deception.

It is surely dubious scholarship to collect quotations (sometimes reduced to half a sentence) from Lenin and Stalin without regard to the time, place, circumstances, composition of the audience and, whenever ascertainable, immediate purposes of such utterances. What results from such compilations, no matter how laboriously and ingeniously put together, is, as a thoughtful critic has pointed out, "a collection of such loose generalizations and so many exceptions and contradictions that few readers can find much guidance in it."[3] Stalin, for example, can be quoted as once having said that "with a diplomat words must diverge from facts" and that "a sincere diplomat would equal dry water, wooden iron"; yet this not too astute observation was made in 1913 in an article dealing with bourgeois diplomacy written by an obscure georgian revolutionary who probably had never met a diplomat. His view in this instance is identifiable as a variant of the classic image of the diplomat as "an honorable gentleman sent abroad to lie for his country." This image may very well have stayed with the congenitally suspicious and pessimistic

---

[2] To cite just one recent source, see V. I. Lisovskii, *Mezhdunarodnoe Pravo* (Kiev, 1955), p. 397.

[3] Marshall Knappen, *An Introduction to American Foreign Policy* (New York, 1956). The quote is from the chapter entitled "Capabilities, Appeal, and Intentions of the Soviet Union" and refers specifically to the well-known effort by Nathan Leites in *A Study of Bolshevism* (Glencoe, Illinois, 1953) to construct, out of thousands of quotes from Lenin and Stalin bolstered with excerpts from nineteenth-century Russian literature, an "image of Bolshevism" and an "operational code" of the Politburo. See also the remarks on "Difficulties of Content Analysis" and "The Problem of Context" in John S. Reshetar, Jr., *Problems of Analyzing and Predicting Soviet Behavior* (New York, 1955). In all fairness to Leites and his prodigious undertaking it must be pointed out that he was aware of a "spurious air of certainty" in his formulations, which were intended to be only "guesses about the mind of the Soviet Politburo" (op. cit., p. 27).

Stalin in later life, and thus might indeed afford us a clue to his "real" nature. However, sound scholarship would seek to reconstruct the attitudes of the Kremlin ruler out of words and deeds of a more relevant period of his life rather than from this loose piece of Djugashvili prose torn out of context.

The Vital Factor of Feasibility

Some objections to the interpretation of Soviet policies in terms of national interest are rooted in the aforementioned line of analysis which conjures up the ghost of Adolf Hitler. The democracies erred, did they not, in initially looking upon Hitler's aims as an expression of "legitimate" (we will return to this phrase in a moment), however distasteful, national aspirations, only to discover later that they were dealing with a maniac whose appetites were unlimited. Since it is generally agreed that Soviet policy, like Hitler's, belongs to the to-talitarian species, would it not be impardonable to repeat the same mistake by looking upon the aims of the Soviet leaders as the expression of the aspirations of a "normal" nation-state?

Two points should be made here. First, Hitler bears comparison with no one; there is no other leader in history who has combined his precise mental make-up with his enormous concentration of power. He was, as his biographer Allan Bullock pointed out, a man "without aims," that is, without *limited* and therefore tractable aims.[4] At one point in his career Hitler began to disregard the cardinal rule of politics—the necessity of aligning ambitions with capacity to trans-late them into reality. He broke the barrier of the *feasible,* motivated by what could most likely be diagnosed as the death-wish. Whatever else may be said about the soviet leaders, no one, including people who suspect them of ideological self-deception, has denied them the quality of caution. Far from seeking self-destruction, they are lustily bent on survival. This in itself, even in the complete absence of scruples, makes their aims *limited.*

Mr. Carew Hunt argues . . . that there are "messianic and cata-strophic elements in the Communist creed which influence . . . the Soviet drive for world power." While there may indeed be a degree of messianism in the Soviet leadership's view of its mission, the "cata-strophic" tendency seems to be held carefully in check. Hitler was

[4] Allan Bullock, *Hitler—A Study in Tyranny* (New York, 1953).

propelled by the absurd notion that he had to accomplish certain aims before he reached the age of sixty—an arrogant and, from the point of view of German national interest, totally irrelevant assumption. Granted that the Soviet leaders aim at "world power" (a concept which in itself should be defined more explicitly than it usually is), they have long since decided not to fix any specific time limit for the achievement of this ultimate aim. Certainly the present generation of leaders has acted to modify (perhaps "refine" is a better word) the aggressive drive for power abroad at least to an extent which will allow some enjoyment at home of the tangible fruits of the revolution this side of the Communist heaven. Even back in the early days of Bolshevik rule, Lenin, though at times carried away by expectations of spreading revolution, never sacrificed practical caution to Missionary zeal; repeatedly he warned his followers to look after the "bouncing baby" (the Soviet state), since Europe was only "pregnant with revolution" (which it wasn't).

An Applicable Concept of Interest

The second point to be made is a crucial one. Reluctance to analyze Soviet aims in terms of national interest is due, in part, to the aura of legitimacy which surrounds the "normal" run of claims of nation-states, giving rise to the notion that the term itself infers something legitimate. However, suggesting that Kremlin moves can best be understood in terms of what the leaders consider advantageous to the Soviet state by no means implies subscribing to their aims or sympathizing with them. In international relations the maxim *tout comprendre c'est tout pardonner* does not apply. The concept of national interest, by focusing attention on the *objective sources of conflict*— that is, those which *can* be explained rationally as issues between nations—permits us to view the international scene in terms of a global problem of power relations rather than a cops-and-robbers melodrama. We can then perceive which are the *tractable* elements in the total equation of conflict, and devote our energies to reducing or altering these factors.

This approach seems to the writer to be indispensable both to the scholar and to the statesman. The scholar who accepts the "natural" (in terms of the nature of international politics) explanation for Kremlin behavior is not likely to violate the "law of parsimony" by unnecessarily piling up hypotheses which are unprovable and which in any case simply confuse the issue, insofar as dealing practically with the Soviet Union is concerned. The statesman finds that he is coping with a phenomenon which he knows how to approach both in accommodation and in opposition, rather than with some occult and other-wordly force.

Those who object to the framework of analysis here proposed would say, as does Mr. Hunt, that there are many cases on record when the Soviet leaders have acted in a way clearly inconsistent with the Russian national interest and intelligible only in terms of ideological dogmatism. The answer to this argument is simple: it does not matter what Mr. Hunt—or anybody else—considers to be the Russian national interest; as the term is defined here, the only view which matters is that held by the Soviet leaders. By the same token it is a rather fruitless thing to speak of "legitimate" vs. "illegitimate" Soviet interests. One of the essential attributes of sovereignty (and the Soviet leaders are certainly jealous where their own is involved!) is that it is up to the sovereign to determine what serves him best.

Yet doesn't this reasoning render pointless the entire conceptual approach proposed? If Soviet national interest is what the Soviet leaders take it to be, and if one agrees—as one must—that their view of the world is derived largely from their adherence to Marxism-Leninism, isn't this another way of saying that Soviet behavior is the result of ideological conditioning? Not quite. The point at issue is whether the "pure" Soviet view of the world is important *as a guide to action,* whether the *ultimate* aims of the Communist creed are operative in policy determinations. In the present writer's view they are not; the fault of the opposing line of analysis is that, in dwelling on the supposed impact of ideology on the leadership, it tends to ignore the degree to which the pursuit of ultimate goals has been circumscribed in time and scope by considerations of *the feasible.* In simple arithmetic, doctrine minus those aspects which are not empirically operative equals empirically determined policy. If a policy action is called "revolutionary expediency," it is still expediency. Why then introduce into the equation an element which does not affect the result?

A supporting view in this respect is W. W. Rostow's characterization of Soviet foreign policy as a series of responses to the outside world which, especially before 1939, "took the form of such actions as were judged most likely, *on a short-range basis,* to maintain or expand the national power of the Soviet regime." Despite the Soviet

Union's vastly greater ability to influence the world environment in the postwar era, says Rostow, "there is no evidence that the foreign policy criteria of the regime have changed."[5] If some instances of Soviet behavior appear to have produced results actually detrimental to the Soviet interest, we must not only refrain from applying our view of Soviet interest but also—as Rostow's viewpoint suggests— judge the policy decisions involved in terms of their validity at the time they were made and not in the light of what happened later (remembering, too, that mistakes and miscalculations are common to all policy-makers, not just those who wear "ideological blinders").

The words "on a short-range basis" have been underscored above to stress that the term policy, if properly applied, excludes aims, ambitions, or dreams not accompanied by action visibly and within a reasonable time capable of producing the results aimed at or dreamed of. In the case of the Soviet leaders, concentration on short-range objectives and adjustment to political realities has, in the brilliant phrase suggested by Barrington Moore, Jr., *caused the means to eat up the ends.*[6]

The objection will still be raised that the Soviet leaders mouth every policy decision in terms of ideological aims. Enough should have been said on this score to obviate a discussion here; as able students of the problem have pointed out, the Soviet leaders' claim to rule rests on their perpetuation of the ideology and their insistence on orthodoxy; they have no choice but to continue paying lip service to the doctrine, even if it is no longer operative. The liberal mind somehow balks at this image of total manipulation, of an exoteric doctrine for public consumption which has no connection with its esoteric counterpart—that is, the principles or considerations which really govern Kremlin behavior. Yet allowance must be made for this possibility.

Moscow and International Communism

One serious argument of those who reject the image of the Soviet Union as a "legitimate" participant in the balance-of-power game played in the arena of international politics is that the Soviet leaders consistently violate the rules of the game by enlisting out-of-bounds

---

[5] W. W. Rostow et al., *The Dynamics of Soviet Society* (New York, 1952), p. 136. Author's italics.
[6] Barrington Moore, Jr., *Soviet Politics: The Dilemma of Power* (Cambridge, Massachusetts, 1950).

help from foreign Communist parties. This point invites the following brief observations:

1. Early in its history the Communist International was transformed into a tool of Soviet foreign policy, at a time when few other tools were available to Moscow.

2. As soon as the Soviet state felt at all sure of its survival (after the period of civil war, foreign intervention, and economic chaos), it reactivated the apparatus of foreign policy along more traditional lines.

3. Under Stalin, the Third International was reduced to a minor auxiliary operation. An index of his attitude toward it is the fact that he never once addressed a Comintern congress. Probably the International was kept up in the interwar period because it seemed to produce marginal dividends in terms of nuisance value. Moreover, Stalin could hardly have divorced himself from it officially at a time when he was jockeying for total power inside Russia, since this would have helped to confirm his opponents' accusations that he was "betraying the revolution." But he certainly did everything to show his belief in the ineffectiveness of the organization and its foreign components as against the growing power of the Soviet state.

4. When the entire record of Soviet success and failure is summed up, the achievements are clearly attributable to Soviet power and diplomacy with no credit due to the international Communist movement. Furthermore, the ties between the Soviet Union and foreign parties have never deterred Moscow from useful alliances or cooperation with other governments—including, from one time to another, the astutely anti-Communist Turkish government of Ataturk, the more brutally anti-Communist regime of Adolf Hitler, and, during World War II, the Western powers. That the Soviet leaders, by virtue of their doctrine, entertained mental reservations about the durability of friendly relations with these governments can hardly be doubted. But it is equally clear that the cessation of cooperation was due in each case to the workings of power politics rather than Soviet ideological dictate—that is, to the historical tendency of alliances to disintegrate when what binds them (usually a common enemy) disappears.

5. Finally, it might be argued that the Soviet appeal to foreign Communist parties is not dissimilar to the practice of various governments of different periods and persuasions to appeal for support abroad on the basis of some sort of affinity—be it Hispanidad, Slav solidarity, Deutschtum, or Pan-Arabism. The

Soviet appeal is admittedly broader and the "organizational weapon" seems formidable, but its importance should not be exaggerated. Actually, there is no way at all to measure the effectiveness of the appeal per se since Communist "success" or "failure" in any situation always involves a host of other variables—including military, geographical, social, political, or economic factors. In the last analysis, virtually every instance where Moscow has claimed a victory for communism has depended on Soviet manipulation of traditional levers of national influence.[7]

An Exception to Prove the Rule

There remains one area of Soviet "foreign policy" where the Soviet leaders have supplemented power politics—or more accurately in this instance naked force—with an attempt to derive special advantage, a sort of "surplus value," from claiming ideological obeisance to the Soviet Union as the seat of the secular church of communism. This area is the so-called Soviet orbit in Eastern Europe.

The term "foreign policy" is enclosed in quotation marks here because Stalin obviously did not consider areas under the physical control of Soviet power as nations or governments to be dealt with in their own right. He was clearly impatient with the claim of at least some Communist parties that their advent to power had changed the nature of their relationship to Moscow, and that the party-to-party level of relations must be separated from the government-to-government level (as Gomulka argued in 1948). In Stalin's thinking, especially after 1947, the East European regimes were not eligible for more real sovereignty than the "sovereign" republics of the Soviet Union. He attempted to extend the principle of *democratic centralism* (a euphemism for Kremlin control) to these countries, allowing them only as much of a facade of sovereignty as was useful for show toward the outside world.

One need not necessarily dig into doctrine to explain this attitude; in fact, doctrine until recently said nothing at all about relations between sovereign Communist states. The explanation lies to a large extent in Stalin's personal predilection for total control, plus the need to tighten Moscow's bonds to the limit, by whatever means or

[7] Samuel L. Sharp, "The Soviet Position in the Middle East," *Social Science* (National Academy of Economics and Political Sciences) 32 (October 1957).

arguments possible, in the face of the bipolarization of global power after World War II.

Stalin's successors began by pressing the same claims of ideological obeisance from the satellites. But rather strikingly—in the same period that their foreign policy has scored substantial successes in other areas in traditional terms of diplomatic advances and manipulation of the economic weapon—they have failed in the one area where they attempted to substitute the ties of ideology for the give-and-take of politics. Communist parties in power, it turned out (first in the case of Yugoslavia, while Stalin still reigned, and later in Poland, not to mention the very special case of China), claimed the right to be sovereign—or at least semi-sovereign—actors on the international scene. Whether or not this makes sense ideologically to the Soviet leaders is unimportant; they have recognized the claim.

It is not necessary to review here the post-Stalin history of fluctuating Soviet relations with Eastern Europe which began with the B. & K. pilgrimage to Belgrade. Let us take only the most recent attempt to reformulate the nature of relations between the U.S.S.R. and other Communist countries—the interparty declaration issued on the occasion of the fortieth anniversary of the Bolshevik revolution. On the surface, the declaration, published in the name of twelve ruling Communist parties, seems to reimpose a pattern of ideological uniformity as well as to recognize the special leadership position of the Soviet Union.[8] However, the circumstances of the gathering and the internal evidence of the declaration, together with the reports of some of the participants, show a far more complex situation.

The following aspects of the conference deserve attention: First, the very fact that the parties representing governments of sovereign countries were singled out for a special meeting and declaration instead of being lumped together with the mass of parties (many of them illegal, some leading no more than a paper existence) is a significant departure from past practice. Secondly, the Yugoslav party, though represented at the festivities, refused to sign the declaration, apparently after long negotiations. Thirdly, attempts to revive in any form an international, Moscow-based organization resembling the Comintern were unsuccessful. Gomulka's report on the meeting

---

[8] The text of the declaration, adopted at a meeting held on November 14–16, 1957, was published in *Pravda* on November 22. A separate "peace manifesto" issued in the name of all of the Communist parties present at the congregation appeared in *Pravda* a day later.

made it clear that the Polish party opposed both a new Comintern (for which it nevertheless had a few good words) and a new Cominform (for which it had nothing but scorn).[9]

A point of particular significance was the revelation that future international gatherings of Communist parties, especially those in power, are to be based on previous agreements concerning the agenda. According to Gomulka, problems which each party thinks it can best solve *"for itself and its country"* will not be decided by interparty conferences.[10]

Perhaps most significant for the purposes of the present discussion was a statement by Mao Tse-tung, who next to Khrushchev and Suslov was the main speaker at the meeting of the "ruling" parties and was billed as cosponsor of the declaration. Mao bolstered his argument for the recognition of the leading position of the Soviet Union in the "socialist camp" with the remark that "China has not even one-fourth of a sputnik while the Soviet Union has two."[11] Now, the possession of a sputnik is a symbol of achievement and a source of prestige for the Soviet Union, but certainly not in terms of ideology. It was Soviet national power to which Mao paid deference.

In sum, the entire circumstances of the gathering indicate a disposition on the part of the Soviet Union to substitute—wherever it has to—the give-and-take of politics for its former relationship with the orbit countries, which relied on naked power to enforce demands of ideological subservience.

From all the foregoing, it should be clear that the task of the non-Communist world is not to worry itself sick over the ultimate goals of the Soviet leadership or the degree of its sincerity, but to concentrate on multiplying situations in which the Soviet Union either will be forced or will choose to play the game of international politics in an essentially traditional setting. How the Kremlin leaders will square this with their Marxist conscience is not really our problem.

---

[9] Gomulka's report was published in *Trybuna Ludu* (Warsaw), November 29, 1957.
[10] Gomulka, ibid, See also an analysis of the conference entitled, "Gescheiterte Komintern-Renaissance" (Failure of Comintern Revival), *Ost-Probleme* (Bad Godesberg), X (January 3, 1958).
[11] Cited in Friedrich Ebert's report to the East German party (SED), published in *Neues Deutschland* (East Berlin), November 30, 1957, p. 4.

IV THE
POSSIBILITIES
OF COEXISTENCE

Nikita S. Khrushchev

PEACEFUL COEXISTENCE: THE RUSSIAN VIEW

The preoccupation of scholars and officials with ideology and the ultimate purpose of the U.S.S.R. in no way eliminated the necessity of facing the ubiquitous Soviet challenges in the world of action with a continuously evolving body of policies designed to permit the two great powers to reside successfully on the same globe. The realization by the mid-fifties that a nuclear stalemate rendered war irrational led Nikita Khrushchev, as leader of the Soviet state, to formulate the concept of "peaceful coexistence" which he defined as "the repudiation of war as a means of solving controversial issues." In this article Khrushchev explained his interpretation of peaceful coexistence in detail. He did not call off the struggle for dominance between the Soviet brand of socialism and Western capitalism; he insisted only that the two systems compete at the level of economic and social performance. Khrushchev followed his disturbing prediction of the ultimate victory of communism with the reasonable assurance that the world could endure the competition indefinitely without resorting to war. Lastly, in a reiteration of the Soviet position on divided Germany, West Berlin, and Eastern Europe, Khrushchev called for a peace treaty as a formal termination of the war in Europe. The West, he wrote, must accept the consequences of World War II.

I have been told that the question of peaceful coexistence of states with different social systems is uppermost today in the minds of many Americans—and not only Americans. The question of coexistence, particularly in our day, interests literally every man and woman on the globe.

We all of us well know that tremendous changes have taken place in the world. Gone, indeed, are the days when it took weeks to cross the ocean from one continent to the other or when a trip from Europe to America, or from Asia to Africa, seemed a very complicated undertaking. The progress of modern technology has reduced our planet to a rather small place; it has even become, in this sense, quite congested. And if in our daily life it is a matter of considerable importance to establish normal relations with our neighbors in a densely inhabited settlement, this is so much the more necessary in the relations between states, in particular states belonging to different social systems.

From "On Peaceful Coexistence," *Foreign Affairs* 38 (October 1959): 1–2, 3, 4–9, 12–18. Copyright 1959 by the Council on Foreign Relations, Inc., New York.

You may like your neighbor or dislike him. You are not obliged to be friends with him or visit him. But you live side by side, and what can you do if neither you nor he has any desire to quit the old home and move to another town? All the more so in relations between states. It would be unreasonable to assume that you can make it so hot for your undesirable neighbor that he will decide to move to Mars or Venus. And vice versa, of course.

What, then, remains to be done? There may be two ways out: either war—and war in the rocket and H-bomb age is fraught with the most dire consequences for all nations—or peaceful coexistence. Whether you like your neighbor or not, nothing can be done about it, you have to find some way of getting on with him, for you both live on one and the same planet.

But the very concept of peaceful coexistence, it is said, by its alleged complexity frightens certain people who have become unaccustomed to trusting their neighbors and who see a double bottom in each suitcase. People of this kind, on hearing the word "coexistence," begin to play around with it one way and another, sizing it up and applying various yardsticks to it. Isn't it a fraud? Isn't it a trap? Does not coexistence signify the division of the world into areas separated by high fences, which do not communicate with each other? And what is going to happen behind those fences?

The more such questions are piled up artificially by the cold-war mongers, the more difficult it is for the ordinary man to make head or tail of them. It would therefore be timely to rid the essence of this question of all superfluous elements and to attempt to look soberly at the most pressing problem of our day—the problem of peaceful competition. . . .

II

From its very inception the Soviet state proclaimed peaceful coexistence as the basic principle of its foreign policy. It was no accident that the very first state act of the Soviet power was the decree on peace, the decree on the cessation of the bloody war.

What, then, is the policy of peaceful coexistence?

In its simplest expression it signifies the repudiation of war as a means of solving controversial issues. However, this does not cover the entire concept of peaceful coexistence. Apart from the commitment to nonaggression, it also presupposes an obligation on the part of all states to desist from violating each other's territorial integrity and sovereignty in any form and under any pretext whatsoever. The principle of peaceful coexistence signifies a renunciation of interference in the internal affairs of other countries with the object of altering their system of government or mode of life or for any other motives. The doctrine of peaceful coexistence also presupposes that political and economic relations between countries are to be based upon complete equality of the parties concerned, and on mutual benefit.

It is often said in the West that peaceful coexistence is nothing else than a tactical method of the socialist states. There is not a grain of truth in such allegations. Our desire for peace and peaceful coexistence is not conditioned by any time-serving or tactical considerations. It springs from the very nature of socialist society in which there are not classes or social groups interested in profiting by war or seizing and enslaving other people's territories. The Soviet Union and the other socialist countries, thanks to their socialist system, have an unlimited home market and for this reason they have no need to pursue an expansionist policy of conquest and an effort to subordinate other countries to their influence. . . .

We say to the leaders of the capitalist states: Let us try out in practice whose system is better, let us compete without war. This is much better than competing in who will produce more arms and who will smash whom. We stand and always will stand for such competition as will help to raise the well-being of the people to a higher level.

The principle of peaceful competition does not at all demand that one or another state abandon the system and ideology adopted by it. It goes without saying that the acceptance of this principle cannot lead to the immediate end of disputes and contradictions which are inevitable between countries adhering to different social systems. But the main thing is ensured: the states which decided to adopt the path of peaceful coexistence repudiate the use of force in any form and agree on a peaceful settlement of possible disputes and conflicts, bearing in mind the mutual interests of the parties concerned. In our age of the H-bomb and atomic techniques this is the main thing of interest to every man.

Displaying skepticism about the idea of peaceful competition, Vice President Nixon, in his speech over the Soviet radio and television in August 1959, attempted to find a contradiction between the Soviet people's professions of their readiness to coexist peacefully with the capitalist states and the slogans posted in the shops of our factories calling for higher labor productivity in order to ensure the speediest victory of communism.

This was not the first time we heard representatives of the bourgeois countries reason in this manner. They say: The Soviet leaders argue that they are for peaceful coexistence. At the same time they declare that they are fighting for communism and they even say that communism will be victorious in all countries. How can there be peaceful coexistence with the Soviet Union if it fights for communism?

People who treat the question in this way confuse matters, willfully or not, by confusing the problems of ideological struggle with the question of relations between states. Those indulging in this sort of confusion are most probably guided by a desire to cast aspersions upon the Communists of the Soviet Union and to represent them as the advocates of aggressive actions. This, however, is very unwise.

The Communist Party of the Soviet Union at its Twentieth Congress made it perfectly clear and obvious that the allegations that the Soviet Union intends to overthrow capitalism in other countries by means of "exporting" revolution are absolutely unfounded. I cannot refrain from reminding you of my words at the Twentieth Congress: "It goes without saying that among us Communists there are no adherents of capitalism. But this does not mean that we have interfered or plan to interfere in the internal affairs of countries where capitalism still exists. Romain Roland was right when he said that 'freedom is not brought in from abroad in baggage trains like Bourbons.' It is ridiculous to think that revolutions are made to order."

We Communists believe that the idea of communism will ultimately be victorious throughout the world, just as it has been victorious in our country, in China and in many other states. Many readers of *Foreign Affairs* will probably disagree with us. Perhaps they think that the idea of capitalism will ultimately triumph. It is their right to think so. We may argue, we may disagree with one another. *The main thing is to keep to the positions of ideological struggle, without resorting to arms in order to prove that one is right.* The point is that with military techniques what they are today, there are no inaccessible places in the world. Should a world war break out, no country will be able to shut itself off from a crushing blow.

We believe that ultimately that system will be victorious on the globe which will offer the nations greater opportunities for improving their material and spiritual life. It is precisely socialism that creates unprecedentedly great prospects for the inexhaustible creative enthusiasm of the masses, for a genuine flourishing of science and culture, for the realization of man's dream of a happy life, a life without destitute and unemployed people, of a happy childhood and tranquil old age, of the realization of the most audacious and ambitious human projects, of man's right to create in a truly free manner in the interests of the people.

But when we say that in the competition between the two systems, the capitalist and the socialist, our system will win, this does not mean, of course, that we shall achieve victory by interfering in the internal affairs of the capitalist countries. Our confidence in the victory of communism is of a different kind. It is based on a knowledge of the laws governing the development of society. Just as in its time capitalism, as the more progressive system, took the place of feudalism, so will capitalism be inevitably superseded by communism—the more progressive and more equitable social system. We are confident of the victory of the socialist system because it is a more progressive system than the capitalist system. Soviet power has been in existence for only a little more than 40 years, and during these years we have gone through two of the worst wars, repulsing the attacks of enemies who attempted to strangle us. Capitalism in the United States has been in existence for more than a century and a half, and the history of the United States has developed in such a way that never once have enemies landed on American territory.

Yet the dynamics of the development of the U.S.S.R. and the U.S.A. are such that the 42-year-old land of the Soviets is already able to challenge the 150-year-old capitalist state to economic competition; and the most farsighted American leaders are admitting that the Soviet Union is fast catching up with the United States and will ultimately outstrip it. Watching the progress of this competition, anyone can judge which is the better system, and we believe that in the long run all the peoples will embark on the path of struggle for the building of socialist societies.

You disagree with us? Prove by facts that your system is superior and more efficacious, that it is capable of ensuring a higher degree of prosperity for the people than the socialist system, that under capitalism man can be happier than under socialism. It is impossible to prove this. I have no other explanation for the fact that talk of violently "rolling back" communism never ceases in the West. Not long ago the U.S. Senate and House of Representatives deemed it proper to pass a resolution calling for the "liberation" of the socialist countries allegedly enslaved by communism and, moreover, of a number of union republics constituting part of the Soviet Union. The authors of the resolution call for the "liberation" of the Ukraine, Byelorussia, Lithuania, Latvia, Estonia, Armenia, Azerbaijan, Georgia, Kazakhstan, Turkmenistan and even a certain "Ural Area."

I would not be telling the full truth if I did not say that the adoption of this ill-starred resolution was regarded by the Soviet people as an act of provocation. Personally I agree with this appraisal.

It would be interesting to see, incidentally, how the authors of this resolution would have reacted if the parliament of Mexico, for instance, had passed a resolution demanding that Texas, Arizona and California be "liberated from American slavery." Apparently they have never pondered such a question, which is very regrettable. Sometimes comparisons help to understand the essence of a matter.

Traveling through the Soviet Union, leading American statesmen and public figures have had full opportunity to convince themselves that there is no hope of sowing strife between the Soviet people and the Communist Party and the Soviet Government, and of influencing them to rebel against communism. How, then, are we to explain the unceasing attempts to revive the policy of "rolling back" communism? What do they have in mind? Armed intervention in the internal affairs of the socialist countries? But in the West as well as in the East people are fully aware that under the conditions of modern military technique such actions are fraught with immediate and relentless retaliation.

So we come back to what we started with. In our day there are only two ways: peaceful coexistence or the most destructive war in history. There is no third choice.

III

The problem of peaceful coexistence between states with different social systems has become particularly pressing in view of the fact that since the Second World War the development of relations between states has entered a new stage, that now we have approached a period in the life of mankind when there is a real chance of excluding war once and for all from the life of society. The new alignment of international forces which has developed since the Second World War offers ground for the assertion that a new world war is no longer a fatal inevitability, that it can be averted.

First, today not only all the socialist states, but many countries in Asia and Africa which have embarked upon the road of independent national statehood, and many other states outside the aggressive military groupings, are actively fighting for peace.

Secondly, the peace policy enjoys the powerful support of the broad masses of the people all over the world.

Thirdly, the peaceful socialist states are in possession of very potent material means, which cannot but have a deterring effect upon the aggressors.

Prior to the Second World War the U.S.S.R. was the only socialist country, with not more than 17 percent of the territory, 3 percent of the population, and about 10 percent of the output of the world. At present, the socialist countries cover about one-fourth of the territory of the globe, have one-third of its population, and their industrial output accounts for about one-third of the total world output.

This is precisely the explanation of the indisputable fact that throughout the past years, hotbeds of war breaking out now in one and now in another part of the globe—in the Near East and in Europe, in the Far East and in Southeast Asia—have been extinguished at the very outset.

What does the future hold in store for us?

As a result of the fulfillment and overfulfillment of the present Seven Year Plan of economic development of the U.S.S.R., as well as of the plans of the other socialist countries of Europe and Asia, the countries of the socialist system will then account for a little more than half of the world output. Their economic power will grow immeasurably, and this will help to an even greater extent to consolidate world peace: the material might and moral influence of the peace-loving states will be so great that any bellicose militarist will have to think ten times before risking going to war. It is the good fortune of mankind that a community of socialist states which are not interested in new war has been set up, because to build socialism and communism the socialist countries need peace. Today the community of socialist countries which has sprung up on the basis of complete equality holds such a position in the development of all branches of economy, science and culture as to be able to exert an influence towards preventing the outbreak of new world wars.

Hence we are already in a practical sense near to that stage in the life of humanity when nothing will prevent people from devoting themselves wholly to peaceful labor, when war will be wholly excluded from the life of society.

But if we say that there is no fatal inevitability of war at present, this by no means signifies that we can rest on our laurels, fold our arms and bask in the sun in the hope that an end has been put to wars once and for all. Those in the West who believe that war is to their benefit have not yet abandoned their schemes. They control considerable material forces, as well as military and political levers, and there is no guarantee that some tragic day they will not attempt to set them in motion. That is why it is so much the more necessary to continue an active struggle in order that the policy of peaceful coexistence may triumph throughout the world not in words but in deeds. . . .

At times, and of late especially, some spokesmen in the West have gone so far as to say that the abolition of the aftermath of the Second World War is a step which would allegedly intensify rather than ease international tension. It is hard to believe that there are no secret designs behind allegations of this kind, especially when attempts are made to present in a distorted light the policy of the U.S.S.R., which is intended to secure a lasting and stable peace, by alleging that it all but leads to war. It seems to us, on the contrary, that the Soviet position on the German question corresponds most of all to the present-day reality.

It now seems that no sober-minded leader in the West is inclined any longer to advance the unrealistic demand for the so-called reunion of Germany before the conclusion of a peace treaty, inasmuch as more and more political leaders are becoming aware of the fact that reunion in the conditions now obtaining is a process which depends upon the Germans themselves and not upon any outside interference. We should start from the obvious fact that two German states exist, and that the Germans themselves must decide how they want to live. Inasmuch as these two states, the German Democratic Republic and the German Federal Republic, do exist, the peace treaty should be concluded with them, because any further delay and postponement of this exceptionally important act tends not only to sustain the abnormal situation in Europe but also to aggravate it still further.

As for Germany's unity, I am convinced that Germany will be united sooner or later. However, before this moment comes—and no one can foretell when it will come—no attempts should be made to interfere from outside in this internal process, to sustain the state of war which is fraught with many grave dangers and surprises for peace in Europe and throughout the world. The desire to preserve the peace and to prevent another war should outweigh all other considerations of statesmen, irrespective of their mode of thinking. The Gordian knot must be cut: the peace treaty must be achieved if we do not want to play with fire—with the destinies of millions upon millions of people.

IV

In this connection it is impossible to ignore also the question of West Berlin. It is commonly known that the German revanchists have made West Berlin the base for their constant undermining and subversive activity directed towards the provoking of war. We resolutely reject any attempts to ascribe to the Soviet Union the intention of seizing West Berlin and infringing upon the right of the population in this part of the city to preserve its present way of life. On the contrary, in demanding the normalization of the situation in West Berlin, we have proposed to convert it into a free city and to guarantee, jointly with the Western states, the preservation there of the way of life and of the social order which suits the West Berlin inhabitants best of all. This shows that the positions of the Government of the Soviet Union and the Governments of the Western states, judging by their statements, coincide on this question. We, and so do they, stand for the independence of West Berlin and for the preservation of the existing way of life there.

It is, therefore, only necessary to overcome the difficulties born of the cold war in order to find the way to an agreement on West Berlin and on the wider question of the conclusion of a peace treaty with the two German states. This is the way to ease international tensions and to promote peaceful coexistence. It would strengthen confidence between states and assist in the gradual abolition of unfriendliness and suspicion in international relations.

Implementation of the Soviet proposals would not injure the interests of the Western powers and would not give any one-sided advantages to anybody. At the same time, the settlement of the German question would prevent a dangerous development of events in Europe, remove one of the main causes of international tension and create favorable prospects for a settlement of other international issues.

The proposals of the Soviet Union were discussed at the Foreign Ministers' Conference in Geneva. The Ministers did not succeed in reaching an agreement, but the Geneva conference did accomplish a great deal of useful work. The positions of the two sides were positively brought closer together and the possibility of an agreement on some questions has become apparent.

At the same time, we still have substantial differences on a number of questions. I am deeply convinced that they are not fundamental differences on which agreement is impossible. And if we still have differences and have not reached agreement on certain important questions, it is, as we believe, with adequate grounds—a result of the concessions made by the Western powers to Chancellor Adenauer, who is pursuing a military policy, the policy of the German revanchists. This is a case of the United States, Britain and France dangerously abetting Chancellor Adenauer. It would have been far better if the NATO allies of Western Germany would persuade Chancellor Adenauer, in the interest of the maintenance of peace, that his policy imperils the cause of peace and that it may ultimately end in irreparable disaster for Western Germany. All this emphasizes again that the representatives of the states concerned must do some more work in order to find mutually acceptable decisions. . . .

V

We are prepared now as before to do everything we possibly can in order that the relations between the Soviet Union and other countries, and, in particular, the relations between the U.S.S.R. and the U.S.A., should be built upon the foundation of friendship and that they should fully correspond to the principles of peaceful coexistence.

I should like to repeat what I said at my recent press conference in Moscow: "Should Soviet-American relations become brighter, that will not fail to bring about an improvement in the relations with other states and will help to scatter the gloomy clouds in other parts of the globe also. Naturally, we want friendship not only with the U.S.A., but also with the friends of the U.S.A. At the same time we want to see the U.S.A. maintain good relations not only with us, but with our friends as well."

What, then, is preventing us from making the principles of peaceful coexistence an unshakable international standard and daily practice in the relations between the West and East?

Of course, different answers may be given to this question. But in order to be frank to the end, we should also say the following: *It is necessary that everybody should understand the irrevocable fact that the historic process is irreversible.* It is impossible to bring back yesterday. It is high time to understand that the world of the twentieth century is not the world of the nineteenth century, that two diametrically opposed social and economic systems exist in the world today side by side, and that the socialist system, in spite of all the attacks upon it, has grown so strong, has developed into such a force, as to make any return to the past impossible.

Real facts of life in the last ten years have shown convincingly that the policy of "rolling back" communism can only poison the international atmosphere, heighten the tension between states and work in favor of the cold war. Neither its inspirers nor those who conduct it can turn back the course of history and restore capitalism in the socialist countries.

We have always considered the Americans realistic people. All the more are we astonished to find that leading representatives of the United States still number in their midst individuals who insist on their own way in the face of the obvious failure of the policy of "rolling back" communism. But is it not high time to take a sober view of things and to draw conclusions from the lessons of the last 15 years? Is it not yet clear to everybody that consistent adherence to the policy of peaceful coexistence would make it possible to improve the international situation, to bring about a drastic cut in military expenditures and to release vast material resources for wiser purposes?

The well-known British scientist, J. Bernal, recently cited figures to show that average annual expenditures for military purposes throughout the world between 1950 and the end of 1957 were expressed in the huge sum of about 90 billion dollars. How many factories, apartment houses, schools, hospitals and libraries could have been built everywhere with the funds now spent on the preparation of another war! And how fast could economic progress have been advanced in the underdeveloped countries if we had converted to these purposes at least some of the means which are now being spent on war purposes!

VI

It is readily seen that the policy of peaceful coexistence receives a firm foundation only with increase in extensive and absolutely unrestricted international trade. It can be said without fear of exaggeration that there is no good basis for improvement of relations between our countries other than development of international trade.

If the principle of peaceful coexistence of states is to be adhered to, not in words, but in deeds, it is perfectly obvious that no ideological differences should be an obstacle to the development and extension of mutually advantageous economic contacts, to the exchange of everything produced by human genius in the sphere of peaceful branches of material production.

In this connection it may be recalled that soon after the birth of the Soviet state, back in the early 1920s, the Western countries, proceeding from considerations of economic interest, agreed to establish trade relations with our country despite the acutest ideological differences. Since then, discounting comparatively short periods, trade between the Soviet Union and capitalist states has been developing steadily. No ideological differences prevented, for instance, a considerable extension of trade relations between the Soviet Union and Britain and other Western states in recent years. We make no secret of our desire to establish normal commercial and business contacts with the United States as well, without any restrictions, without any discriminations.

In June of last year the Soviet Government addressed itself to the Government of the United States with the proposal to develop economic and trade contacts between our two countries. We proposed an extensive and concrete program of developing Soviet-American trade on a mutually advantageous basis. The adoption of our proposals would undoubtedly accord with the interests of both states and peoples. However, these proposals have not been developed so far.

Striving for the restoration of normal trade relations with the United States, the Soviet Union does not pursue any special interests. In our economic development we rely wholly on the internal forces of our country, on our own resources and possibilities. All our plans for further economic development are drawn up taking into consideration the possibilities available here. As in the past, when we outline these plans we proceed only from the basis of our own possibilities and forces. Irrespective of whether or not we shall trade with Western countries, the United States included, the implementation of our economic plans of peaceful construction will not in the least be impeded.

However, if both sides want to improve relations, all barriers in international trade must be removed. Those who want peaceful coexistence cannot but favor the development of trade, economic and business contacts. Only on this basis can international life develop normally.

VII

Peaceful coexistence is the only way which is in keeping with the interests of all nations. To reject it would mean under existing conditions to doom the whole world to a terrible and destructive war at a time when it is fully possible to avoid it.

It is possible that when mankind has advanced to a plane where it has proved capable of the greatest discoveries and of making its first steps into outer space, it should not be able to use the colossal achievements of its genius for the establishment of a stable peace for the good of man, rather than for the preparation of another war and for the destruction of all that has been created by its labor over many millenniums? Reason refuses to believe this. It protests.

The Soviet people have stated and declare again that they do not want war. If the Soviet Union and the countries friendly to it are not attacked, we shall never use any weapons either against the United States or against any other countries. We do not want any horrors of war, destruction, suffering and death for ourselves or for any other peoples. We say this not because we fear anyone. Together with our friends, we are united and stronger than ever. But precisely because of that do we say that war can and should be prevented. Precisely because we want to rid mankind of war, we urge the Western powers to peaceful and lofty competition. We say to all: Let us prove to each other the advantages of one's own system not with fists, not by war, but by peaceful economic competition in conditions of peaceful coexistence.

As for the social system in some state or other, that is the domestic affair of the people of each country. We always have stood and we stand today for noninterference in the internal affairs of other countries. We have always abided, and we shall abide, by these positions. The question, for example, what system will exist in the United States or in other capitalist countries cannot be decided by other peoples or states. This question can and will be decided only by the American people themselves, only by the people of each country.

The existence of the Soviet Union and of the other socialist countries is a real fact. It is also a real fact that the United States of America and the other capitalist countries live in different social conditions, in the conditions of capitalism. Then let us recognize this real situation and proceed from it in order not to go against reality, against life itself. Let us not try to change this situation by interferences from without, by means of war on the part of some states against other states.

I repeat, there is only one way to peace, one way out of the existing tension: peaceful coexistence.

Philip E. Mosely

THE MEANINGS OF COEXISTENCE

Philip E. Mosely, internationally recognized as one of the nation's outstanding authorities on the Soviet Union and after 1955 Director of Studies at the Council of Foreign Relations in New York, served in the State Department during and after the war and took part in several international conferences. In this essay Mosely challenges the acceptability of Khrushchev's concept of peaceful coexistence by contrasting it with the declaration of Soviet policy and intention adopted unanimously by the Twenty-second Party Congress on October 31, 1961. This official statement was heralded as a guide for Soviet thought and action over "the next historic epoch." Peaceful coexistence by Soviet definition, Mosely points out, does not promise stability but rather increasing Soviet pressure, with a wide variety of weapons, for the ultimate triumph of communism. Particularly disturbing in official Soviet statements was the Soviet determination to support "wars of liberation" for the purpose of rescuing "oppressed" people from Western imperialism. The new program, concludes Mosely, is "genuinely Leninist; it lays down not a theory but a set of comprehensive and coherent guidelines for action." To meet this threat the West required new policies.

In the deeply divided world of today, one main obstacle to achieving a genuine state of peaceful coexistence is the gap in the meanings attached to these two words in different societies and political systems. The gap is, of course, just one additional example of the estrangement of vocabularies that besets every effort at direct and sincere exchanges of ideas across or through the ideological and psychological barriers. Words like "democracy," "freedom," "progress" are, as we know only too well, employed in very different and even opposite senses in the two worlds.

Another obstacle lies in the confrontation of absolutes, the insistence on the total good of one ideal and the total evil of the way of life that it seeks to displace and destroy. This sense of serving as a mere instrument of history justifies, in the minds of its champions and supporters, a vast arrogance of self-righteousness. To them, the adversary is not only doomed but is morally wrong in his every act and thought.

Finally, the ideological armor that encases the Communist leaders is wrought of that contradiction in terms, "scientific revelation." Its theoretical bases, which were laid down over one hundred years ago at the beginning of the industrial era, must be proven to be uniquely correct and infallible today; and therefore those who dare reexamine or question any part of its fundamentalist dogmas must be silenced or destroyed.

The most recent and most authoritative statement of Communist dogma is, of course, the new Program of the Communist Party of the Soviet Union, unanimously adopted by the Twenty-second Party Congress on October 31, 1961. Despite its repetitious length and its many internal contradictions, it was carefully designed to serve as the main guide to Soviet thought, policy and action over "the next historic epoch." In the ten weeks between the publication of the draft program and the convening of the Congress, it was "discussed" in tens of thousands of meetings; since the Congress, it has been distributed in millions of copies printed in scores of languages. Hence, its statements on the nature and purpose of coexistence must be studied seriously. First:

> *Peaceful coexistence of the socialist and capitalist countries is an objective necessity for the development of human society. War cannot and must not serve as a means of settling international disputes.*

Excellent! All reasonable people can welcome this position as a basis for a lively and earnest give-and-take discussion on how best to guarantee mankind against the danger of a new and terrible war and especially on how, in practical terms, we can concert our actions so as to diminish, contain or eliminate some or all of the conflicts that threaten to escape our control and balloon into a total struggle.

Here, however, the Program brings its non-Communist partners-in-dialogue up sharp against a flinty dogma of Communist fundamentalism:

> *Imperialism is the only source of the war danger. The imperialist camp is making preparations for the most terrible crime against mankind—a world thermonuclear war that can bring unprecedented destruction to entire countries and wipe out entire nations.*

Here dogma, as so often, takes precedence over reality. After all, the Soviet Union has also been hard at work constructing horrendous weapons systems. Its leaders have, indeed, addressed blackmail notes to more than 30 governments, in which it has threatened their peoples specifically with nuclear destruction unless they abandon certain policies and postures of which Moscow disapproves. Semantically, the Kremlin, like its opponents, argues that it is not preparing for "aggression" but "to deter aggression." The distinction rests in the degree of faith or confidence in the government that makes the threat. Today any nuclear threat raises the level of international tension. This is all the more its effect when the Kremlin stretches the concept of "self-defense" to include the demand for Communist control over West Berlin and for the breaking up of alliances that Moscow views as obstacles to the extension of its own power.

The completely one-sided nature of the Communist interpretation of world politics appears in one small but interesting correction that was inserted in the final version of the Party Program. The draft of August 5 referred with approval to ". . . a growing number of countries that adhere to a policy of neutrality and strive to safeguard themselves against the hazards of participation in military blocs." This wording apparently gave too strong praise to nonalignment. At bottom, Communists are bound by dogma to view nonalignment as a way-station to joining their own power bloc. The words of the draft program might even imply an endorsement of Tito's posture, were it not for his heresy of claiming to be both Communist and uncommitted. And some Communists might have wondered why Khrushchev had used his tanks and artillery, in October 1956, to put down the attempt of the Imre Nágy government to declare Hungary neutral.

The drafters of the final version caught this awkward ideological ambiguity and changed "participation in military blocs" to "participation in aggressive military blocs." Since "aggressive" is an adjective that is applied only to "imperialists" and never to "the countries of socialism," the revised wording modifies the Kremlin's praise of nonalignment and leaves the gate open for presently uncommitted countries to commit themselves later to the "good" military bloc of "socialism."

The pursuit of "peaceful coexistence," in Moscow's view, must not lead to any slackening in the effort to reshape the rest of the world to the Communist pattern. On the contrary, the struggle for the triumph of communism must be pressed even more vigorously and with the wider and more varied arsenal of instruments that is now available:

Peaceful coexistence serves as a basis for the peaceful competition be-
tween socialism and capitalism on an international scale and constitutes
a specific form of class struggle between them. As they consistently
pursue the policy of peaceful coexistence, the socialist countries are
steadily strengthening the positions of the world socialist system in its
competition with capitalism. Peaceful coexistence affords more favorable
opportunities for the struggle of the working class in the capitalist coun-
tries and facilitates the struggle of the peoples of the colonial and de-
pendent countries for their liberation.

The Program specifically warns Communists everywhere against pinning to a new world war their hopes for their worldwide triumph.
Indeed, the expectation of victory through cataclysm might lead them
to relax their efforts and to slacken their discipline. However, in
accord with a long Leninist tradition, the Soviet leadership is not
against all types of wars:

The CPSU and the Soviet people as a whole will continue to oppose all
wars of conquest, including wars between capitalist countries, and local
wars aimed at strangling people's emancipation movements, and consider
it their duty to support the sacred struggle of the oppressed peoples and
their just anti-imperialist wars of liberation.

This reservation leaves a wide range of military actions open to
Soviet arms, for the Kremlin reserves to itself the right to decide what
peoples are "oppressed" and which wars are "wars of liberation."
Despite the great risks that may accompany its participation, direct
or indirect, in a variety of wars, the Program affirms the self-
confident belief of the Soviet leadership that it can achieve complete
victory without becoming involved in a nuclear war:

The growing superiority of the socialist forces over the forces of im-
perialism, of the forces of peace over those of war, will make it actually
possible to banish world war from the life of society even before the
complete victory of socialism on earth, with capitalism surviving in a part
of the world. The victory of socialism throughout the world will do away
completely with the social and national causes of all wars. To abolish war
and establish everlasting peace on earth is the historic mission of com-
munism.

In the Soviet view, "peaceful coexistence" is the correct policy in
"an epoch," more or less prolonged, during which "capitalism" (the
label the Kremlin attaches to those who resist its embrace) is to be

compelled to retreat from one position to another until it finally gives up the ghost. The means for enforcing each such retreat are to be varied according to the local and international balance of power.

In some countries the transition to socialism (i.e., to rule by the Communist Party) may take place by peaceful, in others by "nonpeaceful," means. Of course, even if "the working class" (those who obey and support the Communist Party) manages to ". . . win a solid majority in parliament . . . ," it must also ". . . launch a broad mass struggle outside parliament, smash the resistance of the reactionary forces, and provide the necessary conditions for a peaceful socialist revolution." Since the Communists would then hold the monopoly of force, they would also be able to define "the reactionary forces" to suit their own interests. In any case they would have no further interest in providing conditions of "peaceful coexistence" with any groups or individuals that they considered hostile or recalcitrant to that monopoly of power.

The Program emphasizes that the struggle must be waged untiringly and relentlessly, with a rapid succession of tactics, in order to keep the various opposing forces off balance and disunited:

The success of the struggle which the working class wages for the victory of the revolution will depend on how well the working class and its party master the use of all forms of struggle—peaceful and nonpeaceful, parliamentary and extra-parliamentary—and how well they are prepared to replace one form of struggle by another as quickly and unexpectedly as possible.

In the end, of course, all roads lead to Rome, to the dictatorship of the proletariat, i.e., of the Communist Party:

. . . Whatever the form in which the transition from capitalism to socialism is effected, that transition can come about only through revolution. However varied the forms of a new people's state power in the period of socialist construction, their essence will be the same— dictatorship of the proletariat, which represents genuine democracy, democracy for the working people.

It is essential, of course, for the main center of the Communist movement to assure the unquestioning unity of "the working class," in order to lead a well-orchestrated offensive against "capitalism." In recent years this has not proved easy or simple even within those countries and Parties that acknowledge Moscow's hegemony. In fact,

> *Revisionism, Right opportunism, which is a reflection of bourgeois influence, is the chief danger within the Communist movement today. The revisionists, who mask their renunciation of Marxism with talk about the necessity of taking account of the latest developments in society and the class struggle, in effect play the role of pedlars of bourgeois-reformist ideology within the Communist movement.*

However, "dogmatism and sectarianism, unless steadfastly combated, can also become the chief danger at particular stages in the development of individual parties."

Finally, who is to define "revisionism" and "dogmatism"? Obviously Khrushchev is determined to keep this "lever of power" in his own hands. He demonstrated this most dramatically at the Twenty-second Party Congress, where he made his famous attack on the Albanian Party leaders, only to be rebuffed by Chou En-lai, who protested the bringing into the open of this bitter interparty quarrel, and then departed for Peking. The Chinese leadership could, had it been so minded, have cited the very words of the Soviet Party Program on this crucial point:

> *The Communist Parties are independent and they shape their policies with due regard to the specific conditions prevailing in their own countries. . . . The Communist Party of the Soviet Union . . . regards it as its internationalist duty to abide by the appraisals and conclusions which the fraternal parties have reached jointly concerning their common tasks in the struggle against imperialism, for peace, democracy and socialism. . . .*

Apparently the Soviet leadership has been unusually sensitive to the accusation that it dictates its policies unilaterally to other Parties, for it inserted a significant rewording in the final version of the Program. The draft of August 5 stated:

> *The CPSU will continue to strengthen the unity and cohesion of the ranks of the great army of Communists of all countries.*

This could be read to mean that the CPSU will, by its direct action within or upon those Parties, strengthen their "unity and cohesion" and assure their obedience to Moscow. In the final draft this slip of the drafters was softened:

> *The CPSU will continue to direct its efforts to the unity and cohesion of the ranks of the great army of Communists of all countries.*

Indeed, it is becoming increasingly difficult for Khrushchev to exercise over a wide diversity of regimes and Parties Stalin's "internationalist discipline." As the Program states in another context: ". . . not only the big states, but also the small ones . . . are in a position, irrespective of their strength, to pursue an independent foreign policy." The forces of division seem to be working within "the camp of socialism" as well as beyond its bounds. The impact of fissiparous trends may be all the more serious for Khrushchev's policy just because these tendencies run directly counter to Communist dogma as well as to Soviet ambition.

II

It is important to know the new Party Program. It is not mere rhetoric or a pious affirmation of hopes or aspirations. Lenin and his successors have prided themselves on "the unity of theory and practice," and since the new Program, despite Peking's carpings, is genuinely Leninist, it lays down not a theory but a set of comprehensive and coherent guidelines for action.

Modern practices of scientific analysis also affirm "the unity of theory and practice," but this means something quite different to the West. Under conditions of free inquiry it means that theories are formed on the basis of carefully examined facts for the purpose of giving order to larger and more complex bodies of facts. Then, when new or previously unexamined facts can no longer be explained or contained within existing theories, these comprehensive concepts must be revised, sometimes radically. Thus, the generalizing role of theory in a system of free inquiry means that all theories have a utility value rather than a moral value, that many theories are competing to establish their validity as scientific tools, and that they are basically tentative rather than absolute in character.

Despite the recent and modest enlargements of the sphere of inquiry in Soviet scientific thought, the fundamental duty of the political leadership to define the limits of inquiry and to state in advance the conclusions it must reach has been strongly reaffirmed in the 1961 Program:

> The investigation of the problems of world history and contemporary world development must disclose the law-governed process of mankind's advance toward communism, the change in the balance of forces in favor

of socialism, the aggravation of the general crisis of capitalism, the break-up of the colonial system of imperialism and its consequences, and the upsurge of the national-liberation movement of peoples.

In Soviet theory and practice, what is desired is stated as already proved "scientifically." The only purpose of inquiry is to prove again what has already been affirmed by political authority to be "true." The Soviet insistence that new data, or facts that cannot be fitted to the only valid theory, are "non-facts" is a continuing obstacle to any genuine freedom of discourse. The habit of raising each disagreement to a quarrel between "sin" and "virtue" also remains strong. This means that the examination of new or unwelcome facts is regarded, not as an interesting exercise in scientific skill, but as another form of political combat.

The rigidities of Communist thought make it very difficult (outside the natural sciences and technology) for the shapers of policy to have available the findings of objective research. Nevertheless, the range of useful investigation is definitely wider today in domestic policy than it is in the analysis of world affairs. The Soviet leaders have made numerous adjustments in their domestic economic policy: breaking up the machine-tractor stations, cutting back long-range investment in hydroelectric power plants in favor of more numerous and less costly thermal plants, and so forth.

The quality of rational inquiry has been improved substantially in those fields where its validity is of direct advantage to the decision-makers. Unfortunately, even in this area of policy many of the major decisions seem still to be based primarily on deeply rooted prejudice. What will the Soviet people do with all the steel that has been promised by 1980? What can it do with a vast flow of petroleum if the output of private cars remains as low as is planned? Can agriculture possibly meet the growing and more varied needs of the Soviet people without a far larger investment of resources?

In the study of foreign countries and world politics, on the other hand, there has been almost no relaxation of political rigidities. Everything is painted in black and white. On one side, angels; on the other, devils. If dialectical materialism can provide a scientific basis for analysis, it should make it possible for Soviet experts to examine more objectively than they now do the causes of the high rate of growth in several of the free-world economies. It should actually encourage them to state calmly and without indignation why other systems operate differently from the Soviet one. A strong and powerful country needs objective information and conscientious analysis, and its rulers should not be afraid to permit the full use of scholarly inquiry if they want to be well served.

Because "science" had become a magic word in his time, Karl Marx baptized his theory of economic history with the name of "scientific socialism," and the same honorific adjective has been claimed by Lenin, Stalin and Khrushchev for their political programs. In practice, however, many of the judgments made by Soviet leaders have chiefly reflected ingrained ideological prejudices and strong political ambitions. As often as not, Soviet appraisals have fallen wide of the mark.

By the late 1920s the Comintern, along with some "bourgeois" economists, was predicting the onset of an economic crisis in Western Europe and North America. On the other hand, the first Five Year Plan was drawn up on the assumption that world prices of foodstuffs and raw materials, Russia's main exports, would remain stable. Moscow's oracles insisted, in the face of obvious facts, that the depression of 1929 was driving the United States down the path of fascism. In 1941 Stalin assumed that, if Hitler attacked the Soviet Union, Britain would make a compromise peace with him because of common "class interests." Fortunately for the people of the Soviet Union, Churchill and Roosevelt had already concerted a policy of alliance with Russia against the common enemy. In 1948 Stalin thought he could take West Berlin by a cruel blockade, and since 1958 Khrushchev has made several misjudgments of the Berlin question. Until recent months Soviet spokesmen have had little or nothing to say about the rapid steps that Western Europe has been taking toward economic unification; the "law" of capitalist competition made this historic process, in Moscow's eyes, an absurdity. The record of Soviet predictions suggests that it is more faith or habit than practical performance that supports the Kremlin's claim to possess the sole "scientific" and "infallible" instrument for predicting the future course of events.

III

Since 1953 many things have changed for the better in Soviet life. The improvements in food, housing, clothing and household conveniences have been widespread and substantial. In literature new themes of individual love and suffering, together with a cautious criticism of recent Stalinist "excesses," have become almost fashionable. More than at any time since the early 1930s the Party and the press seem to be trying to remedy some of the most callous features of Soviet administration and to improve the workings of Soviet justice.

All this is extremely welcome. The people of the Soviet Union, as they approach the forty-fifth anniversary of the October Revolution, have earned over and over the right to a modest return for their vast sacrifices and patience. Through this long travail they have preserved many fine qualities of friendliness, hospitality and patriotism. The modest comforts many of them have now attained, the pride in the scientific and material achievements of their country, and a burning memory of the Second World War combine to make them deeply and genuinely eager for peace and coexistence. They are now confident of the good intentions of their new rulers toward themselves, and therefore they accept more readily the Kremlin's protestations that only Soviet policy is "peace-loving" and that the sole risks of war now arise from the "imperialists" and their conspiracies.

"Making a peace treaty" with East Germany, "putting an end to the occupation regime in West Berlin"—all this sounds very reasonable to Soviet people. They are not aware that the people of West Berlin regard the token garrison as their protector and that they resent profoundly Ulbricht's insistence on "liberating" them from their hard-won freedom and prosperity. If people in the Soviet Union did know this, with whom could they discuss it? All they can do is hope that Khrushchev, who seems to them a human sort of man, knows what he is about and will, as he promises, safeguard peace.

The same old attempt to maintain a low level of strain at home and a high level of tension abroad has again been standard Soviet tactics in recent years. For many months Soviet readers heard all about the 400 or so American military advisers in Laos and the supply of American military materiel and economic support. It was many months before one relatively obscure Soviet newspaper gave one solitary hint that Soviet supplies and planes were engaged on the Communist side. Even now Soviet readers have no inkling that in Laos a major part of the fighting has been conducted by North Vietnamese units. Similarly, after the Soviet Government had announced on August 31, 1961, the forthcoming renewal of hydrogen bomb tests, it gave no further information to Soviet readers for some six weeks. Even so, the news apparently spread rather widely, at least in the major cities, and gave rise to a good deal of muted anxiety.

A fierce patriotism, a defensive resentment of any condescension on the part of foreigners, a strong pride in Soviet strength and achievements—these emotions are widely shared. They make it easy for many Soviet people to accept a messianic ideology of Russia's unique mission, without thinking very much about the historic foundations of this notion or about its intellectual inconsistencies. The extreme self-righteousness of the Kremlin's boasts and demands is more troubling to many thoughtful Soviet people. Sometimes they wonder whether there is not a contradiction between Russia's being "the strongest power" in the world, as Khrushchev often claims, and the strenuous effort to protect its people against all but carefully screened and denatured information about the "imperialist" world.

Coexisting on the same globe with a one-eyed and angry giant is dangerous rather than exhilarating. In one breath he demands "friendship" and describes the many achievements, mainly material, that he admires in American life. In the next, he explains with "scientific" certainty why communism will inevitably "bury" this much envied America. Even without benefit of Freud, it is not hard to see the power lust bursting out from behind the appeals for "peace and friendship."

We must, nevertheless, deal with the world as it is, and two of the facts of the world are the Soviet messianic fantasy and the power the Soviet leaders wield. It is, of course, a sign of good judgment that the Soviet leadership recognizes the mutually suicidal character of a nuclear war, and we must welcome its stated intention to contain the conflict with a rather elastic definition of "peaceful coexistence." As the Soviet spokesmen have made clear at Geneva, however, the Kremlin is not actively interested in bringing nuclear arms under control, and it believes it can gain more political advantages by continuing the arms race at a high pitch.

Moscow regards the present period of "peaceful coexistence" as a prolonged contest in which it must exert its full strength and will in order to make decisive gains by all means short of nuclear war. By the leverage of its strategic, political and economic power it hopes, within a few years, to bring about a great shift of political power in its favor. In contrast to Stalin's cautious peripheral probings, Khrushchev's declared ambitions, and the current Soviet programs of action, now extend to all continents except, perhaps temporarily,

Australia. Since Soviet military and economic strength will be growing rapidly in coming years, it is not going to be enough for the countries that cherish freedom to repeat old and tried formulas that have served them well in previous crises. They must seek actively for new ways to bring their great political, economic and strategic resources to bear in the balance if they are going to survive in freedom the multiple challenge that is posed by Khrushchev's program of "peaceful coexistence."

Frederick L. Schuman

THE RUSSIAN RIDDLE

Frederick L. Schuman, long Professor of Political Science, Williams College, adopting a more hopeful view of coexistence, finds the bases of Soviet action less in words than in a variety of Russian traditions. For him the Soviet challenge remains limited and finite. The United States, moreover, has no choice but to accept the challenge of coexistence even on Soviet terms because the only alternative is war. Professor Schuman reminds the reader that Soviet achievements seldom bear any resemblance to Soviet intentions. There is no relationship, he continues, between the Russian mission of saving the world from social injustice and Russia's actual role in world affairs. He sees a continuity between the foreign policies of the Tsars and those of the Soviet leaders, for all have been concerned primarily with a quest for power, productive capacity, and security. Russia has always responded to external pressures, he writes, with political autocracy, intolerable orthodoxy, territorial aggrandizement, and a messianic universalism. Russian ambitions have included the strengthening of frontiers, not the subjugation of Europe or the conquest of the earth. Since Russia can be contained, Schuman sees no reasonable alternative to the mutual diplomatic acceptance of a partition of the globe into spheres of influence.

Panslavism is a movement which endeavors to undo what a thousand-year-old history has created. It cannot achieve its aim without sweeping Turkey, Hungary and half of Germany off the map of Europe. Should this result ever be accomplished, it could be made to last by no other means than the subjugation of Europe. Panslavism has now transformed itself from an article of faith into a political program. By now, it is no longer only Russia, but the whole panslavistic plot which threatens to found its realm on the ruins of Europe. This leaves Europe only one alternative—subjugation through slavery or the lasting destruction of the center of its offensive strength.

So wrote, a hundred years ago, a staunch defender of the West against Eastern darkness. The writer was shrewd and well informed. Yet his stark "either-or" was to prove false, as comparably grim "alternatives" may well prove false today. The quotation is from the *Neu Oderzeitung* of April 1855. The writer was Karl Marx.

Students of foreign policy (and of a closely related, albeit far less tangible, phenomenon usually labeled "national character") are con-

Reprinted by permission from Frederick L. Schuman, "The Russian Riddle," *Current History* 28 (February 1955): 65–69.

stantly searching for a golden key to unlock all mysteries, simplify all choices, and bring into intelligible relationship a bewildering variety of attitudes and acts which, considered separately, appear to be a jumble of paradoxes. Some among the searchers have sought to explain the United States in terms of "Manifest Destiny," the "Frontier," or the "American Dream." The secret of modern Germany, by the same logic, is said to be "militarism"; of Britain, the "balance of power"; of France, the glory of *La Grande Nation;* and so forth. Since no nation fully understands itself, pretensions to understanding others by reducing them to a formula may well be dismissed as presumptuous. Since all men and mankind *in toto* are bundles of ambivalences, all efforts to reduce chaos to order may be deemed vain. Yet such efforts often furnish insight and supply some semblance of the hypotheses upon which all human groups must act in dealing with other groups.

The enigma of Russia has long fascinated the imaginations of Russians and non-Russians alike. Attempted answers have embraced such diverse explanations as the Russian Soul, the Great Plain, the Third Rome, Infant Swaddling, Byzantinism, Barbarism, Geopolitics, Panslavism, Muscovite Imperialism, Marxist Messianism, Total Depravity and sundry combinations of these and other stereotypes. Cautious scholars may grant to each of these interpretations an element of truth. But few can regard such verbalizations as reliable guides to the past or prospective conduct of the polyglot people and successive power-holders in the vast realm known through the centuries as Kiev-Rus, the Khanate of the Golden Horde, the Grand Duchy of Muscovy, the Romanov Czardom, and the Soviet Union. To offer another explanation is a work of supererogation. To offer no explanation is to despair of the possibility of knowledge and to render Russia terrifyingly unintelligible. Insofar as the second objective is both unthinkable and unnecessary, the first is worthy of further exploration.

Truth and Consequences

Since man is the animal who makes ends of his means, his achievements often bear little resemblance to his intentions. Many Russians in 1917 hailed the October Revolution in the name of the new freedom, pure democracy, an end of exploitation and oppression, world unity and peace, and the cooperative commonwealth of the classless society destined to bring salvation to humanity. Their survivors or successors of 1955, while still bewitched by heroic phrases, live in a highly stratified society under a despotic and intolerant oligarchy in a world stubbornly refusing to be "saved" and therefore divided into the hostile camps of the Cold War. How did this come out of that? This eternal question of the historian is answerable, if at all, only in many thick volumes of record and analysis. Meanwhile a simpler, more obvious, and, I suspect, more significant paradox may serve as a point of departure for the present briefer inquiry.

Russia's "mission" in the minds of most of Russia's rulers, from Ivan the Great to Malenkov, has been to "save the West" from its crimes and follies by leading it back to the true faith and the good life. In borrowing the Western creed of Marxism (concocted by Heresiarch St. Karl in the library of the British Museum), Russia's revolutionary leaders were more determined than their forebears to rescue the West, by example or World Revolution, from the evils of social injustice. This purpose was no facile rationalization but a deep spiritual conviction.

Russia's actual role in the world society of our century has been of a wholly different order. Through totalitarian dictatorship and socialist economic planning, the Marxist masters of Muscovy have lifted Russia to the stature of a "Super-Power" and demonstrated how a primitive community, through immense sacrifice and suffering, can "raise itself by its bootstraps" to the level of a highly industrialized, urbanized society. The demonstration inspires loathing and fear in the wealthy West. But in the Eastern slum-lands of the earth it evokes admiration and emulation. The message to the West falls on deaf ears. It finds eager Oriental listeners, for whom it was never meant in the wildest imaginings of Marx and Engels or even of Lenin. The causes and results of this unintended reversal of roles is a major clue to foreign policy and domestic developments in contemporary Russia.

Voices of the Past

Space is lacking to elaborate the argument. A few generalizations must serve as keys to the events of dubious yesterdays and problematical tomorrows. They should be judged in the light of the adage that all generalizations are false, including the generalization that all generalizations are false. . . .

1. Russia, vis-à-vis the West, has long been economically backward and militarily weak, thanks chiefly to the Mongol yoke (1240–1480) which cut off the Russian community from the cultural stimulation of medieval Europe and the dawn of the Renaissance and Reformation.

2. Unlike America expanding westward over an empty continent, Russia expanding eastward over an empty continent was ever exposed to attack by more efficient land powers—Turkey, Poland, Sweden, Prussia, France, Germany. From a time antedating 1571, when Turks and Tartars last burned Moscow, to a time following 1941, Russia experienced more destructive invasions and interventions than any other modern nation-state.

3. Under Dukes, Czars, Commissars and Ministers, the Russian community has always responded to external threats and internal weakness with the devices of political autocracy, intolerant orthodoxy, territorial aggrandizement and messianic universalism, all coupled with frantic attempts to catch up with Western technology. Such were the goals of Ivan the Terrible, Peter the Great, Catherine the Great, and Alexander I. Such were the goals of Lenin and Stalin. The most revealing single statement of purpose in Soviet politics was made by Stalin on February 4, 1931 (ten years after the end of the Allied intervention and ten years before the Nazi invasion) to the First All-Union Conference of Managers of Socialist Industry:

> *Those who fall behind get beaten. . . . Old Russia was beaten by the Mongol Khans. She was beaten by the Turkish Beys. She was beaten by the Swedish feudal lords. She was beaten by the Polish and Lithuanian gentry. She was beaten by the British and French capitalists. She was beaten by the Japanese barons. All beat her—for her backwardness, for military backwardness, for cultural backwardness, for political backwardness, for industrial backwardness, for agricultural backwardness. . . . You remember the words of the pre-Revolutionary poet: "You are poor and abundant, mighty and impotent, Mother Russia." These words of the old poet were well learned by those gentlemen. . . . Such is the law of the exploiters—to beat the backward and the weak. . . . That is why we must no longer lag behind. You must put an end to backwardness in the shortest possible time and develop genuine Bolshevik tempo in building up the socialist system of economy. There is no other way. . . . Either we do it, or they crush us.*

4. In the great tests of power Russia's rulers, when they have acted wisely, have left the initiation of hostilities to the enemy even when "preventive war" offered decisive strategic advan-

tages. This passive policy is attributable to awareness of Russian feebleness and knowledge that Russia's masses fight heroically against foreign invaders but indifferently in ventures of conquest abroad. The prelude and outcome of the "Great Patriotic Wars" of 1812 and 1941 support the point, as does the very different course of other conflicts unleashed by Russian decisions.

When Russia opens hostilities, Russia is usually defeated. When other powers attack, Russia is usually victorious. Invaders of Russia who pursue circumscribed political and territorial objectives sometimes attain them, at least temporarily, as in 1856, 1905 and 1917–1918. But all invaders of Russia (since the Mongols) who pursue unlimited aims of national annihilation and subjugation are invariably vanquished.

5. Russian annexations in Europe have more often been the consequences of unsuccessful Western aggression against Russia than of successful Russian aggression against the West. Relations between Russia and Sweden, Lithuania, Poland and Turkey bear early witness. The French assault of 1812, the Allied intervention of 1918, the Polish invasion of 1920, and the Nazi attack of 1941 bear later witness. In each case Russian lands were less extensive before the assault from abroad than they became in the wake of the foe's defeat.

6. Muscovite aggrandizement, though looming as limitless to Western alarmists fearing Russian intentions and capabilities of "conquering the world," has always aimed at specific strategic frontiers or areas of influence suitable for defense in depth against anticipated future attacks and never at unlimited objectives of subjugating Europe, Asia and all the earth.

Medieval Kiev sought control of the "water road" from the Baltic to Byzantium and of the Western reaches of the "steppe road" out of Mongolia. Early Muscovy sought mastery of the great river valleys of the Volga, Don, Dnieper and Western Dvina, all arising in central Russia. Later Muscovy sought to reach the seas washing the shores of the Great Plain. Subsequent control of most of the Eurasian "Heartland" has never meant mastery of the "World Island" and of the World, as the pundits of Geopolitics have argued.

The great drive westward in 1945 and thereafter in pursuit of the beaten Wehrmacht was aimed at control of the triangle of Slavic borderlands between the Baltic, Black and Adriatic Seas and the conversion of this vast area into a carapace or "cordon sanitaire" in reverse against the West. Yugoslav defection and satellite unrest suggest overextension. Now, as in the past, Russian aggrandizement is self-limiting or in any event capable of "containment" by equivalent Western power, now centered in America rather than in Western Europe.

7. Because of geographic locus and chronic fear of a combination of all other powers against the Muscovite Behemoth, Russia has never been able to afford the nineteenth-century American luxury of "isolationism," but has ever striven to form alliances with the weaker or remote or less menacing of the Western powers against the stronger or nearer or more menacing. Ivan IV, four centuries ago, strove in vain for an alliance with Elizabethan England against Poland, as Molotov seeks in vain today to reactivate an old alliance with France against a resurgent Reich. In the interim, many effective alliances have been negotiated by Russian diplomats with other powers feeling equally menaced by the strongest continental power of the day.

The Shape of the Future

Ancient attitudes and habits, born of painful experience, change slowly even in new times. What is novel and what is the same in 1955 in the time-worn patterns of Russian relations with the West? What do the constants and the variables suggest regarding the probable determinants of future Russian behavior?

The Russian community, by mastering industrial, military and atomic technology, is no longer weak and backward but stands second only to the United States in economic and martial power. It can no longer be menaced by any present or imaginable coalition of European States, regardless of German rearmament. Insofar as insecurity promotes aggression and aggrandizement, the new security tends to mitigate and mellow old fears and ambitions, the more so as the costs and risks of overexpansion are self-evident.

Yet the conclusion is not a certainty. The United States is vastly wealthier, more powerful and more secure than Russia. Americans nonetheless feel less secure than ever before in their national experience and act accordingly in foreign policy. Russians may do likewise. The possibility is enhanced by the fact that their creed imbues them with a conviction, stronger than that of even the most ardent of "world-saving" Americans, that their sacred mission is to "liberate" mankind through conspiracy, subversion and, conceivably, an armed crusade. Aside from messianism, which long antedates the Marxist era, Russia's rulers cling tenaciously, with only a modicum of "mellowing" since Stalin's demise, to other antique formulas for "safety," i.e., political despotism, dogmatic conformism, secretiveness, xenophobia, and Byzantine equivocation in diplomacy.

But the grand design of communizing the world has no timetable. It is likely to be pursued with circumspection, expediency and calculation. The Soviet totalitarian elite is not led by madmen, inexorably driven toward war by domestic schisms admitting of no other resolution. Unlike some other peoples, Russians have never found in war a primrose path to prosperity and national unity, but only a vale of tears in which wander the ghosts of ruin and death, mass misery, disaffection, revolution, anarchy and mortal danger to the whole community. Russia's rulers, unlike the late potentates of Germany, Italy and Japan, do not regard suicide as the only honorable alternative to mastery of the planet.

They may be expected to resist by arms any armed effort to wrest from their control the lands east of the Elbe and the Danube. They may be expected to resist by diplomacy, propaganda and counterbalancing armaments, but not by overt resort to force, the rearming of the Western Reich. In the new bi-polar pattern of world politics, they have little prospect of exploiting disunities in the Western coalition to a point making possible new bargains with some Western Powers against other.

In their obsession with the "American Menace," they will strengthen, not unskillfully, their political, economic and military bonds with their European satellites and their Chinese ally. They still seek to restrain their ebullient confrères in Peking, Pyongyang and Hanoi from rash adventures. Their creed will make many more converts in Asia and Africa, but few in the Occident. Under no circumstances, present or predictable, will they undertake a war of aggression against the West.

Russian efforts by military means to foster revolution abroad spell war. Western efforts by military means to "liberate" Russia or the Soviet satellites spell war. War in the atomic age spells coextinction. War is never unleashed by sane policy-makers, moreover, when no illusions of decisive superiority are possible and no strategic plans promising triumph are available.

The alternative to war is peace. The only possible basis of peace is "coexistence" or a modus vivendi, grounded in mutual acceptance of the prevailing partition of the globe. Many Americans will deem this immoral or dangerous. Russia's rulers will share this judgment, for motives of their own, but will remain more aware of the tragic lessons of a longer past. They will thus accept such a settlement, as will most West Europeans and Asians.

Communist acquiescence in the status quo will be a temporary expedient, pending new opportunities to promote the "collapse of capitalism." But what is provisional can become enduring if the West keeps its house in order. On these foundations will be built the world settlement of the days to come.

V RESTRAINTS OF A CHANGING ENVIRONMENT

Norman A. Graebner

THE LIMITS OF CHOICE

As early as 1950 Dean Acheson developed the theme of negotiation from strength. The purpose of United States power, including nuclear power, was that of creating the foundations of international stability from which the United States might negotiate satisfactory arrangements with the U.S.S.R. Unfortunately, negotiation from strength, short of war, can achieve no more than the legitimatizing of the status quo, for the mere possession of destructive power, without some clear demonstration of the will to use it, can effect little or no change in established conditions. Clearly the United States never intended to use power to revise the political and territorial realities of East-Central Europe. This fact reduced power to an end in itself which underwrote, not negotiations, but brinkmanship. What encouraged this behavior was the assumption that the destructiveness of modern weapons had really rendered war irrational. That the repeated confrontations did not result in conflict reflected, first, an appreciation of the ultimate cost of a nuclear conflict and, second, the realization that the issues in conflict were better left unresolved than settled through war. To Norman A. Graebner the great powers served no useful purpose in avoiding negotiations over realities which they could not and would not change.

Few writers and scientists of the past decade have regarded a nuclear war as a reasonable and acceptable alternative to peace. The English philosopher, Bertrand Russell, has warned that there is no escape from the choice that faces humanity; there will be peace or the annihilation of the species. Officials of the major powers, saddled with the responsibility for the proper control of such forces of destruction, have acknowledged repeatedly the obligation to neglect no avenue to peace. Yet the diplomatic history of the postwar era has scarcely reflected the prodding of such necessity. Through eighteen years of almost unceasing tension and arms expansion, powerful spokesmen of the great Cold-War rivals, anchoring their hopes and expectations to convictions of ideological superiority, have predicted with disturbing regularity the total collapse of their adversaries. They have framed their external objectives on such illusions of omnipotence, demanding, on most critical issues, nothing less than the total capitulation of those who oppose them. Clinging as they have to

From Norman A. Graebner, "Can a Nuclear War Be Avoided?" *The Annals of the American Academy of Political and Social Science* 351 (January 1964): 133–139. Used by permission.

inflexible positions, they have appeared, at least on the level of rhetoric, to ignore the inescapable fact that the only long-term alternative to war is negotiated settlement.

It is strangely ironic that the powers of destruction which should encourage compromise actually have a corrosive effect on diplomacy. The very assumption that the destructiveness of modern weapons renders war irrational has encouraged national leaders to live dangerously, heralding brinkmanship—the employment of a strategy of terror in lieu of negotiation and compromise—as the essence of successful diplomacy. . . . It is significant that, despite the sword of Damocles that hangs over them, the great powers have managed to negotiate away no major issue in conflict throughout the period of the Cold War. That the West has moved successfully through crisis after crisis since 1945, neither compromising its established diplomatic positions nor experiencing attack, has reflected the existence of several essential stabilizing factors in world politics. Not the least of these is a general appreciation of the ultimate costs involved in a nuclear conflict.

Soviet and American officials alike have attempted to encourage a fundamental caution among their detractors at home and abroad by citing the threat to civilization inherent in the nuclear arms race. "A full-scale nuclear exchange, lasting less than 60 minutes, with the weapons now in existence," President Kennedy warned the nation on July 26, 1963, "could wipe out more than 300 million Americans, Europeans and Russians, as well as untold numbers elsewhere." Such an exchange, added Secretary of State Dean Rusk a month later, "could erase all that man has built over the centuries." Similarly, Chairman Nikita Khrushchev warned the Russian people that over a half billion people would be killed in the initial stages of a nuclear war. There would be no escape. Writing in October 1959, the Soviet leader observed that "with military techniques what they are today, there are no inaccessible places in the world. Should a world war break out, no country will be able to shut itself off from a crushing blow." Those that survived, Khrushchev has predicted, would envy the dead, for the world they would inherit would be so devastated by explosions, poison, and fire that one could hardly conceive of the horrors. Nor would the survivors have any assurance that they had experienced the last of such catastrophes.

That such predictions of disaster have been a force for peace seems undeniable. Many writers and statesmen would agree with the observation, phrased by Vice-President Richard M. Nixon following the initial tests of the hydrogen bomb, that "the very existence of this new weapon may in itself prove to be the greatest force for peace in world history." Not all weapons races have terminated in war; not all concentrations of power have resulted in peace. The record is less than reassuring. . . .

No wall of power, whatever its magnitude, has ever prevented war without the benefit of diplomacy. If the world has avoided a major conflict since 1945, the answer cannot be found in weapons alone. The continued absence of war suggests that the unresolved questions between East and West have been considerably less than vital for one side or the other. The stability of Europe, especially, reflects the realization among Western and Soviet leaders alike that the issues of the Cold War are better left unresolved than disposed of through war. The crisis will come when one side discovers that it has expected too much of time. It is then that the world will produce statesmanship of the highest order or pay the consequences of drift. As President Kennedy suggested, nations will not go down leaving their nuclear arsenals unused.

Meanwhile, the capacity of humankind to escape nuclear destruction appears hopeful enough. The balance of power in Europe has succeeded in establishing and perpetuating a stable division of the continent. As James Reston of the *New York Times* has written, "At no period of history have enemies faced each other for so long over so vast an area and yet shown more restraint than the Western powers and the Communists." There have been innumerable incidents and provocations, even some minor wars, but no nation possessing nuclear striking power has passed, or perhaps approached, the point of no return. Most lines of demarcation have been well established through tradition and practice, if not by diplomatic agreement; few, if any, can be tampered with without setting off a war.

What has characterized world politics in the postwar era, therefore, has been a remarkable stability, produced partially by the dangers of thermonuclear war but especially by the relative absence of conflicting interests whose resolution would be worth the risk of general destruction. The history of the Cold War has demonstrated that no human wants dictate the necessity or wisdom of another Armageddon. There are no apparent problems which lie outside the power of astute diplomacy to compromise, provided that governments are permitted the freedom to maneuver. Yet the forces that lead to war are varied and illusive, and the ultimate decision to fight and fight totally is more often the product of fears and emotions than of clear and measured judgments of national interest. In the long run, therefore, peace rests on the ability of nations to distinguish with considerable accuracy their essential rights, upon which hinge their security and welfare, from demands of secondary importance which are always proper questions for negotiation and compromise.

These minimal standards of national action have not been achieved. If the day-to-day policies of the superpowers have recognized the limits of their capacity to perform, their ultimate goals have been attached to abstractions which have little relationship to their national interests. If the Soviets have introduced uncertainty and abused the normal privileges and methods of diplomacy by maintaining a varied political, economic, and psychological assault on the non-Communist world, the United States has warred on the Soviet bloc through appeals to the doctrine of self-determination. It was against such tendencies that William Graham Sumner, the noted Yale sociologist, warned over a half century ago. He wrote:

> *If you want war, nourish a doctrine. Doctrines are the most frightful tyrants to which men are ever subject, because doctrines get inside of a man's own reason and betray him against himself. . . . Doctrines are always vague; it would ruin a doctrine to define it, because then it could be analyzed, tested, criticized, and verified; but nothing ought to be tolerated which cannot be so tested. . . . What can be more contrary to sound statesmanship and common sense than to put forth an abstract assertion which has no definite relation to any interest of ours now at stake, but which has in it any number of possibilities of producing complications which we cannot foresee, but which are sure to be embarrassing when they arise!*

Arguing from the principle of self-determination, the West has refused to recognize the Soviet sphere of influence in East-Central Europe, established with the destruction of German power in 1944 and 1945. Throughout World War II, Western leadership did nothing to prevent this transferal of power to the Soviet Union, yet it refused to accept it as the basis of negotiation at the conclusion of the war. In large measure, the Kremlin, in establishing Soviet political and economic control over Slavic Europe, was mistaken in its wartime and postwar estimate of Western purpose. Since 1947 Western policies have been defensive in nature. Yet the persistent attachment of containment policies to the rhetoric of rollback and liberation sustains the impression of an offensive purpose which appears to deny to the Russians the tangible fruits of victory and to aim at the actual destruction of Soviet influence in European affairs. What this posture of not recognizing the massive changes that have occurred in Eastern Europe has achieved beyond its contribution to postwar tensions is not clear. It has liberated no one. And it is conceivable that many of the unfortunate aspects of the Cold War, including the nuclear arms race itself, might have been avoided by more realistic policies based on interests rather than doctrines which have never really been applicable. The United States has demonstrated its capacity to maintain the status quo where it appears essential; it has not demonstrated any power—moral, economic, or military—to alter it appreciably. The West, under the mantle of American preparedness, can have what it needs; it cannot have much more.

Nor is more demanded. The United States and the West have coexisted with the Kremlin and the satellite empire for almost two decades with remarkable success. It would be well for the Cold-War antagonists to dwell less on the failure of their ideals and doctrines in the unfolding history of the postwar era and more on the age's unprecedented achievements. By almost every standard of accomplishment, the world is passing through one of the greatest periods of history. This is true not only for the developments in science and technology and in material progress but also for the genuine gains in the realm of politics and even of self-determination. This era has been marked less by the antagonism between the Western and Communist worlds than by the creation of dozens of new nations, comprising a billion people, as well as by sheer economic expansion on both sides of the Iron and Bamboo curtains.

Even the more mundane diplomacy of the Cold War has been characterized by an essential and hopeful conservatism. Eighteen years after the Versailles Treaty, the world was inescapably on the road to war. Without the benefit of any general postwar settlement, the great powers since 1945 have maintained a reasonable peace. With all its confusion of interests with abstractions, post-war diplomacy has performed far more successfully than did the diplomacy of the interwar period. There remain many arrangements in the world which defy the principle of self-determination; no American takes any pleasure in their existence. But the United States lacks the power, and therefore the obligation, to serve mankind in general. Any attempt to eliminate from the world those factors which, to many

Americans, appear immoral would terminate in the destruction of a civilization which has reached unprecedented achievements in most areas of human endeavor. Could big-power diplomacy reflect a satisfaction with the past and present rather than a pursuit of utopian ambitions which transcend the achievable, the future would appear far more secure. . . .

Neither side in the Cold War can escape responsibility for bringing the world crisis to its present state. Before there can be a genuine relaxation of tension, both sides must free their policies of ideological, universal objectives. As long as Khrushchev proclaims the right to the Soviet Union, under conditions of coexistence, to wage war on the values of the Western world until they are destroyed, Western leaders can hardly regard coexistence as a hopeful arrangement. Unfortunately, the choices confronting the West are limited. Whatever the disagreement on the meaning of peaceful coexistence, the West has no alternative to coexistence, even on Soviet terms, but war. There is, moreover, a vast discrepancy between Soviet rhetoric and the Soviet capacity to achieve a Communist society. It remains well within the power of the West to preserve a world that is, in the words of Dean Rusk, "safe for freedom."

Those who from fear of Soviet intention would borrow the words of Abraham Lincoln to rationalize an unrelenting assault on the Communist world might remember that the world can exist half slave and half free. It has always done so. The abstract ideals of universal freedom and justice can never establish the foundations of national policy. To sunder the control of one people over another does not guarantee political progress or even the survival of freedom. The world is replete with examples of political and economic retrogression which followed the achievement of self-determination. To free a people from its external masters, moreover, requires nothing less than war, and to establish a vital interest in the freedom of a nation or group of nations, long held in subjugation, is never simple. The price required under conditions of nuclear stalemate might come high indeed.

That the United States has had no genuine stake in the destruction of the Soviet hegemony in East-Central Europe or in the elimination of the Peking regime, for which it was willing to risk a war, was amply demonstrated through eighteen years of carefully sustained inaction during moments of crisis behind the Iron and Bamboo curtains. This experience, spanning as it did a period of unprecedented material progress and almost untrammeled freedom, demonstrated that any war fought over the future of East-Central Europe . . . would scarcely reflect the vital interests of the United States. There is no guarantee that war will not return to the world through accident, provocation, or deliberate attack. And any war which involved the major powers could easily escalate into a grand nuclear confrontation. Secretary Rusk warned in August 1963: "A local conflict anywhere around the globe in which the interests of the great powers are engaged might suddenly pose the prospect of nuclear war."

Nothing would demonstrate so clearly the limited choices confronting the great powers than the outbreak of war. Military conflicts in the contemporary world can be limited only by an unequivocal declaration for the continuance of the status quo as the object of the involvement—as was done in Korea. But if a nation at war, fighting under the immediate threat of nuclear escalation, faces the simple alternative of announcing the limits of its intentions or inviting a thermonuclear attack, then it is not unreasonable to suggest that it regard as negotiable in time of peace what it must, in time of war, regard as negotiable or suffer general destruction. As Duff Cooper once observed, it would be interesting to collect historical instances of harm that has been done by the reluctance of men to accept readily what they knew they would of necessity accept in the end.

Hans J. Morgenthau

CHANGING ISSUES, CONDITIONS, AND PERSPECTIVES

By the early seventies it was clear to some that changes in world politics and altered perceptions of danger had created the foundations for a new era in Soviet-American relationships. For Hans J. Morgenthau, the well-known student of international affairs long associated with the University of Chicago, the objective factors in international life raised a serious question: "Is it possible to move from sterile confrontation to meaningful negotiations?" Morgenthau cited five factors which, he believed, had transformed relations between the United States and the U.S.S.R. These factors, in general, revealed the declining influence and ambition of the superpowers. For the U.S.S.R. the essential limitation was the growing hostility of China. Morgenthau recognized the continuing ideological conflict, as demonstrated by Vietnam, but he believed that peace hinged less on ideology than on the actual Soviet-American conflict of interests and purposes in the European and non-European worlds.

Our reactions to Soviet foreign policy have a way of jumping from one extreme to another, both in the long and short run, with more regard for changing superficial appearances than permanent objective factors. During the last year of the Second World War, we tended to idealize the Russians, Stalin became "Uncle Joe" to be charmed by Roosevelt into cooperation, and the United Nations, having done away with "power politics," was supposed to be the vehicle of that cooperation. From 1947 onwards, the Kremlin was perceived as the headquarters of the devil on earth, causing all that was wrong with the world and, more particularly, scheming the destruction of the United States. These extreme swings of the pendulum can also be observed in much shorter time spans. . . .

Yet beneath these fluctuations of mood and tactics the perennial question about the future of Amerian-Soviet relations persists in demanding an answer: Is it possible to move from sterile confrontation to meaningful negotiations? While 20 years ago such a question was purely rhetorical since the negative answer was a foregone conclu-

From Hans J. Morgenthau, "Changes and Chances in American-Soviet Relations," pp. 429–41. Excerpted by permission from *Foreign Affairs* 49 (April 1971). Copyright 1971 by the Council on Foreign Relations, Inc.

sion, it can now be asked seriously, and it deserves a serious answer, derived not from the changing mood of the day but from the objective factors which in the long run determine the relations among nations. What has happened during the last 20 years to account for the possibility of posing that crucial question seriously?

II

Five factors have transformed the relations between the United States and the Soviet Union: the rejection of nuclear war as an instrument of national policy; the ideological decontamination of foreign policy at least with respect to each other; the failure of the competition for the allegiance of the third world; the implicit recognition by the United States of the status quo in Eastern Europe; and the Chinese threat to the Soviet Union.

The fear of mutual destruction through nuclear war has imposed effective restraints upon the foreign policies of the superpowers in two respects: the avoidance of direct military confrontation and, when it inadvertently occurs, its speedy liquidation. The United States has fought in Korea and Vietnam wars for limited objectives, falling short of military victory, because of the fear of such a confrontation. It has kept its hands off a series of East European revolts against Soviet domination. For the same reason, the Soviet Union has not followed up with action its repeated demands—twice in the form of ultimatums with a precise time limit—for a change in the status quo of West Berlin. In the Middle East, Russia has come close to a military confrontation with America, but the latter has not responded in kind, and both powers have joined in an initiative to restore peace. When there was military confrontation during the Cuban missile crisis of 1962, both sides went as far as they dared without compelling the other side to take steps that might lead to nuclear war, and retraced their steps in partial retreat.

Sharing the conviction of the suicidal irrationality of nuclear war, the United States and the Soviet Union have thus in a sense helped each other to avoid it; they appear to have concluded that the sole legitimate purpose of nuclear arms is not to win a nuclear war but to deter it. Nevertheless, they have continued an unlimited nuclear arms race as though there did not exist an optimum of nuclear preparedness sufficient for deterrence, beyond which to go is utterly irrational. They have thus pursued the rational goal of nuclear deterrence with the irrational means of an unlimited nuclear arms race. Recognizing this irrationality, they have joined in the Strategic Arms Limitation Talks (SALT), searching for an agreement which could bring the nuclear arms race under control.

While the United States and the Soviet Union have begun to deal with each other as one great power with another, having certain interests in common and being at loggerheads with regard to others, there was a time, not much more than a decade ago, when we took the Communist dogma much more seriously as a guide to policy than did, for instance, Stalin, who with utter cynicism and brutality used communism and Communists as a means to further the traditional ends of the Russian state. Yet we saw in Stalin the heir of Trotsky who was out to accomplish the communization of the world, begun in Eastern Europe at the end of the Second World War, while in truth Stalin was the heir of the Tsars, seeking the traditional goals of Imperial Russia with the new instruments communism put at his disposal. The Russians, in turn, interpreted our insistence upon democratic governments in Eastern Europe and our verbal commitment to "rollback" and "liberation" as evidence of the undying hostility of capitalism which since 1917 had used every opportunity to try to destroy the Soviet Union.

The emancipation of American and Soviet foreign policies from these dogmatic ideological stereotypes—again I must emphasize, limited to their mutual relations—has been the result of the impact the facts of life have made upon the thoughts and actions of the governments concerned. Foremost among these facts has been their failure to win the ideological allegiance of the nations of the third world in Africa, Asia and Latin America. The third world was supposed to be the decisive battleground in the struggle for men's minds, a struggle which would decide the fate of the world. Khrushchev, for instance, used to assure us that the third world would follow the lead of the Soviet Union and thereby seal the doom of the West. Nothing of the kind happened. The new nations of the third world have apparently preferred to be miserable in their own way to being made happy by the United States or the U.S.S.R.

This failure of ideological competition has led both superpowers to the conclusion that it is not worth the expense and the risk of a direct military confrontation, and they have given it up. The absence of any ideological reference and the explicit disavowal of ideological commitment in President Nixon's message to Congress on the state of the world of March of last year at least provides verbal evidence of this fundamental change in our approach to certain aspects of foreign policy. On the other hand, the Soviet Union has banished, a few exceptions to the contrary notwithstanding, ideological considerations from its policies in the third world. It has very close relations with the United Arab Republic whose Communists are in jail, and it supports Latin American dictators against their Communist parties, which are in turn supported by Cuba, the ally of the Soviet Union. That is to say, it practices old-fashioned power politics, unencumbered by ideological considerations.

It is part and parcel of this victory of the facts of life over ideological blinders that the United States has for all practical purposes recognized the Soviet predominance in Eastern Europe. True enough, we have contained the Soviet Union at the line of military demarcation of 1945; but now we and the Soviet Union realize that the United States, too, has been contained at that very same line. This realization has removed from the cold war its main issue: the territorial status quo, especially with regard to the two Germanys. The recent treaty between the Soviet Union and West Germany makes explicit what had been implicit in the policies of the two superpowers: the recognition by all concerned of the territorial boundaries established at the end of the Second World War. This normalization of East-West relations in Europe has also deprived the status of West Berlin of much of the leverage which Stalin and Khrushchev used against the West. They threatened the status quo of West Berlin in order to compel the West to recognize the territorial status quo in Eastern Europe. Since that recognition has now been forthcoming, the status of West Berlin as a pawn in the hands of the Soviet Union has markedly decreased, although it still retains its usefulness as an instrument of annoyance.

Finally, even if these two developments had not greatly contributed to stability in Europe, the Soviet Union would have a vital interest in such stability. For the Soviet Union must cope at its Chinese frontier with endemic instability which might well escalate into war, and in such a contingency it must be reasonably certain that its western frontiers are secure. It needs that certainty in particular because its elite is obsessed with the fear the Americans will gang up with the Chinese. The Russian leaders suffer from the same *cauchemar des coalitions* which disturbed Bismarck's sleep (only he had better reasons than they). Thus they are not likely to provoke the

United States in Europe as long as the insecurity at their eastern frontiers persists.

Considering the beneficial impact these factors have had on the relations between the United States and the Soviet Union, it is tempting to conclude that, undisturbed by contrary tendencies, these factors will continue to exert their pacifying and normalizing effect. This conclusion is particularly tempting for those who have conceived of our relations with the Soviet Union primarily, if not exclusively, in ideological, that is, anti-Communist terms. Since we do not need to worry any more about the Soviet Union as the spearhead of communism bent upon destroying us, so the argument runs, there is really nothing at all to worry about. This position, simple if not simplistic and superficially attractive since it caters to our wishes, is, however, vulnerable to three arguments: the elimination of ideological considerations from our foreign policy is partial, and tenuous where it exists; the power politics of the Soviet Union contains residues of ideological commitment; the U.S.S.R. is a great power whose interests and the policies serving it, regardless of ideology, may run counter to the interests of the United States and the policies serving it.

Nor does the ideological decontamination of our relations with the Soviet Union signify that our foreign policy has been altogether freed of its ideological ingredients. We still think about foreign policy in demonological terms and allow our actions to be influenced by them. Why are we fighting in Indochina? In order to prevent the Communist takeover of South Vietnam is the official answer. Why did we send our troops to the Dominican Republic? Because we cannot have another Communist government in the Western Hemisphere, said President Johnson. Thus it appears that the struggle against communism still influences our actions. Only the devil's place of residence has changed. He could at a moment's notice move back to the Kremlin, and his reappearance in his old haunts would rekindle the ideological animosity between the United States and the Soviet Union. As William Graham Sumner put it: "The amount of superstition is not much changed, but it now attaches to politics, not religion," and, one can add, it attaches to one locale rather than another as circumstances seem to require.

This propensity for political demonology finds support in the nature of the Soviet state and the foreign policies it pursues. It is true that since Stalin the Soviet Union has used ideological factors as means to the end for the Soviet state and in consequence has been able to switch with great alacrity its ideological preferences and stigmatizations from one country to the other. Thus the German "fascist beasts" became comrades-in-arms against Western imperialism after the Molotov-Ribbentrop pact of August 1939, and the "neo-fascists" and "revanchists" of West Germany transformed themselves into respectable partners, once they were willing to recognize the territorial status quo. China was embraced as a junior partner in the world Communist movement as long as it was satisfied with that junior position. It was read out of the Marxist-Leninist camp altogether when it struck out on its own in competition with the Soviet Union.

But it is also true that the Soviet Union regards itself not only as one nation among others but also as the "Fatherland of Socialism," the leader of all "progressive" forces throughout the world. It is this position, now to be maintained against China's competitive claims, that imposes upon Soviet foreign policy certain ideological burdens which the Soviet Union would not need to bear if it conceived of its national interests in strictly traditional terms. What happens in Cuba has no bearing upon the interests of the Russian state traditionally conceived, but it bears heavily upon the position of the Soviet Union as leader of the "progressive" forces of the world. For that reason, the Soviet Union subsidizes Cuba to the tune of approximately $1 million a day even though Castro supports subversion and civil war against the very Latin American governments with which the Soviet Union deals on a pragmatic basis. It is for the same reason that the Soviet Union supports North Vietnam with military aid, carefully limited so as not to provoke the United States to escalate the war, but sufficient to prevent an American military victory.

Thus the ideological conflict between the United States and the Soviet Union is not dead but only dormant. As long as the interests of the two superpowers do not openly clash, the ideological conflict may remain in its present state of suspended animation. But if and when one superpower shall again openly encroach upon the interests of the other, the ideological demons are also likely to be awakened from their slumber. Here is indeed the crux of the future relations between the United States and the Soviet Union. Can they pursue their respective interests without encroaching upon each other's?

III

Since the downfall of Khrushchev, the Soviet Union has unobtrusively and effectively expanded its political and military influence in the eastern Mediterranean, the Middle East, South Asia and the Indian Ocean in the best tradition of great-power politics and has enhanced its economic influence throughout the world in the best tradition of a capitalist trading nation. The pattern of that expansion has been constant: Russia has moved into the spaces left by the liquidation of the British and French Empires, thereby bringing close to consummation the Tsarist aspirations which during the better part of the nineteenth century had pitted Russia against Great Britain over the "Eastern Question.". . .

Instead of remembering how in the sixteenth century the center of power shifted from the Mediterranean to the nations bordering on the Atlantic in consequence of the opening of new trade routes, we have been hypnotized by the ideological aspects of the Indochina war. While we put our minds to beating the Russian Communists to the moon and keeping the Vietnamese Communists out of Saigon, the Soviet Union has occupied much of the middle ground between these cosmic and parochial goals. Thus the absence of open conflict between the United States and the Soviet Union or, to put it in positive terms, the improvement in U.S.-Soviet relations is in good measure the result not of the settlement of outstanding issues or of the absence of points of conflict, but of American failure to compete with and oppose a Soviet Union steadily expanding its power throughout the world. What looks to the naive and the wishful thinkers as a new harmonious phase in American-Soviet relations is in truth a by-product of our military involvement in Indochina. We have been too busy with trying to save Indochina from communism to pay much attention to what the U.S.S.R. was doing in the rest of the world and to compete with it or oppose it as our interests require.

As long as our main national energies and human and natural resources remain absorbed by Indochina, we will continue to enjoy "good" relations with the Soviet Union. The "good" quality of these relations will be the result not of the identity or the parallelism of interests derived from the settlement of outstanding issues, but of letting the defense and promotion of our interests go by default. After all, it takes two to quarrel. If one side does not object to what the other is doing, there will be harmony, but it can be harmony at the former's expense. Thus, paradoxically enough, the lack of controversy in American-Soviet relations results in good measure from the pathological inversion of our national priorities caused by our involvement in the Indochina war. Once we terminate that involvement and conduct our foreign policies again on the basis of the rational assessment and ordering of our national interests, we are likely to find ourselves again in competition and conflict with the Soviet Union.

IV

Four issues, if they are not settled, are likely to revive the competition and opposition between America and Russia: the nuclear arms race, the status of Germany, the balance of power in the Middle East, and the ferment in the third world.

The restraints which the fear of mutual destruction has imposed upon the foreign policies of the United States and the Soviet Union are predicated upon the certainty of that destruction. That is to say, they depend upon what Churchill called a "balance of terror," in which B, after having suffered unacceptable damage from nuclear attack by A, would still be able with what remained of its retaliatory nuclear force to inflict unacceptable damage upon A, and vice versa. It is this psychological conviction that a nuclear war is a genocidal and suicidal absurdity which has preserved the peace and at least a modicum of order in the relations of the superpowers.

However, the indefinite persistence of this conviction cannot be taken for granted. It is threatened by two assumptions: that one or the other side has acquired a first-strike capability which would destroy the enemy's retaliatory capability or at worst reduce it to tolerable proportions, and that one or the other side or both sides have developed a defensive system which at worst would reduce nuclear damage to tolerable proportions. It is irrelevant for the purpose of this discussion whether or not these assumptions are correct; it is sufficient that they might be held. If they were held, they would be bound to exacerbate drastically the nuclear competition between the United States and the Soviet Union; for then the question before us would no longer be the relatively simple one of maintaining mutual deterrence, but how to assure for oneself, and deny to the enemy, the ability to wage a successful nuclear war. The restraints which, as we have seen, have characterized the foreign policies of the superpowers would then follow mutual deterrence into oblivion; for the avoidance of nuclear war appears no longer as a precondition for physical survival if a nation is convinced that it can win a nuclear war either through irresistible attack or impenetrable defense.

It is this dire possibility that makes the success of the SALT talks, seeking a way to control the nuclear arms race, so crucially important for the future of American-Soviet relations. If they fail, a drastic deterioration of these very relations is likely to result. If they succeed, they will not only have stabilized the nuclear arms race on a level sufficient for mutual deterrence, though not for a first strike or effective defense, but they will also have demonstrated the ability of the two superpowers to translate their common interest in survival into operative policies.

While this issue, overshadowing all others, is still in the balance, the normalization of the relations between West Germany and the Soviet Union through the former's recognition of the territorial status quo has brought to the fore a conventional issue which touches the vital interests of both the United States and the Soviet Union: the future orientation of West Germany. Almost 20 years ago, West Germany joined the Western alliance in order to contain the Soviet Union and to assure powerful backing for its claim to be the sole legitimate representative of the whole German people, East and West. It succeeded in the first, and failed in the second, objective. That failure was due to the East German government's staying power and the Soviet determination to contain the West at the 1945 demarcation line.

For West Germany, however, the relations with East Germany and West Berlin have remained crucial. Bonn has come to recognize that the only power which can improve and secure these relations is the Soviet Union. By the same token, the Soviet Union knows that the security of its European empire depends upon West Germany's position. A West Germany which is the dissatisfied spearhead of a hostile alliance is a constant threat; a neutralized and friendly West Germany is an invaluable asset. For a Russo-German combination would become the master of the Eurasian land mass, reducing what remains of Western Europe to an insignificant promontory. This has been the long-range aim of Soviet foreign policy at least since Khrushchev. Khrushchev expressed time and again in private conversation his conviction that there would be another Rapallo, that is, another understanding between Germany and the Soviet Union after the model of the Rapallo Treaty of 1922; that it would come not under him and not under his successor but under his successor's successor; that it was inevitable; and that the Soviet Union could wait. The Soviet Union, in the treaty with West Germany recently concluded, has taken the first step in the direction sketched by Khrushchev.

This treaty, on the face of it, performs the function of a peace treaty—a quarter of a century overdue—in which West Germany recognizes explicitly the territorial status quo of 1945. This recognition has been implicit in the policies which West Germany and the United States have pursued for two decades vis-à-vis the Soviet Union and the nations of Eastern Europe, but the revisionary rhetoric accompanying it, especially in the 1950s, could not help but create doubts as to whether that implicit recognition could be relied upon if opportunities for a change in the territorial status quo should arise. These doubts have now been laid to rest.

However, it is hardly necessary to point out that the development so confidently predicted by Khrushchev would run counter to the interests of the United States and would nullify the policies Washington has pursued in Europe since the end of the Second World War; for it was the major aim of these policies to prevent all of Germany from being drawn into the Russian orbit. In the course of such a development, the Soviet Union, by replacing the United States as the predominant power in Western Europe, would achieve another of its long-term aims: the expulsion of the United States from Europe. . . .

At present it is the Middle East which appears the most obvious point at which the interests and policies of the United States and the Soviet Union appear to collide. The Soviet Union seeks to maintain and expand its predominant presence in the region, while the United States tries to contain it. In order to realize its aim the Soviet Union must support the Arab aspirations up to the point where the survival of Israel is in jeopardy; for much of the Soviet leverage in the Arab world depends upon the continuation of the enmity between the Arabs and Israel. Paradoxically enough, the Soviet Union has an interest in the survival of Israel, however precariously placed in the midst of continuing Arab hostility. On the other hand, the United States, too, is interested in the survival of Israel, secured through the acceptance of the Arab states; for such acceptance would reduce the Soviet leverage to a minimum and improve the chances for American influence reasserting itself. Thus American and Soviet interests with regard to Israel are both contradictory and run for quite different reasons along parallel lines. They make for conflict as well as cooperation.

The third possible point of friction between the United States and the Soviet Union, the revolutionary ferment in the third world, differs from the others in that it is highly speculative. In theory, both superpowers are committed to incompatible positions on this issue. The Soviet Union has repeatedly come out in favor of "wars of national liberation," while the United States favors stability, which means in concrete terms the defense of the status quo against revolution from the Left. In consequence of these incompatible positions, the United States and the Soviet Union have found themselves on opposite sides of the fence in the Congo, the Middle East, Cuba, Vietnam. But, as pointed out before with regard to Latin America, the Soviet Union has not hesitated to abandon this position in favor of a pragmatic pursuit of its national interests as a great power. And the United States, after the Indochinese experience, is not likely to intervene openly in Africa or Latin America in order to defend the established order against revolutionary change. In view of the abatement of ideological commitment on both sides, this source of friction may appear remote at present, but it might become acute overnight if an unforeseen event, domestic or international, should suddenly awaken the slumbering ideological passions. . . .

Thus the future of American-Soviet relations is shrouded in uncertainty. Neither amity nor enmity is foreordained. Those who proclaim the inevitability of conflict on ideological grounds are as wrong as are those who assert the inevitability of peace, or even friendship, because the United States and the Soviet Union have become more restrained in words and deeds in dealing with each other. The future depends first of all upon how the two governments conceive of their respective interests and how they will go about defending and protecting them. If they conceive of them in compatible terms and pursue them with appropriate concern for each other's sensibilities, the future might well witness the realization of Roosevelt's dream, Stalin's grand design, and Mao's nightmare: the cooperation of the United States and the Soviet Union in establishing and maintaining a modicum of order in the world. Otherwise, the world will continue to hover on the brink of self-destruction.

The outcome, however, will no longer depend exclusively upon the actions of the superpowers vis-à-vis each other, but to an increasing extent upon the actions of secondary power centers—China, Japan, West Germany, either alone or in concert with a politically and militarily united Europe—and the reactions of the two superpowers to them. Thus the issues dividing the two superpowers will remain susceptible to peaceful settlements only in the measure that the superpowers are able to prevent their relations with the secondary power centers from exacerbating their relations with each other. When they deal with each other, they must also, as it were, look over their shoulders to see what other nations are doing and to anticipate what they are likely to do. While the freedom of maneuver which the secondary power centers are likely to enjoy will introduce a new element of uncertainty and risk into the relations between the super-powers, concern with the interests and policies of the secondary powers may well strengthen the self-restraint with which America and Russia have been dealing with each other because of the fear of nuclear war.

George F. Kennan

"X" TWENTY-FIVE YEARS LATER

On the twenty-fifth anniversary of the publication of the "X" article (re-printed earlier in this book), the editors of Foreign Policy *invited George Kennan, through answers to a series of specific questions, to comment on the impact of a quarter century of historical evolution on Soviet power and purpose. In his* Memoirs, 1925–1950 *Kennan analyzed his own reaction, as well as that of official Washington and the press, to his article, but did not reflect on the changes that had occurred in Soviet conduct. In the following essay Kennan noted the decline of political and ideological stability in the areas surrounding the U.S.S.R. since 1947, as well as the decline of Soviet influence in much of Asia (matched by a decline of United States influence as well). These changes, he concluded, contributed to Russian political in-security. No longer did Russian policies toward China, the United States, and Western Eruope represent a unified approach, for Soviet interests could no longer be identified with a clear division of the world into Communist and non-Communist blocs. Much of the Soviet effort in 1972 was aimed at containing China. In the absence of serious political and territorial conflict, Kennan believed, the Soviet-American military rivalry moved largely on its own momentum. Still, at the level of ideology, politics, and diplomacy Ken-nan could not foresee any intimate United States relationship with the U.S.S.R. In building its naval power Russia was merely behaving like a great power, giving the West little choice but to accept it.*

The conditions to which Soviet policy-makers had to address them-selves in 1947 have changed drastically over these 25 years.

In 1947, the Soviet Union, though seriously exhausted by the war, enjoyed great prestige. Stalin's hold on the international Communist movement was monolithic and almost unchallenged. There was still, in the major Western countries and to some extent elsewhere, a strong contingent of the pro-Soviet intellectuals and fellow-travellers who were amenable to Soviet influence and could be counted on to give general support to Soviet policies. All around the Soviet fron-tiers, on the other hand, there was great instability. This applied to East Asia as well as to Europe and the Middle East. For the Soviet leadership, this presented both opportunity and danger: opportunity for taking advantage of this instability, danger that if they did not do so, others would. Their foreign policy, in these circumstances, was

Excerpted from George F. Kennan, " 'X' Plus 25," reprinted by permission from *Foreign Policy* 7 (Summer 1972): 5–21.

directed to two main objectives: one, the elimination, to the extent possible, of all other great-power influence—and this meant primarily American influence—everywhere on the Eurasian land mass, so that the Soviet Union would overshadow everything that was left, in power and prestige; and, two, the achievement and consolidation of effective strategic glacis in East, South, and West.

Compare that with the situation the present generation of Soviet leaders has before it today. The international Communist movement has broken into several pieces. They retain, beyond the limits of their own military-occupational power, the overt loyalty of only a portion of it. This is a not insignificant portion; but the facade of solidarity can be maintained, today, only by extensive concessions to the real independence of the respective Communist parties. Meanwhile, a great deal of the erstwhile liberal following in other countries, disillusioned by Soviet repressive measures at home and in Eastern Europe, has lost confidence in Soviet leadership. As a military power, the U.S.S.R. has great prestige—greater, in fact, than in 1947—but as a political power it has less than it did then.

The instability in the areas surrounding the Soviet Union has in part disappeared. The Chinese and Japanese have put an end to it in East Asia. Economic recovery, NATO, and the movements towards unification have largely done so in Western Europe, although there are disturbing symptoms of an underlying instability in Western Germany, and a state of semi-chaos in Italy that is only slightly less alarming because it is chronic.

The East Asian glacis was largely taken away from them by the Chinese. The Middle Eastern one they are gradually gaining; but it is precarious, undependable, and expensive to keep. The European one, i.e., the satellite area of Eastern and Central Europe, they continue to hold (Yugoslavia excepted) either by occupying it or by overshadowing it militarily. It is flawed by a certain potential instability in the form of the positions taken by the Rumanians; but it has won acceptance in the West, and does not appear, at the moment, to be seriously threatened. It may be said, generally, that the southern and western glacis are fulfilling their function, as does the remaining one—Outer Mongolia—in East Asia; and the Soviet leaders undoubtedly derive from this fact a certain heightened sense of security.

The effort to expel American influence and presence from the Eurasian land mass has also been largely successful, though rather by the force of circumstance than as a response to anything the

Russians themselves have done. Yet the result is only in part satisfactory from the Soviet point of view. In Northeast Asia, the Americans never did play a role, except in South Korea and Japan; and they have now largely forfeited their influence over the Japanese. On the other hand, Russia now finds herself confronted there by two local great powers—China and Japan—both capable of making more trouble for her in that region than the Americans ever did. In the Middle East, the American presence and influence are pretty well eliminated everywhere except in Israel, Jordan, and Saudi Arabia. As for Western Europe: the American guaranty remains, as does the American military presence. Moscow would still like to eliminate both—just to be on the safe side. But the need for doing so has been reduced by the general Western acceptance of the Soviet hegemony in Eastern Europe. And the agreements concluded with the Brandt government, if ratified, will relieve the Soviet leaders of their greatest single anxiety: that of an association of American military power with a *revanchiste* and revisionist Western Germany.

If, then, today the Soviet leaders have a sense of military insecurity, it is not—for the first time in Russian history—primarily with relation to stronger forces just beyond their land borders, but rather in relation to the nuclear weapons race, which is a subject in itself. Where they really feel most insecure is politically. The Chinese inroads on their international prestige and on their influence in the world Communist movement have really hurt and alarmed them, because they leave them no alternatives except isolation or alliance with capitalist countries, which could undermine the legitimacy of their power at home. They are also insecure at home, because they are dimly conscious, as was the Tsar's regime 70 years ago, that they have lost the confidence of their own intellectuals, and don't know how to recover it. Finally, there is the continuing hostility of the populations in most of Eastern Europe to the Soviet hegemony, a hostility which even with full control of the media over 25 years they have not been able to overcome.

What, in the face of these environmental conditions, are their policies? These no longer represent a unified whole, or reflect any unified concept. The Party priesthood exerts itself mightily to recover ground lost to the Chinese in the foreign Communist communities. The Foreign Office pursues a policy of détente with France and Germany and Italy in order to prove to the Chinese that Russia has an alternative to good relations with them, and can easily arrange for security on her Western front. The military-industrial complex, as real there as in Washington, struggles to match the United States in the cultivation of nuclear weaponry. The hotheads in their military establishment appear to be obsessed with the hope of breaking the long-standing supremacy of the Anglo-Americans on the high seas, and this strikes me, incidentally, as the most irresponsible and dangerous, at the moment, of all Soviet undertakings, comparable to the Kaiser's effort to out-balance the British in naval forces before World War I.

These policies present a sharp contrast to those of 1947. The Soviet-American conflict has been largely removed geographically from the Eurasian land mass and relegated to the struggle for the control of the high seas and the fantasy world of nuclear weaponry. A great part of the energy of Soviet foreign policy is today devoted to the effort to "contain," politically, another Socialist state—China. The anti-American propaganda and the competition with the United States for favor and influence in the Third World continue; but this is more of a force of habit than a policy, and the few successes achieved to date have come from American mistakes far more than from Soviet brilliance. "World revolution" has simply faded out of the picture, as a concrete aim of Soviet foreign policy. In general, the situation of the Soviet Union is such that were it not for the dangerous nuclear and naval rivalry, the outside world, and particularly, the United States, would have little more to fear from Russia today than it did in 1910. The ideological factor makes itself felt today almost exclusively in the Soviet relationship to the French and Italian Communist parties, which, if they were to come into power, would easily destroy NATO and upset the power balance in Europe. But these parties are reflections of long-term internal crises within the respective countries, and their influence cannot be treated as primarily a problem of international relations. . . . What all this means for Soviet-American relations is this: that the United States, having accepted the Soviet domination of Eastern Europe as well as the situation in all of Asia other than its southeastern extremity, has today, for the first time, no serious territorial-political conflict with the Soviet government, the one exception being the Middle East. But the Middle Eastern situation is, by common agreement, not worth a war between the two powers, and both hope to avoid its leading to one. This means that today the military rivalry, in naval power as in nuclear weaponry, is simply riding along on its own momentum, like an object in space. It has no foundation in real interests—no foundation, in fact, but in fear, and in an essentially irrational fear at that. It is carried not by any reason to believe that the other side *would,* but only by an hypnotic fascination with the fact that it *could.* It is simply an institutionalized force of habit. If someone could suddenly make the two sides realize that it has no purpose and if they were then to desist, the world would presumably go on, in all important respects, just as it is going on today.

There is a Kafkaesque quality to this encounter. We stand like two men who find themselves confronting each other with guns in their hands, neither with any real reason to believe that the other has murderous intentions towards him, but both hypnotized by the uncertainty and the unreasoning fear of the fact that the other is armed. The two armament efforts feed and justify each other.

Admitting that it is unreasonable to expect either side to disarm suddenly and unilaterally, one must still recognize that this curious deadlock, devoid of hope, replete with danger, is unlikely to be resolved just by carefully negotiated contractual agreements: these latter will have to be supported by reciprocal unilateral steps of restraint in the development of various forms of weaponry.

If one could begin to work this process backward, and eventually reduce the armed establishments of the two countries to something like reasonable dimensions—for both have, of course, ulterior military obligations and commitments as well—then there is no reason why the Soviet Union should be considered a serious threat to American security.

Should this happen, however, the United States would do well not to indulge itself in unreal hopes for intimacy with either the Soviet regime or the Soviet population. There are deeply rooted traits in Soviet psychology—some of old-Russian origin, some of more recent Soviet provenance—that would rule this out. Chief among these, in my opinion, are the congenital disregard of the truth, the addiction to propagandistic exaggeration, distortion, and falsehood, the habitual foulness of mouth in official utterance. So pernicious has been the effect of 50 years of cynicism about the role of objective truth in political statement that one begins to wonder whether these Soviet leaders have not destroyed in themselves the power to distinguish truth from falsehood. The very vocabulary in which they have taught themselves to speak, politically, with its constant references to the American imperialists and monopolists," is confusing and offensive, and constitutes in itself a barrier to better international understanding. Add to this the hysterical preoccupation with espionage, the continued fear of foreigners and effort to isolate the Soviet population allowed to play in the conduct of Soviet diplomacy, and one is obliged to recognize that it is simply unrealistic for Americans to look for any great intimacy or even normalcy, as we understand it, of relations with the Soviet Union. As is also the case with China, though for somewhat different reasons, relations can be reasonably good, but they must also be reasonably distant; and the more distant they are, in a sense, the better they will be. . . . It seems to me . . . that Russia is behaving . . . like a great power. [One can] list a number of things she is doing: naval deployments in distant oceans, military and economic aid programs, treaties with Egypt and India, expanded trade relations with many countries. . . . But is there any reason why a country of Russia's size and economic potential should not do these things? Are there, in fact, any of them that we do not do—any of them in which we have not set the example?

It seems to me that those who see a danger in these activities are predicating, just as in the case of the weapons race, some underlying political conflict which may not be there at all. I admit that Soviet activities in many of these countries are impregnated with anti-American attitudes, and one of their objectives, if not the leading one, seems to be at least the discrediting and the isolation of the United States—a purpose at which, I must say, we connive with an adeptness little short of genius. As a traditionalist who does not believe that this country is well constituted, anyway, to play a very active role in world affairs, I find myself less frightened than others over the fact that Soviet policies are so inspired.

It would be a very sad and hopeless situation if we were to convince ourselves that the peace of the world depended on the ability of the rest of us to prevent the Soviet Union indefinitely from acting like a great power. Would it not be better to avoid assuming that all Soviet activities are aimed primarily against us—unless, at least, it is proved otherwise—and to see whether there are not some areas of assistance to other nations, and constructive involvement with their affairs, where we and the Russians could work together instead of separately? . . . The Nixon-Kissinger policies fit the conceptions of the "X" article, it seems to me, only indifferently.

Those policies continue to give great attention, geographically, to what I viewed in 1947, and have always viewed, as a secondary area from the standpoint of our interest: Southeast Asia.

While the SALT talks are certainly a significant and welcome step in advance, a great deal of American governmental attention and energy continues to be riveted to the sterile and dangerous effort to excel the Russians in the nuclear arms race. That had no place in my scheme of things. . . .

Finally, there is the obvious partiality for summit meetings with Communist leaders, a procedure which may have its domestic political dividends but which I regard as at best irrelevant, and potentially pernicious, to a sound handling of relations with the great Communist governments.

So far as the Soviet Union itself is concerned, I do not see a great deal that the Nixon Administration could do that it is not now doing. I think—though it may not be of major importance—that we should at once agree to the cessation of underground testing. I think that we could well take certain further unilateral measures of restraint in the development of nuclear weapons and their carriers, with a view to encouraging the others to do likewise. I think we should press talks with the Russians to see whether we could not agree with them on putting a stop to the childish and dangerous mutual shadowing of naval vessels that now goes on all over the high seas. I think we should bend every effort to develop technical collaboration with them—in space activities as well as in international environmental undertakings. We should keep in communication with them—constantly—concerning the situation in the Middle East, with a view to avoiding misunderstandings. Beyond that, there is not much we can do. . . .

The importance of the "X" article was of course distorted out of all reasonable proportion by the treatment it received at the hands of the press. The American mass media produce upon any given event an effect analogous to that produced on a man's shadow by the angle of the sun—causing it normally to be either much greater or much less than life-size. In the case of this particular article it was much greater.

But the principle enunciated in it—that our differences with the Russians are not ones which it would take a war to solve—is still sound. What we need mostly to do is to free ourselves from some of our fixations with relation to the military competition—to remind ourselves that there is really no reason why we and the Russians should wish to do frightful things to each other and to the world—and to address ourselves vigorously, and with some degree of boldness, to the enormous danger presented by the very existence in human hands, and above all the proliferation, of weapons such as the nuclear ones. Somewhere between the intimacy we cannot have—either with the Russians or the Chinese—and the war there is no reason for us to fight, there is a middle ground of peaceful, if somewhat distant, coexistence on which our relationship with the great Communist powers could be considerably safer and more pleasant than it now is. We cannot make it so by our own efforts alone; the Russians and Chinese will have to help. But we could do better, in a number of respects, than we have been doing.

Marshall D. Shulman

NEW FORCES AND THE DECLINE OF THE SUPERPOWERS

In this essay Marshall Shulman, the noted Student of Soviet affairs at Columbia University, poses the central issue of the seventies: the impact of the intense preoccupation of all countries with burgeoning domestic concerns on the future of Soviet-American relations. Amid the tendencies toward economic chaos and human disaster the two superpowers were clearly of declining significance to the world and to each other. The new conditions, believed Shulman, established, not détente, but a "limited adversary relationship." This ruled out war but not political competition in which the U.S.S.R. would attempt, however slowly and carefully, to extend its influence. Nevertheless he advised the Congress to accept détente as a promising arrangement and certainly the best that the United States could achieve in the immediate future. Shulman warned, as did Graebner in the twelfth reading, that the two superpowers, in their avoidance of key settlements, had relied too heavily on the destructiveness of modern weapons to prevent war. Thus he favored not only a more realistic acceptance by both powers of what they could not change but also a greater restraint in their military competition. For too long, he believed, the United States had focused on containment of Soviet power and influence whereas the grave issues before the world had no answer in weapons at all.

The fundamental conditions of international life are being transformed with extraordinary rapidity; we cannot foresee what the world will look like even a few years from now. New patterns are emerging, the nature of which is still unclear. Diverse forms of power—economic and political, as well as military—are shifting previous

Detente: Hearings Before the Committee on Foreign Relations, United States Senate, 93rd Cong., 2nd Sess., on United States Relations with Communist Countries, August 15, 20, and 21, September 10, 12, 18, 19, 24, and 25, and October 1 and 8, 1974 (Washington: U.S. Government Printing Office, 1975), pp. 102–10.

balances among nations. Under the pressure of forces of change, many nations are experiencing domestic upheavals or at least intense domestic preoccupations. Assumptions once widely accepted that nuclear war and worldwide recession were remote contingencies are beginning to be questioned. Beyond these challenges to traditional nation-state relations are emergent problems of global proportions. The prospect of famine on an unimaginable scale confronts us immediately, inadequate food for a growing world population has become an imminent reality, and the time when conditions for human life on the planet will become increasingly difficult does not appear far distant.

The present system of relations among nations has so far not been able to cope with problems of this magnitude constructively and cooperatively; instead, it shows tendencies of regressing toward international anarchy. The United States and the Soviet Union are called "superpowers" because of their unprecedented capabilities for destruction, but they can neither command nor direct the forces of change now transforming the world.

In this somber perspective, it is clear that the Soviet Union is a complicating factor rather than a prime cause of the problems we must address. The immediate and overriding requirement in our relations with the Soviet Union is to do all that is humanly possible to reduce the possibility of nuclear war. Over the longer run, our objective must be to draw the Soviet Union into constructive participation in a strengthened international system, however remote this possibility may seem today.

There is a widespread misunderstanding in this country about the nature of our present relationship with the Soviet Union, which partly stems from the ambiguities of the word "détente." We have what I believe is best described as a "limited adversary relationship" with the Soviet Union. It is limited by the interest of both countries in the avoidance of general war. It is an adversary relationship because the two countries are engaged in a serious political competition, and it seems likely that this competition will continue for some time, though it may be conducted at high, medium, or low levels of tension, with varying degrees of restraint, and mixed with some elements of cooperation. The Soviet leadership has moved a certain distance toward a policy of reduced tension and a moderate degree of restraint in its competition with the United States—a policy which it calls peaceful coexistence—because it perceives the need to consolidate its situation at home and its relations with Eastern Europe and China, and also because it believes it can more effectively and more safely increase its influence in the world under conditions of reduced tension. There should be no misunderstanding that the Soviet political strategy of peaceful coexistence does not imply that the Soviet Union renounces its ultimate commitment to the further advancement of communism, or that the Soviet Union will not take advantage of opportunities that present themselves for an increase of Soviet influence; it does, however, signify a lower tension policy and a reliance upon longer term developments to validate Soviet aspirations.

From the point of view of the United States, this represents a desirable turn in Soviet policy, provided that we understand it correctly and respond to it appropriately, even though it presents some serious problems for us as it does for the Soviet Union. Under conditions of reduced tension, it is more difficult for our people to support the maintenance of the military equilibrium which is a necessary condition for international stability. It is also more difficult for us to sustain a harmonious relationship with our allies. Despite these difficulties, however, the paramount consideration for us is that the current phase of Soviet policy offers at least the possibility of reducing the danger of nuclear war by damping down the military competition and by encouraging moderation in the continuing competition between the two countries. We can compete effectively under conditions of reduced tension while at the same time working to strengthen safeguards against a nuclear catastrophe. In this crucial respect, our interests and Soviet interests are not in conflict.

No one, I believe, would argue that it is in our interest to see a return to the intense and dangerous tensions of an earlier period, but in the course of our national debates, some measures have been proposed which could have that effect. For example, there are some in this country who argue that we should not accept what is sometimes called a limited détente, that we should accept nothing less than what they call a true or a comprehensive détente, which they define as a relationship in which the Soviet Union gives up the "ideological struggle," accepts an agreed settlement of our political and military competition, and grants a greater degree of human rights to its citizens. The difficulty with this view in my opinion is that it seeks as an immediate objective that which can at best be accomplished over a longer period of time, and by posing conditions which the present Soviet regime cannot but regard as terms of surrender and of self-liquidation, it sacrifices the possibility of a more modest but more realizable moderation of the danger of war. It appears to me to be a clear case of "the best being the enemy of the good." They fear that a limited détente is an advantage to the Soviet and would be against our interests, but this would only be the result if, misled by overblown rhetoric, we allowed ourselves to believe that a few summit meetings could achieve a millenial transformation in a deeply rooted adversary relationship.

Because the symbolism and the atmospherics of the summit meetings created unreal expectations which were bound to be disappointed in practice, and because the regulation of the military competition has proved more difficult than had been hoped, there has been a tendency to underestimate the limited but nevertheless significant distance the United States and the Soviet Union have come toward establishing channels of communication which would have been impossible a few years ago and toward some beginning understanding of the desirability and the possibility of avoiding the costs and dangers of an unregulated political and military competition. As a consequence of the negotiations of the past two years, there has emerged a multilevel relationship between the two countries. In place of the old "hard-soft" dichotomy, it is necessary to bring to bear a more differentiated analysis of the various aspects of the relationship, such as the strategic military competition, the conventional military competition, the political competition with occasional cooperation, the economic competition and cooperation, cultural relations, the various forms of functional cooperation—such as environment, health, oceanography, space, science, etc.—and the ideological competition. In addition, we have become aware of how deeply each country is affected by the domestic politics of the other.

Why is it that the logic for limiting the strategic military competition has not seemed more compelling? There can be no advantage for either country in an unregulated competition in nuclear weapons. There can be no doubt that both countries and the rest of the world would be more secure if the level of Soviet and American strategic weapons were half of what it now is. Both countries pay lipservice to this objective, but in neither the Soviet Union nor the United States have the political leaders been able and willing to control pressures from within their respective societies to drive on this irrational competition. The strategic arms limitation talks have not prevented, and may even have stimulated, the continuing development and deployment of new weapons.

One reason why this is so, I believe, is that there is a widespread complacency about the inconceivability of a nuclear war, which does not seem warranted by the present situation. We have not yet faced up to the probability of the spread of nuclear weapons to other countries and even to groups of people. The possibility that local conflicts can escalate into a nuclear conflict without either the United States or the Soviet Union intending this to happen is too lightly dismissed. The development of greater mobility, firepower, and accuracy of conventional weapons and the eruption of many situations of political instability around the world present an increasing danger of conventional war. The sale and transfer of conventional weapons to less-developed countries amounts to billions of dollars each year. The line between conventional and nuclear weapons is being blurred, and some of the inhibitions on the use of, or at least the deployment of, tactical nuclear weapons, are being weakened. Technological innovations which have the effect of increasing the instability of the present nuclear balance are being introduced without a thought of the consequences. The stability of the present deterrent balance is also being undermined by actions in both the United States and the Soviet Union which seem intended to develop the capability to wage various levels of nuclear war. Although no one in his right mind on either side could rationally opt for nuclear war, the consequence of these developments is that an unintended war cannot be regarded as a remote possibility.

Although a serious burden of responsibility for this state of affairs rests upon the Soviet Union, it cannot be said that the United States has done all that it can or should do to bring reason and sanity into the military competition. On the Soviet side, the extreme and endemic secrecy which shrouds its actions and its intentions arouses fear and anticipatory reactions to potential threats that are often not realized. If the Soviet Minister of Defense were to publish a posture statement similar to that issued by the Secretary of Defense in the United States, it would help greatly to remove at least some of the uncertainties regarding Soviet intentions. . . .

As for the United States, we do not yet perceive clearly how our actions in the military field produce responses in the Soviet Union which are adverse to our security interests. The Secretary of Defense talks of parity, or what he prefers to call essential equivalence in the military balance as a necessary condition for international stability, and this seems a reasonable proposition. But our actions do not seem to correspond to this principle. We have forced the pace of development in multiple warheads and missile accuracy, with the consequence that the military balance has become more unstable and more difficult to bring under control. We have proposed weapons programs to the Congress on the grounds that they would serve as incentives for the Soviets to negotiate, and then announced that we would go ahead with these programs in any case. We have announced a proposal shift in our strategic doctrine away from a reliance upon a deterrent balance to a counterforce posture which would involve not only a change in our targeting doctrine to give us a range of warfighting capabilities, but also a development program to give our missiles the degree of accuracy necessary to knock out Soviet missiles. From the Soviet point of view, this is taken to signal an American intent to work toward a first-strike capability, and the consequence is to give ammunition to the Soviet military in their demands for larger appropriations.

It is striking how differently the strategic balance is perceived from Moscow and from Washington. In the Soviet view, the United States appears to have a strong advantage in technological superiority, and despite Soviet efforts to catch up, the American technological lead continues to lengthen. From Washington, these Soviet efforts to catch up are observed in the form of accelerated programs of development and testing, and are regarded with alarm for the potential capabilities they could give the Soviet when and if the new weapons are procured and deployed in large numbers. This in turn is used to argue for new systems and new development programs on the American side, and the cycle continues. Under these circumstances, it appears unlikely that a plateau of essential equivalence can ever be reached.

If we ask why our defense policy has followed this course, the explanation must be sought at two levels. At the level of conceptualization, there has been a lingering assumption in many quarters that our security is best served by seeking to maintain clear superiority over the Soviet Union. This approach is a carryover from the prenuclear age. It has not yet come to terms with the fact that nuclear superiority in any practically significant sense cannot be achieved by either side, and that the quest for superiority can only result in a further decline in real security for both sides. A more reasonable approach would seem to be that our optimum security interests would be best served by working toward a military equilibrium—necessarily, a symmetrical balance—at as stable and moderate a level as can be managed by negotiation. If this is genuinely accepted as our conceptual objective, it would give us a criterion now lacking for measuring our present and proposed military programs. . . .

How does the internal situation in the Soviet Union affect Soviet-American relations? In the course of our national debates, one aspect of this broad question has been raised regarding the effect of Soviet internal politics upon Soviet foreign policy. In recent years, we have been learning how much each country is affected by the other's domestic politics. In the Soviet Union over the past 20 years, we have observed repeated efforts of the Khrushchev and the Brezhnev leadership to move toward a low-tension policy in response to national-interest requirements, only to be effectively resisted by groups that saw their interests as adversely affected by the political strategy of "peaceful coexistence." At the 24th Party Congress in 1971, Brezhnev was successful in winning support for the "peaceful coexistence" line in foreign policy, but despite assurances and concessions to the skeptics, the course is not without its influential domestic opponents. They appear to be found mainly in the Soviet security apparatus, the military services, and in the orthodox, doctrinaire wing of the party bureaucracy. For them, a prolonged period of low tension, summits with the "imperialist" arch adversary, a weakening of Soviet economic autarchy, foregoing militant exploitation of political targets of opportunity abroad, discussion of limitation of armaments—all these are seen as threatening to the system of political control and the group interests they represent.

This debate goes on, often veiled in indirect language. It is difficult to judge the relative strength of these challenges to the present policy, but given this uncertainty and the age of the present Soviet leadership, we clearly cannot extrapolate a projection of the present policy into the indefinite future. This has two implications for our policy: One is that we must be conscious of the effect of what we say and what we do upon the internal balances in the Soviet Union; and the other is that we should expect from time to time variations in the degree of tension, and in the degree of risks accepted in the exploitation of conflict.

A second aspect of the question concerns the extent to which we can legitimately and effectively influence the evolution of the Soviet system toward a fuller realization of human rights. We have observed that the powerful and influential Soviet security apparatus, concerned to limit the effect of low-tension relations with the target of its ideological hostility, has convulsively tightened its controls, seeking to crush the expression of dissident opinion, and to narrow the range of creative life in the Soviet Union.

This has raised in the minds of many people in this country the question whether by entering into improved relations with the Soviet Union we share a moral complicity in the heightened repressive accompaniment to the policy of "peaceful coexistence," the most favorable condition for long-term evolution of the Soviet system to-ward less repressiveness is a prolonged period of reduced tension. The Soviet Union is not immune to forces of change in the world. There are many forces for change in the complex spectrum of Soviet politics, and it seems reasonable to believe that effective change is most likely to come from within, provided the international situation does not stimulate a return to high levels of domestic mobilization. We cannot be sure of the outcome of this complex process, but we can at least reduce counterproductive effects by avoiding frontal public confrontations of the Soviet leadership by demands from our Government for concessions in their system which exceed a reason-able scale of feasibility. It does, however, seem reasonable and legitimate for individuals and private groups to draw to world public attention and to express our humanitarian concern over the egre-gious violations of human rights in the Soviet Union, as we should do with equal vigor in our own country and elesewhere, including countries that are allied to us.

As a government, our priority concern is to bring the Soviet Gov-ernment, as it is, without waiting for millenial transformation, into a limited relationship in which the danger of nuclear war can be re-duced. This does not require us to blind ourselves to the realities of Soviet life, nor does it depend upon trust. It is based solely upon the self-interest of both governments in the avoidance of war, despite other conflicts of interest. In the longer perspective of decades, the movement toward a greater degree of genuine cooperation between the two countries in constructive efforts to strengthen the interna-tional system will depend upon some profound transformation in the Soviet outlook, which will in turn depend upon the effectiveness of our foreign policy as a whole.

This brings us to a few concluding words about the place of our policy toward the Soviet Union in relation to the larger aspects of our foreign policy. As we reminded ourselves at the outset, the Soviet Union is a complicating factor, rather than a prime cause of many of the most urgent problems facing us in the world. For too long, we allowed the military aspects of the effort to contain the expansion of Communist influence to be the central touchstone of our foreign policy. Now it should be evident to all of us that the survival of democracy if not of human life itself upon the planet requires a larger perspective than we have yet realized as a nation. Unless we are successful in dealing with such problems as inflation, recession, unemployment, and monetary chaos, with famine and the growing impoverishment and desperation of the less developed countries, with the spread of nuclear weapons and the wholesale traffic in conventional weapons, we cannot hope to preserve democratic values in our domestic life, no matter how great is our capability for nuclear destruction.

Formidable as this agenda may be, we cannot escape the realization that these problems, if unresolved, offer a temptation to the Soviet Union to seek a militant exploitation of our differences and our troubles. If we wish to encourage a continued movement in Soviet policy from restraint to responsible cooperation, the indispensable condition is evidence of progress by the United States toward an effectively functioning society at home, and toward a foreign policy which shows awareness of and responsiveness to the aspirations of the people of the world.

Suggestions for Additional Reading

Through three decades of cold-war experience the accumulation of writings on the American-Russian conflict has reached enormous proportions. The very complexity of the struggle, the difficulty in determining its nature or measuring its significance, has undoubtedly stimulated this vast quantity of research and writing. Fortunately for the student, the ideas and essential facts on a subject even as illusive as the cold war are limited. With few exceptions the postwar writings on Russian-American relations fall into a series of clearly defined schools of thought. Each additional volume, whatever the impressiveness of the research on which it is based, tends to demonstrate the validity of some specific interpretation of the cold war already suggested by others.

Historians agree generally that the cold war had its origins in the wartime disagreements over the future of Eastern Europe. Two standard works on Allied diplomacy during World War II, both somewhat critical of the lack of realism in the western position, are William Hardy McNeill, *America, Britain and Russia: Their Cooperation and Conflict, 1941–1946* (London, 1953) and Herbert Feis, *Churchill, Roosevelt, Stalin: The War They Waged and the Peace They Sought* (Princeton, N.J., 1957). John L. Snell's *Wartime Origins of the East-West Dilemma over Germany* (New Orleans, 1959) traces the emergence of the German question as a central issue in the Soviet-Western conflict. Among the many writings on the burgeoning disagreement over Eastern Europe are Edward J. Rozek, *Allied Wartime Diplomacy: A Pattern in Poland* (New York, 1958); Roman Umiastowski, *Poland, Russia and Great Britain, 1941–1945* (London, 1946); and W. W. Kulski, "The Lost Opportunity for Russian-Polish Friendship," *Foreign Affairs* 25 (July 1947): 667–84. The major account of the Eastern European question in wartime diplomacy is Lynn Etheridge Davis, *The Cold War Begins: Soviet-American Conflict over Eastern Europe* (Princeton, N.J., 1974).

Three critical analyses of Roosevelt's wartime leadership and diplomacy are Gaddis Smith's *American Diplomacy during the Second World War, 1941–1945* (New York, 1965), Robert A. Divine's *Roosevelt and World War II* (Baltimore, 1969), and James McGregor Burns's *Roosevelt: The Soldier of Freedom, 1939–1945* (New York, 1970). General John R. Deane has written a significant personal account of wartime United States-Soviet relations in *The Strange Alliance* (New York, 1947). Another important personal history of wartime diplomacy is Robert E. Sherwood, *Roosevelt and Hopkins: An Intimate History*

(New York, 1948). Three volumes which agree that the West gave nothing away at Yalta are Edward R. Stettinius, Jr., *Roosevelt and the Russians: The Yalta Conference* (Garden City, N.Y., 1949), John L. Snell, ed., *The Meaning of Yalta* (Baton Rouge, La., 1956), and Diane Shaver Clemens, *Yalta* (New York, 1970). Books which assume that other Western policies might have limited Soviet expansion are Chester Wilmot, *The Struggle for Europe* (New York, 1963), and the far more critical Felix Wittmer, *The Yalta Betrayal* (Caldwell, Idaho, 1953). Athan G. Theoharis, in *The Yalta Myths* (Columbia, Mo., 1970), traces the impact of Roosevelt's alleged sellout at Yalta on American thought and politics. Stressing economic factors in the Soviet-American friction is Albert Z. Carr, *Truman, Stalin, and Peace* (Garden City, N.Y., 1950).

Since 1947 a large body of historical literature has traced the general evolution of United States—Russian relations. Three volumes which place the cold war in historical perspective are Vera Micheles Dean, *The United States and Russia* (Cambridge, Mass., 1947); Thomas A. Bailey, *America Faces Russia: Russian-American Relations from Early Times to Our Day* (Ithaca, N.Y., 1950); William Appleman Williams, *American-Russian Relations, 1781–1947* (New York, 1952). Among the general assessments of postwar Soviet-American relations, differing widely in their assignment of guilt, are Kenneth Ingram, *History of the Cold War* (New York, 1955); John Lukacs, *A History of the Cold War* (Garden City, N. Y., 1961); Henry L. Roberts, *Russia and America: Dangers and Prospects* (New York, 1956); Desmond Donnelly, *Struggle for the World: The Cold War, 1917–1965* (New York, 1965); André Fontaine, *History of the Cold War* (2 vols; New York, 1968–1969); and Louis J. Halle, *The Cold War as History* (New York, 1967). A briefer and more original study is Paul Seabury's *The Rise and Decline of the Cold War* (New York, 1967). Adam B. Ulam's *The Rivals: America and Russia Since World War II* (New York, 1971) is a thoughtful account, rather critical of United States policy toward Russia. Several general studies of the postwar world, analyzing the relationship of the Soviet-American conflict to broad international issues, are J. Hampden Jackson, *The World of the Postwar Decade: 1945–1955* (Boston, 1956); Hugh Seton-Watson, *Neither War Nor Peace* (New York, 1960); Louis Fischer, *Russia, America, and the World* (New York, 1961); and Pauline Tompkins, *American-Russian Relations in the Far East* (New York, 1949).

Stimulated by the cold war, American and British scholarship has produced a wide range of impressive studies of Soviet foreign policy. The standard work on prewar Soviet diplomacy is Max Beloff, *Foreign Policy of Soviet Russia, 1929–1941* (2 vols.; New York, 1947–1949). Two perceptive surveys by George F. Kennan, *Soviet Foreign Policy, 1917–1941* (Princeton, N.J., 1960) and *Russia and the West under Lenin and Stalin* (Boston, 1961), are generally sympathetic with the Soviet point of view. Tracing the rebirth of Russian nationalism during the war years is Walter Kolarz, *Stalin and Eternal Russia* (London, 1944). Critical of Soviet policy are the well-known volumes of David J. Dallin, *Soviet Russia's Foreign Policy, 1939–1942* (New Haven, 1942), *The Big Three* (New Haven, 1945), and *The New Soviet Empire* (New Haven, 1951). Edward Hallett Carr's *The Soviet Impact on the Western World* (New York, 1947) contains six cogent essays on the meaning of Soviet policy. Another interesting study of Russian behavior is Paul Winterton's *Inquest on an Ally* (London, 1948). Isaac Deutscher's *The Great Contest: Russia and the West* (New York, 1960) is sympathetic to the Soviet view. More balanced, and in large measure the standard account, is Adam B. Ulam's *Expansion and Coexistence: The History of Soviet Foreign Policy, 1917–1967* (New York, 1968). Two studies of Stalin are Marshall D. Shulman, *Stalin's Foreign Policy Reappraised* (Cambridge, Mass., 1963), and Richard D. Warth, "Stalin and the Cold War: A Second Look," *South Atlantic Quarterly* 59 (Winter 1960): 1–12. Three useful anthologies, revealing the complexity of Soviet foreign policy, are Alexander Dallin, ed., *Soviet Conduct in World Affairs* (New York, 1960); Alvin Z. Rubinstein, ed., *The Foreign Policy of the Soviet Union* (New York, 1960); and Ivo J. Lederer, ed., *Russian Foreign Policy: Essays in Historical Perspective* (New Haven, 1962). Frederick C. Barghoorn, *The Soviet Cultural Offensive* (Princeton, N. J., 1960) analyzes the nature and significance of Soviet cultural diplomacy.

Several studies of Soviet diplomatic method are extremely useful in tracing the breakdown of the Grand Alliance. Raymond Dennett and Joseph E. Johnson, eds., *Negotiating with the Russians* (Boston, 1951) is a highly instructive symposium by ten Americans. Another excellent volume by a participant is Philip E. Mosely, *The Kremlin in World Politics* (New York, 1960). A perceptive article on wartime Soviet diplomacy is John C. Campbell, "Negotiating with the Soviets: Some Lessons of the War Period," *Foreign Affairs* 34 (January 1956): 305–19. Admiral C. Turner Joy, in *How Communists Negotiate* (New York, 1955), reveals Communist diplomacy during the Korean armistice negotiations. Another helpful study is Stephen D. Kertesz,

"Reflections on Soviet and American Negotiating Behavior," *Review of Politics* 19 (January 1957): 3–36.

On Soviet policy in Eastern Europe are Hugh Seton-Watson, *The East European Revolution* (New York, 1951); Reginald R. Betts, ed., *Central and Southeast Europe, 1945–1948* (London, 1950); Stephen D. Kertesz, ed., *The Fate of East Central Europe* (Notre Dame, Ind., 1956); Reuben Henry Markham, *Rumania under the Soviet Yoke* (Boston, 1949); Stanislaw Mikolajczyk, *The Pattern of Soviet Domination* (London, 1948); John A. Lukacs, *The Great Powers and Eastern Europe* (New York, 1954); and Stephen D. Kertesz, "The U.S.S.R. and the Communist Bloc," *Current History* 41 (November 1961): 280–85. On Czechoslovakia is Dana Adams Schmidt, *Anatomy of a Satellite* (Boston, 1952). On the problem of divided Germany are John P. Nettl, *The Eastern Zone and Soviet Policy in Germany* (New York, 1951); Hugh Seton-Watson, "Eastern Europe and the German Problem," *20th Century* (March 1953), pp. 195–202; and Philip E. Mosely, "The Dismemberment of Germany," *Foreign Affairs* 28 (April 1950): 487–98. On the economic relations of the Soviet bloc is Margaret Dewar, *Soviet Trade with Eastern Europe, 1945–1949* (London, 1951). Zbigniew Brzezinski suggests techniques for creating diversity within the Communist camp in "The Challenge of Change in the Soviet Bloc," *Foreign Affairs* 39 (April 1961): 430–43.

Scholarly opinion on the role of ideology in Soviet foreign policy is sharply divided. Among the studies which view the U.S.S.R. as controlled, not by ideology but by a pragmatic response to traditional Russian objectives and the problems of survival are Vera Micheles Dean, *Russia: Menace or Promise* (New York, 1947); Louis Fischer, *The Great Challenge* (New York, 1946); and N.S. Timasheff, "Soviet Ideology for the 1960s," *Current History* 43 (October 1962): 224–28, 245. Stressing the traditionally imperialistic nature of Soviet foreign policy are two articles by M. S. Handler, "The Cominform: Instrument of the Kremlin," *New York Times Magazine,* October 9, 1949, and "The New Pattern of Soviet Aggression," ibid., October 1, 1950. Hans J. Morgenthau's perceptive study, "The Real Issue between Russia and the United States," *University of Chicago Magazine* (April 1951), compares the Soviet challenge to that of France in the days of the French Revolution. He thus identifies the issue as imperialism and not world revolution. Edward Crankshaw attributes Soviet purpose to Russian nationalism and the quest for security in a series of articles which include "The Great Contradiction in Russia," *New York Times Magazine,* September 25, 1949; "Russia's Power: Not Ideas But

Force," ibid., June 3, 1951; and "Russia's Imperial Design," *Atlantic Monthly* (November 1957), pp. 39–45. Of special importance in assigning to power rather than ideology the chief determinant in Soviet policy is Barrington Moore, Jr., *Soviet Politics—The Dilemma of Power* (Cambridge, Mass., 1950).

An opposing and impressive body of literature interprets Soviet policy and intention within the universal framework of Marxist-Leninist-Stalinist dogma. Walter Bedell Smith, American Ambassador to Moscow from 1946 to 1949, leaves little doubt that the Kremlin goal is world domination in *My Three Years in Moscow* (Philadelphia, 1950). A similar judgment can be found in E. Day Carman, *Soviet Imperialism: Russia's Drive Toward World Domination* (Washington, 1950). A thoughtful symposium which also views the Soviet problem as grim is C. Grove Haines, ed., *The Threat of Soviet Imperialism* (Baltimore, 1954). Another symposium, edited by Waldemar Gurian, *Soviet Imperialism: Its Origins and Tactics* (Notre Dame, Ind., 1953), as well as Gurian's special study, *An Introduction to Soviet Communism* (Notre Dame, 1953), deal with international aspects of the Communist creed. Impressive in their scholarship and accepting the theme that a Communist world state is the operative goal of Kremlin policy are Nathan Leites, *A Study of Bolshevism* (Glencoe, Ill., 1953); Elliot R. Goodman, *The Soviet Design for a World State* (New York, 1960); J. M. Mackintosh, *Strategy and Tactics of Soviet Foreign Policy* (New York, 1962); and Bertram D. Wolfe, *Communist Totalitarianism: Keys to the Soviet System* (Boston, 1961). Two volumes by Zbigniew Brzezinski which seek a balance between power and ideology in Soviet action are *The Soviet Bloc: Unity and Conflict* (Cambridge, Mass., 1960) and *Ideology and Power in Soviet Politics* (New York, 1962).

Writings on American policy in the cold war have been as voluminous and impressive as those on the Soviet Union. In large measure the writings on United States policy and the beginnings of the cold war fall into three categories. Some writers have accepted the official American view that United States policy was never more than a defensive effort to stop the encroachments of an expansive Soviet Union. An excellent and judicious study of the factors that determined American policy for the first postwar decade, as seen through official eyes, is that of William Reitzel et al., *United States Foreign Policy, 1945–1955* (Washington, 1956). Joseph M. Jones, *The Fifteen Weeks* (New York, 1955), is a perceptive study of the formulation of the Truman Doctrine and the Marshall plan by an insider.

Herbert Feis's two noted works on postwar American policy adopt a generally pro-Truman administration viewpoint: *Between War and Peace: The Potsdam Conference* (Princeton, N. J., 1960) and *From Trust to Terror: The Onset of the Cold War, 1945–1950* (New York, 1970). Perhaps the best defense of United States policy can be found in Dean Acheson, *Present at the Creation: My Years in the State Department* (New York, 1969). Two more specific volumes on United States-Russian relations are Harry B. Price, *The Marshall Plan and Its Meaning* (Ithaca, N. Y., 1955), and W. Phillips Davison, *The Berlin Blockade: A Study in Cold War Politics* (Princeton, N. J., 1958).

Another body of writing, secondly, criticizes American policy for its lack of realism in refusing to accept what the war had wrought. Volumes that accept this view in varying degrees are John Lewis Gaddis, *The United States and the Origins of the Cold War* (New York, 1972); Hans J. Morgenthau, *In Defense of the National Interest* (New York, 1951); two books by George F. Kennan, *American Diplomacy, 1900–1950* (Chicago, 1951) and *Memoirs, 1925–1950* (Boston, 1967); Norman A. Graebner, *The New Isolationism* (New York, 1956); Emmet John Hughes, *America the Vincible* (Garden City, N. Y., 1959); C. L. Sulzberger, *What's Wrong with U.S. Foreign Policy* (New York, 1959); Kenneth W. Thompson, *Political Realism and the Crisis of World Politics* (Princeton, N. J., 1960); William L. Neumann, *After Victory: Churchill, Roosevelt, Stalin and the Making of the Peace* (New York, 1967); William G. Carleton, *The Revolution in American Foreign Policy: Its Global Range* (New York, 1964); and Stephen E. Ambrose, *Rise to Globalism: American Foreign Policy since 1938* (Baltimore, 1971). Suggesting the requirements for new policies toward the Afro-Asian world are Max F. Millikan and W.W. Rostow, *A Proposal: Key to an Effective Foreign Policy* (New York, 1957), and two volumes by Chester Bowles, *The New Dimensions of Peace* (New York, 1955) and *Ideas, People and Peace* (New York, 1958).

The third coherent body of literature comprises the New Left school. Members of this group agree generally that the United States, not Russia, was the expansive force, and that this nation, in the interest of peace, should have accepted Russia's postwar position as an expression of insecurity. Leading revisionist works include W. A. Williams's *The Tragedy of American Diplomacy* (New York, 1962); D. L. Fleming's *The Cold War and Its Origins, 1917–1960* (2 vols.; Garden City, N. Y., 1961), a massive and important contribution to revisionist writing; Gar Alperovitz's *Atomic Diplomacy: Hiroshima and Potsdam* (New York, 1965); Martin F. Herz, *Beginnings of the Cold*

War (Bloomington, Ind., 1966); David Horowitz's *The Free World Colossus* (New York, 1965); Walter LaFeber's *America, Russia, and the Cold War* (2nd ed.; New York, 1971); Neal D. Houghton, ed., *Struggle against History: U. S. Foreign Policy in an Age of Revolution* (New York, 1968); two volumes by Gabriel Kolko, *The Politics of War* (New York, 1968) and (with Joyce Kolko), *The Limits of Power: The World and United States Foreign Policy, 1945–1954* (New York, 1972); Lloyd C. Gardner's *Architects of Illusion: Men and Ideas in American Foreign Policy, 1941–1949* (Chicago, 1970); and Thomas G. Paterson, ed., *Cold War Critics* (Chicago, 1971). A good summary is Gar Alperovitz's review of Herz's book in "How Did the Cold War Begin?" *New York Review of Books* 8 (March 23, 1967): 6-12. Three more radical studies are Carl Marzani, *We Can Be Friends: Origins of the Cold War* (New York, 1952); Joseph P. Morray, *From Yalta to Disarmament: Cold War Debate* (New York, 1961); and Herbert Aptheker, *American Foreign Policy and the Cold War* (New York, 1962). Arthur M. Schlesinger, Jr. has offered a criticism of the New Left historians in "Origins of the Cold War," *Foreign Affairs* 46 (October 1967): 36–52. Robert J. Maddox has presented a broader critique in *The New Left and the Origins of the Cold War* (Princeton, N. J., 1973).

To terminate the sharp division of Europe, George F. Kennan argued for a program of military disengagement in his *Russia, the Atom, and the West* (New York, 1958). A detailed defense of the concept of disengagement can be found in Eugene Hintherhoff, *Disengagement* (London, 1959). Hugh Gaitskell, former head of the British Labour Party, accepted the need for some new basis of negotiation in"Disengagement: Why? How?" *Foreign Affairs* 36 (July 1958): 539–56. Dean Acheson attacked the concept of disengagement in "The Illusion of Disengagement," ibid. (April 1958): 371–82, and Kennan defended his initial program in "Disengagement Revisited," ibid. 37 (January 1959): 187–210.

Another group of American writers, attributing nothing less than global conquest to Soviet intentions, condemned the concept of containment as well as all proposals designed to stabilize world politics as inadequate and dangerous. Unless the United States discovered the means to undermine the Soviet structure through policies of liberation ran the argument, the free world would eventually succumb to world communism. In a struggle for the globe there could be only winners and losers. William C. Bullitt, former United States Ambassador to Russia, in his *The Great Globe Itself* (New York, 1946), demanded a total response commensurate with the gigantic Soviet plan for world conquest. Hamilton Fish, in *The Challenge of World Communism* (Milwaukee, 1946), called for a policy to destroy communism. Similarly James Burnham, in *The Struggle for the World* (New York, 1947) and *Containment or Liberation?* (New York, 1953) argued that the United States must prepare for a showdown with the U.S.S.R. In two books William Henry Chamberlain suggested, without clarifying alternative courses, that the United States must achieve more: *Beyond Containment* (Chicago, 1953) and *Appeasement: Road to War* (New York, 1962). Thomas I. Cook and Malcolm Moos, in *Power through Purpose* (Baltimore, 1954), attacked the concept of realism and suggested that the United States encourage discontent within the Soviet Union and the satellites. Similarly Thomas K. Finletter's *Foreign Policy: The Next Phase* (New York, 1958) emphasized the need for new strategies to drive the Soviets back. Perhaps the studies that pictured most thoroughly the need for a "forward strategy" to meet the unrelenting pressure of Soviet aggressiveness are Stefan T. Possony, *A Century of Conflict* (Chicago, 1953); William S. Schlamm, *Germany and the East-West Crisis: The Decisive Challenge to American Policy* (New York, 1959); Robert Strausz-Hupe et al., *Protracted Conflict: A Study of Communist Strategy* (New York, 1959); Robert Strausz-Hupe et al., *A Forward Strategy for America* (New York, 1961); and William R. Kintner and Joseph Z. Kornfeder, *The New Frontier of War: Political Warfare, Present and Future* (Chicago, 1962).

Students of the Soviet Union have studied thoroughly the changes in Soviet policy wrought by the death of Stalin in 1953 and the eventual accession of Nikita Khrushchev to power. Perhaps the most detailed and balanced account of Khrushchev's impact on Soviet strategy is David J. Dallin's *Soviet Foreign Policy After Stalin* (Philadelphia, 1961). In his *Peaceful Coexistence: An Analysis of Soviet Foreign Policy* (Chicago, 1959), Wladyslaw Kulski stresses Soviet policy in the underdeveloped areas of the world. On the new Soviet policies of aid and trade are Joseph S. Berliner, *Soviet Economic Aid: The New Aid and Trade Policy in Underdeveloped Countries* (New York, 1958); Klaus Eugene Knorr, *Ruble Diplomacy: Challenge to American Foreign Aid* (Princeton, N. J., 1956); Averell Harriman, "Soviet Challenge and American Policy," *Atlantic Monthly* (April 1956), pp. 42–47; Willard L. Thorp, "American Policy and the Soviet Economic Offensive," *Foreign Affairs* 35 (January 1957); 271–82; N. B. Scott, "Soviet Economic Relations with the Underdeveloped Countries," *Soviet Studies* 10 (July 1958): 36–53; and Zbigniew

Brzezinski, "The Politics of Underdevelopment," *World Politics* 9 (October 1956): 55–75.

For some students of the Soviet Union, Khrushchev's policies of competitive coexistence offered little more hope for peace and relaxation than did the more rigid, power-based policies of Stalin. Julian Towster, for example, in "The Soviet Union after Stalin: Leaders and Policies," *American Slavic and East European Review* 13 (December 1954): 471–99, offered little assurance for better American relations with the U.S.S.R. G. F. Hudson developed the same thesis in "The Return to Wishful Thinking: Has International Communism Really Changed?" *Commentary* 17 (January 1954): 1–8; "Negotiating an End to the Cold War: The Hazards," ibid. 20 (September 1955): 193–99; and "Moscow's Aims Have Not Changed: Khrushchev's 'Peace Offensive' Imperils NATO," ibid. 25 (March 1958): 209–16. Bertram D. Wolfe warned that the Kremlin under Khrushchev was more irreconcilable than ever before in *Khrushchev and Stalin's Ghost* (New York, 1956); "Stalinism Versus Stalin: Exorcising a Stubborn Ghost," *Commentary* 21 (June 1956): 522–31; and "The Durability of Soviet Despotism: Forty Years of Revolution," ibid. 24 (August 1957): 93–104. Philip E. Mosely, in a series of articles published after Stalin's death, insisted that long-range Soviet strategy had not changed: "The Kremlin's Foreign Policy Since Stalin," *Foreign Affairs* 32 (October 1953): 20–33; "How 'New' Is the Kremlin's New Line?" ibid. 33 (April 1955): 376–86; "Soviet Foreign Policy: New Goals or New Manners?" ibid. 34 (July 1956): 541–53; and "Soviet Myths and Realities," ibid. 34 (April 1961): 341–54.

Other writers in their late fifties, while anticipating no cessation of the cold war, stressed the importance of accepting the challenge of competitive coexistence, even on Khrushchev's terms. They believed, first, that the West has no realistic alternative except war, and, second, that the West, whatever the Soviet intention in the competition, could meet the challenge successfully. Several writings that viewed the changes in Soviet policy quite optimistically are Thomas P. Whitney, "What We Can Expect of the Russians," *New York Times Magazine,* May 22, 1955, as well as two volumes by Isaac Deutscher, *Russia—What Next?* (New York, 1953) and *The Great Contest* (New York, 1960).

Less sanguine over post-Stalinist Soviet policy, but convinced that the United States could accept the challenge of competitive coexistence with some assurance of success are Edward Crankshaw, *Russia Without Stalin* (New York, 1956); C. L. Sulzberger, *The Big Thaw*

(New York, 1956); Hugh Gaitskell, *The Challenge of Coexistence* (Cambridge, Mass., 1957); G. L. Arnold, *The Pattern of World Conflict* (New York, 1955); Averell Harriman, *Peace with Russia?* (New York, 1959); John Scott, *Political Warfare: A Guide to Competitive Coexistence* (New York, 1955); Michael Lindsay, *Is Peaceful Coexistence Possible?* (East Lansing, Mich., 1960); Alvin Z. Rubinstein, "The Problem of Coexistence," *Current History* 41 (November 1961): 273–79; Walter Millis, "How to Compete with the Russians," *New York Times Magazine,* February 2, 1958; and Ross N. Berkes, "American Fears of the Soviet Union," *Current History* 42 (May 1962): 287–90, 301. George F. Kennan, in "Peaceful Coexistence: A Western View," *Foreign Affairs* 38 (January 1960): 171–90, pleaded that both sides in the cold war forget the past and proceed to eliminate the more intolerable elements in world affairs. Developing a similar theme, that the danger of communism was overshadowed by the danger of international anarchy, is Frederick L. Schuman's *The Cold War: Retrospect and Prospect* (Baton Rouge, La., 1962). Stressing the limited Western alternatives in the cold war and the absence of major Soviet gains are Norman A. Graebner, "The Cold War: An American View," *International Journal* 15 (Spring 1960): 95–112; Graebner, *Cold War Diplomacy, 1945–1960* (Princeton, N.J., 1962); and Thomas W. Wilson, Jr., *Cold War and Common Sense* (Greenwich, Conn., 1962). Of special significance on the problem of adapting an American foreign policy, established on the assumption of a bipolar world, to the actual conditions of change is Edmund Stillman and William Pfaff, *The New Politics: America and the End of the Postwar World* (New York, 1961).

Three books by members of the Kennedy administration and generally favorable in their treatment of the Kennedy policies are Arthur M. Schlesinger, Jr., *A Thousand Days: John F. Kennedy in the White House* (Boston, 1965); Theodore Sorenson, *Kennedy* (New York, 1965); and Roger Hilsman, *To Move a Nation* (Garden City, N.Y., 1967). Still many of the appraisals of the Kennedy policies toward Europe have been critical. This is true for Robert Kleiman's *Atlantic Crisis* (New York, 1964) and William G. Carleton's "Kennedy in History: An Early Appraisal," *Antioch Review* 24 (Fall 1964): 277–99. The Cuban missile crisis, a major event in the Kennedy record, has produced a large body of literature. Three well-known accounts are Elie Abel's *The Missile Crisis* (Philadelphia, 1966), Robert F. Kennedy's *Thirteen Days* (New York, 1969), and Henry Pachter's *Collision Course* (New York, 1963). Also of value is the collection of articles in

Robert A. Divine, ed., *The Cuban Missile Crisis* (Chicago, 1971).

Much of the writing on United States-Russian relations after the mid-sixties assumed a changing relationship which reflected international stability and restraint. Among the writings which reflected the changes are W. Averell Harriman, *America and Russia in a Changing World* (Garden City, N.J., 1971); Paul Y. Hammond, *The Cold War Years* (New York, 1969); George F. Kennan, *Memoirs, 1950–1963* (Boston, 1972); David S. McLellan, "The Changing Nature of Soviet and American Relations with Western Europe," *Annals of the American Academy of Political and Social Science* 372 (July 1967): 16–32; Merle Fainsod, "Some Reflections on Soviet-American Relations," *American Political Science Review* 62 (December 1968): 1093–1103; and Michael P. Gehlen, *The Politics of Coexistence* (Bloomington, Ind., 1967). Studies of Soviet foreign policy in the late sixties include Foy D. Kohler, *Understanding the Russians* (New York, 1970): Alexander Dallin and Thomas B. Larson, eds., *Soviet Politics Since Khrushchev* (Englewood Cliffs, N.J., 1968); William Zimmerman, *Soviet Perspectives on International Relations, 1956–1967* (Princeton, N.J.,1969); and Marshall D. Shulman, "Recent Soviet Foreign Policy: Some Patterns in Retrospect," *Journal of International Affairs* 22 (1968):26–47. Walter Z. Laqueur analyzed the impact of change on world communism in "The End of the Monolith: World Communism in 1962," *Foreign Affairs* 40 (April 1962): 360–73. Donald S. Zagoria's *The Sino-Soviet Conflict* (New York, 1962) remains a standard work on that subject.

By 1965 some students of United States-Soviet relations believed that the cold war, especially as it applied to Europe, had ceased to exist or at least had been modified beyond recognition by evolving restraints on Soviet and American behavior. Richard J. Barnet and Marcus G. Raskin suggested this in *After Twenty Years: Alternatives to the Cold War in Europe* (New York, 1965). Marshall D. Shulman's *Beyond the Cold War* (New Haven, 1966), as well as his "Europe versus 'Détente'?" *Foreign Affairs* 45 (April 1967): 389–402, also recognized the possibilities for a new and improved Soviet-American relationship. Brian Thomas argues that all that is left of the cold war is the refusal of the superpowers to admit it in "What's Left of the Cold War?" *Political Quarterly* 40 (April 1969): 173–86. James Chace's *A World Elsewhere: The New American Foreign Policy* (New York, 1973) comprises a basic evaluation of the Nixon foreign policies.